INDIAN PRIME MINISTERSHIP
A Comprehensive Study

About the Author

Jagdish Chandra Sharma was born in Lahore (now in Pakistan, then called *The Paris of India*). He migrated to India in 1947 as a penniless refugee after the Partition of India. He received his M.A. degree in Political Science in 1953, M.A. in English in 1955 from the Punjab University, Chandigarh.

He served as a lecturer in Political Science at Guru Ram Rai College, Nahan (H.P.) (now Government College) from 1956 to 1962; Head of the Political Science Department at D.A.V. College, Ambala from 1963 to 1968; Head of the Post-Graduate Department of Political Science at Dayanand (Evening) College, Hissar, from 1968 to 1972; Principal Mewat Degree College, Nagina (now Government College) from 1972 to 1975; Assistant Chief Editor, Section, Encyclopaedia of Indian Literature, National Sahitya Academy, New Delhi from 1975 to 1979; Editor, The Lions International, Delhi Branch; Chief Consultant, Chandra Export Agencies, New Delhi.

He also contributed from time to time to *Caravan; Illustrated Weekly of India,* Bombay; *Organisor*, Delhi.

His publications; *Gandhi The Humanist* (1964); *Nehru the Humanist* (1965); *The Political Philosophy of Jawaharlal Nehru* (1966); *Gandhi and Nehru* (1966).

He also contributed short stories in Urdu in *Pasbaan* an Urdu weekly published from Chandigarh.

INDIAN PRIME MINISTERSHIP
A Comprehensive Study

Jagdish Chandra Sharma
(Principal)

CONCEPT PUBLISHING COMPANY, NEW DELHI - 110059

ISBN 81-7022-924-3

First Published 2002

Published and Printed by
Ashok Kumar Mittal
Concept Publishing Company
A/15-16, Commercial Block, Mohan Garden,
NEW DELHI - 110059 (India)

Phones : 5648039, 5649024
Fax : 091-11-5648053
E-mail : publishing@conceptpub.com

DEDICATED
TO

PANDIT JAI DEV	—	FATHER
SHRIMATI MAYA DEVI	—	MOTHER
SHRIMATI SUMITRA DEVI	—	MOTHER-IN-LAW

Preface

The inherited tradition of Parliamentary government has come to stay in India. The head of the State—The President of the Republic—is the legal repository of the powers of the State but the centre of gravity of the real powers has shifted, as a corollary, to the Prime Minister who presides over the whole power structure of the State.

The office of the Prime Minister of India, in the modern sense, is a recent development. The rapidly increasing significance of this most important political luminary has provoked much debate and discussion. The novel constitutional experiment—federal-cum-unitary and Parliamentary set-up—has been a success. It has weathered many a storm *viz.* war with China, two wars with Pakistan and the imposition of emergency. The Prime Minister has borne the brunt of all these devastating tempests.

I hope the present research work on the office of the Prime Minister of India will fill in the void which has been unwittingly left by the scholars of Political Science, though a great amount of research has been conducted on Indian government and politics. An attempt has been made to bring to light the full significance of the office of the Prime Minister together with a critical appraisal of the powers, functions and the status it has come to enjoy in due course of time.

I must take this opportunity to sincerely thank my mentor and guide Dr. K.C. Gupta but for whose guidance I could not have succeeded in my present venture.

I must also thank the librarians of the following libraries who rendered great help to me in my onerous task:

The ICWA Library, Sapru House, New Delhi.

The American Centre Library, New Delhi.
The British Council Library, New Delhi.
The Parliament Library, New Delhi.
The National Sahitya Akademi Library, New Delhi.
The India International Centre Library, New Delhi.
Meerut University Library, Meerut.
The Punjab University Library, Chandigarh.
Nehru Memorial Library, New Delhi.
Gandhi Peace Foundation Library, New Delhi.
Allahabad University Library, Allahabad.
The District Library, Hissar.
The State Library, Chandigarh.
The District Library, Ambala.

I shall be failing in my duty if I do not mention the source of my inspiration, my wife Principal K. Chandra whose immense assistance needs no formal praise.

I must also acknowledge my debt to Dr. K.K. Bhutani of Allahabad University and Dr. (Mrs.) Sunita Bhutani who rendered valuable assistance to me from time to time. Thanks are also due to Dr. V.M. Nagpaul and Dr. (Mrs.) Sudesh Nagpaul whose suggestions at different occasions proved to be quite useful. My thanks remain incomplete if I make no mention of Doctors Vijay Kakkar and Sangita Kakkar, Shri Sunil Bhatia and Smt. Sumita Bhat who by their utmost sympathy kept me on the right track towards success. Shri Manu Chandra and Smt. Renu Chandra deserves special thanks as they kept me free from domestic worries to enable me to devote all my time to the project in hand.

Jagdish Chandra Sharma

Contents

1
Introduction

Some people think that India is not a country but a sub-continent, not a nation but a plurality of nations. For most of us India is a country, a nation, a federation though with a unitary bias. India, as a matter of fact, like Russia, is a nation of multi-lingual, multi-racial and multi-religious people. It is a nation composed of many nationalities. The outward diversity conceals within it the strong chord of cultural unity. "But it is interesting and rather wonderful to think of this long range and continuity of Indian culture and civilization, right from the dawn of history, through long ages, down to us."[1] Our country having been welded into a Federation in 1950, when the Indian Constitution was introduced, bears a resemblance with Russia, turning a unitary system into a Federation. But it has nothing in common with the Russian political system. On the other hand, it possesses some features in common with the American system. The political system that our forefathers chose to adopt in 1947 resembles mostly that of Britain, a unitary state. Our plural society having no monolithic communist organisation is bound to have a multi-party system.

Our ancestors with full sense of responsibility introduced in 1950 through the Indian Constitution a hybrid democratic system borrowing from America and heavily from Britain.

India might have had a long record of monarchy but she has never been alien to democracy, if by democracy we mean, "it is the temper of peaceful discussion. It is the temper of arriving at decisions after peaceful discussions which are adhered to by even those who disagree. It is the way of majority functioning, tempered by the minority, and taking into consideration the feelings of the minority."[2] Indian society like that of the United Kingdom has been democratic in character. The core of the teachings of all the reformers and leaders has been democratic ideals *i.e.* brotherhood and equality. It was this spirit that motivated our national leaders to introduce democracy despite the stout opposition by some. Dr. Ambedkar, Chairman of the Drafting Committee on the Indian Constitution, also described democracy as the 'top dressing soil'. Whether the nursling will grow into a tree taking deep roots in the Indian soil, he was skeptical about it. Generally, most of the leaders concurred on the acceptance of democracy. The proceedings of the Constituent Assembly debates show that the tide was favourably tilted in its favour. The Indian masses though poverty-stricken and illiterate were trusted with the most difficult of arts of democracy.

Historians like Altekar and Beni Prasad have tried to prove that there was a time when many republics existed in India. During the Vedic period many republics flourished in different parts of India. Even after the *Mahabharata* many republics appeared in different regions of Bharat. Even when republican states disappeared by the 5th Century A.D., democratic institutions in the form of "*Gram Panchayats*" and "*Paur Sabhas*" remained as vestiges of democracy. The vitality of village *Panchayats* as late as 1853 is testified by Charles Metcalf, the Governor of the then North West Province (modern U.P.) of British India, who described the self-governing villages of Uttar Pradesh as "republics in miniature".[3] "These villages were almost independent and were governed by their elected *Panchayats*."[4]

Different forms of government including democracy

were tried by the Indians long before anything of the kind was even conceived by the ancient Greeks and Romans. That is why Will Durant considers "Mother India" to be the mother of democracy as well.

An ancient republic had '*Sabha*' and '*Samiti*', two popular bodies which assisted the Vedic kings in the art of government. Both the institutions were called "twin daughters of Prajapati". From *Sabha* to the present Lok Sabha is a long journey.

The chronicles relating to Alexander's invasion bear out the fact that at the time Alexander invaded India in the 4th century B.C. a number of republics existed in the Punjab and Sindh, which offered such a stiff resistance to the Greek forces that the latter rebelled and refused to go any further. "It is interesting to observe that these Bactrian and Turki rulers in parts of India did not make much difference to Indo-Aryan society. These rulers, being Buddhist, followed the Buddhist Church organisation, which was itself based on the old Indo-Aryan plan of democratic village communities. Thus India continued to be, even under these rulers, largely a collection of self-governing village communities or republics, under the central power."[5]

Lord Buddha was also convinced about the true democratic character of the republics which existed in his time. He was a friend of kings but he liked the republican administrations. "As a matter of fact, he modelled his own monastic order on the broad-based democratic policy of the republics."[6]

The republican states disappeared from the Indian soil after 4th century A.D. but the republican tradition continued.

The Indian political thinkers never visualized an omnipotent state seeking to guide and control every aspect of man's life nor was it divorced from ethical and moral values that governed the life of the people in society. "The aim and purpose of state was to promote *Dharma*, moral and ethical basis of every individual's behaviour in society; *Artha*, the economic welfare; *Karma*, the satisfaction of human urges; and *Moksha*, the spiritual end of life."[7] J. L. Nehru expresses similar feelings. "It is interesting, however, to see that the idea of kingship in ancient India meant service of the people. There was no divine right of kings, no autocratic power. And if the king misbehaved, his people had the right to remove him and put another in his place."[8]

All this belongs to very remote period of history the record whereof is not available. The period with a record reveals that the emphasis has always been on the strong but benevolent monarchy. There had been '*Chakravarti*' kings in the past. It was considered to be a matter of great pride and jubilation for a king to attain to that much-coveted status. It implied a strong centre, and a strong centre meant a prosperous and glorious India. It was a common experience that a weak centre foreboded a chaotic and degenerate India.

In ancient times when communications were difficult and education was quite limited there was little scope for frequent experiments in the political field. Even then Indians ventured to launch republics which lasted for centuries, monarchy was the only system that ensured unity, prosperity and peace. There appeared many enlightened kings on the national scene, who did not stand in the way of progress. India under such monarchs made abiding contribution to human civilization. "These men who could rise to the loftiest heights of philosophical speculation, produced immortal works of art and literature, and contributed significantly to the advancement of science and technology, were, however, content to advocate monarchy as the best form of Government."[9] They did so under a compelling civil and military necessity. A vast and wealthy country frequently exposed to external aggressions and internal disruptions needed an authority that could act swiftly and decisively. The political thinkers of the time perceived that only a mighty king could perform the yeoman's task of controlling this vast land riven by religious, caste and linguistic rivalries. It goes to the credit of our forefathers that side by side of kingship they produced a sizable number of republics which flourished in different parts of the country for over one thousand years till 400 A.D. These republics, however, remained confined to small areas. None of them could acquire an all-India character. The business in such states was conducted through popular assemblies where free and frank discussions were held. There was liberty but no brilliance and glory. "It may be said with much truth that polity of the republics of ancient and medieval India answered to Abraham Lincoln's famous definition of democracy, namely, government of the people, by the people, for the people."[10]

Kautilya who wrote about statecraft in his *Arthashastra* advocated the rule by one strong personality because it was his belief that a monarchical state was far better than a state controlled by a multitude of deputies. On the issue of government he anticipated Hegel, the German political thinker, by many centuries.

Early Aryans did not believe in the divinity of kings. The responsibilities of the rulers of the earlier period were strictly contractual. The chief was honoured and maintained comfortably for leading his community in war and for keeping peace within during peace time. But the centre of power shifted with change in time. The emperors of the Mauryan period had little in common with their remote Vedic ancestors. The Mauryan kings declared themselves to be higher than ordinary mortals and adopted the title of *Devanamapriya* or beloved of gods, thus making them look like semi-divine beings.

Royal divinity is openly advocated in works like the Epics and the Laws of Manu. The exaltation of monarchy has scriptural support as was the case everywhere in the world. It was no wonder that out of historical needs it had transformed itself into a part of national tradition.

Despite emphasis on monarchy, ancient India's political thinkers never favoured a tyrant on the throne who could claim divine right to misgovern. They always insisted that the king must be the first servant of the people. It was imperative that the king be guided by a body of ministers headed by a strong prime minister. Chanakya was such a powerful prime minister of Chandragupta Maurya. He was the real architect of the Mauryan empire. In spite of his high position he regarded his post as a trust and never exploited it for his self-aggrandisement. He refused to live in palatial mansions, preferred a hut (like a true servant of the people) which was often visited by the emperor for personal consultations. The prime ministers and the ministers were usually able men who took the oath to serve the king and the people loyally. Akbar had a talented team of ministers who actually made him Akbar the Great. Chandragupta also had a gifted team of ministers called *nav-ratna* (nine diamonds). Kalidas the immortal poet of Sanskrit was one of them.

> "India would never have attained the summit of civilization if the government of the land had been a nightmare of oppression. Her contribution to science and technology, to medicine and astronomy has substantially advanced human knowledge in these realms."[11]

Let me quote Prof. Basham who recalled what Syrian astronomer monk Severus Sebokt wrote about India in 662 A. D. "I shall now speak of the knowledge of the Hindus.... of their subtle discoveries in the science of astronomy—discoveries even more ingenious than those of the Greeks and Babylonians—of their rational system of mathematics, or of their method of calculation which no words can praise strongly enough. I mean the system of using nine symbols. If these things were known by the people who think they alone have mastered the sciences because they speak Greek, they would perhaps be convinced, though a little late in the day, that other folk, not only Greeks, but men of a different tongue, knew something as well as they."

It was not for nothing that the civilization of the Hindus spread to many parts of the world, enriching and enlarging the local cultures of one-fourth of the human race. This shows there is nothing wrong with any form of government if the show is managed well. We remember Pope's following lines:

> For the forms of Government let fools contest;
> What'er is best administer'd is best;"

India rose to great heights under enlightened despots like Asoka the Great. Such like kings accelerated considerably the social, religious, economic and cultural well-being of the Indian people. Monarchy became blameworthy only when there was no central ruler and the multiplication of small kings generated a cockpit of competing sovereignties and exposed the country to foreign invasions.

England is still a monarchy but it is called the mother of democracy. England also strode like a colossus on the map of the world under the patronage of monarchs. The English built an empire on which the sun never set. They became the centre of the world. London was one time the virtual capital of the world, guiding the politics of other countries. All these rapid strides in politics, religion, economic order and culture became possible under kings. Even now this politically awakened country cannot do without the crown. Walter Bagehot spoke about the British monarchy thus: "The use of the Queen, is a dignified capacity, is incalculable. Without her in England, the present English government would fail and pass away."[12]

Oddly enough, all the King's powers have fallen in the hands of the British Prime Minister who can be easily dubbed as the 'Elected King'.

Truly speaking, kingship has been the most intelligible government in the world, most so in India where there is even now only thirty per cent literacy. The common man easily understands and puts no question if we tell him that the President or the Prime Minister is the king of India, as the case may be. Walter Bagehot writing about monarch says:

> "The mass of mankind understands it, and they hardly anywhere in the world understand any other. Will you be governed by a king, or will you be governed by a constitution. The inquiry comes out like this. Will you be governed in a way you understand or will you be governed in a way you do not understand?"[13]

It is quite appropriate to cite from *'The Economist'* to confirm the virility of monarchical democracy. "The two (Holland and Belgium) monarchies have kept their societies rather better together despite the inconveniently frequent interregna when they cannot have a government, while in republican Italy the wrangling over the formation of new governments tends to make society's splits already worse."[14] The advent of the Britishers in India was the important landmark in the history of India. For the first time personal rule was replaced by a government of laws. It proved to be a blessing in disguise. The warring principalities had turned India into a land of lawlessness and anarchy. The Britishers brought about unity and peace.

Liberal leaders like Raja Ram Mohun Roy and Gopal Krishna Gokhale openly hailed the establishment of the British Raj in India.

In a small country the things tend to evolve towards

a sort of decisiveness but in a big and pluralistic society as of India the things have got to be pushed towards finality. Upto certain extent the imposition has to be resorted to in the initial stage. The Aryans imposed Sanskrit and the cultural unity evolved in due course of time. The Muslims imposed Persian and again a new synthetic order evolved. The Britishers forced English down our throats and a new pattern of political and cultural unity evolved in due course of time. Now Hindi is in the waiting when will the consensus in favour of Hindi evolve, God alone knows? It may take centuries.

Before coming to the topic 'Why Parliamentary Government?' I shall be failing in my duty if I do not mention the most essential steps towards constitutional development upto 1947. The birth of the National Congress in 1885 was an important milestone on the road towards self-rule.

The Home Rule Scheme of 1889 formulated by the Congress is historically an important document because it was drafted under the presidentship of Sir William Wedderburn. A skeleton constitutional scheme providing for the creation of representative institutions in India was drawn up at the Congress session. According to that scheme both the central and provincial legislatures were to consist of members not less than one-half of whom were to be elected. All elections were to be by ballot.

Constitutional Framework in India's Parliamentary and Federal System in a Multi-Party Set-up

The Constitution of India Bill 1896 is a comprehensive document. It was probably inspired by Lokmanya Bal Gangadhar Tilak and was acclaimed by Annie Besant, the gifted Irish woman who had made the Indian cause her own, as the Home Rule Bill for India. It envisaged a bicameral legislature to be called the Parliament of India whose members were to be the representatives of the "Indian Nation". It was laid down that all the supreme legislative judicial and executive powers should be vested in the national legislature. The executive functions were to be exercised by a cabinet of ministers under the chairmanship of a Prime Minister.

Under the Government of India Act 1919, the principle of provincial autonomy was narrowly recognised. The Indians were sought to be associated though grudgingly, for the first time, with the administration. An opening was made for further increased participation by the Indians in the government of their country.

The Swaraj Constitution (1928-1929) embodied the proposal, "there was to be an Executive Council consisting of the Prime Minister and not more than six ministers."

The Government of India Act 1935 is the most important document which has left its deeply indelible impress on the present Constitution of India. It was a cunning move by the British diplomats. "It made an impossible attempt at convincing Indians that all that they demanded has been conceded to them, while telling the British public at home that nothing substantial has been lost."[15]

Under the Government of India Act 1935 barely 30 million people were enfranchised in 1937. This number rose to 40 million during the 1946 elections which provided the basis for representation in the Constituent Assembly. The provincial autonomy in full was conceded for the first time. The next step was now the national autonomy. The constitutional development set in motion by this Act culminated in the Government of India Act 1947, creating two dominions, the Dominion of India and the Dominion of Pakistan.

The 15th August, 1947 introduced a new turn in the efforts at constitution-making. The previous constitutional developments were marked by discussions by the British representatives sitting in the

British Parliament at Westminster Abbey. The new development was to be characterised by deliberations by the Indian representatives sitting in the Indian legislature in New Delhi. After a humiliating experience of 200 years, the Indians could breathe in free air for the first time. They became the architect of their own fate. On the battlefield of the Constituent Assembly after winning the first battle of democracy the warring camps engaged themselves in the second fight for the parliamentary type of government. "There was a considerable body of opinion in the Constituent Assembly of India in favour of the Presidential system."[16]

K. T. Shaw addressing the Constituent Assembly on December 10, 1948 argued that there should be as little dependence between these two bodies as possible. "The Executive is in a position to influence the votes of the members by the number of gifts or favours they have in their power to confer in the shape of offices, in the shape of consulships, and any number of offices which the Executive has in its power to bestow."[17]

Commending the American type, the professor suggested that the powers of the Indian President should be clearly defined. He did not, however, contemplate the abrogation of the parliamentary system and made his position clear by saying that the President should function only in Emergency. He was, however, of the opinion that this high dignitary should not be a 'mere gramophone' of the Prime Minister.

Along with K. T. Shaw a good number of members of the Constituent Assembly believed that a powerful national executive, independent of the legislature, could muster sufficient strength to secure and promote stability.

K. Santhanam was also at first in favour of the Presidential type, but later, like others, on second thought, he veered round to the Parliamentary type. The Parliamentary government had also been criticised on the ground that the Parliamentary government has been replaced by cabinet dictatorship and the latter has succumbed to bureaucracy which thrives behind the cloak of ministerial responsibility.

Gandhi had once called Parliament a 'Prostitute' and the staunch Gandhians in accordance therewith had opposed the Parliamentary form of government. Their plans for a decentralized system were, however, too vague to be seriously considered.

The matter was, anyhow, fully debated and the majority in the end gave its verdict in favour of the Parliamentary form. Dr. K. M. Munshi has given the following reasons for the adoption of the Parliamentary type:

> "The strongest government and the most elastic executive have been found to be in England and that is because the executive powers vest in the cabinet supported by a majority in the Lower House which has financial powers under the Constitution. As a result, it is the rule of the majority in the legislature, for it supports its leaders in the cabinet, which advise the head of the state, namely, the King. The King is thus placed above the party. He is made really the symbol of the impartial dignity of the Constitution. The Government in England is found strong and elastic under all circumstances. We must not forget a very important fact that, during the last hundred years, Indian public life has largely drawn upon the traditions of British Constitutional Law. Most of us have looked up to the British model as the best. For the last thirty or forty years, some kind of responsibility has been introduced in the governance of the country. Our Constitutional traditions have become Parliamentary and we have now all our provinces functioning more or less on the British model. Today, the Dominion Government of India is functioning as a full-fledged parliamentary government. After this experience, why should we

> go back upon the tradition that has been built for over a hundred years and try a novel experiment?"[18]

R. N. Mishra argues, "It ensures harmony between the Executive and the Legislature. The responsibility of the Executive is daily and periodic. The daily assessment is done by members of parliament through questions, resolutions, no-confidence motions, adjournment motions and debates on addresses. Periodic assessment is done by the electorate at the time of elections."[19]

Dr. Ambedkar while making comparison remarked,

> "Under the non-Parliamentary system of government the assessment of responsibility was periodic. Where the Parliament system of government prevailed the assessment of responsibility of the executive was both daily and periodic. The daily assessment or responsibility was far more effective than the periodic."[20]

Dr. Alladi Krishnaswamy Aiyar, that Vedic Brahman with astonishing memory, made an impassioned plea for parliamentary democracy and concluded: "The Union Constitution Committee and this Assembly have all adopted what may be called the Cabinet system of government. The infant democracy could not afford to take the risk of a perpetual cleavage, feud or conflict or threatened conflict between the executive and the legislature.... there were many Indian states which would form units of the Indian federation and there was no intention of "effacing" the rulers from the various states. Those rulers should not again be vested with real executive powers free from the control of the legislatures because that would be against the marked tendency of the times.[21]

It was widely believed that the Prime Minister and the whole Cabinet are members of the legislature. The conflict between authority wielding the executive power and the legislature is reduced to the minimum.

The adoption of Parliamentary system was not a surprise for the Indians. The Indians because of their long association with the Britishers had acquired a belief in the soundness and responsible character of this system. "The draft constitutions published by groups of the Left, Centre, and Right,—those of 'the' Marxists M. N. Roy, of the Socialist Party, and of the Communal Hindu Sabha—were also all Parliamentary centralised institutions (M. N. Roy, *Constitution for Free India*, 1944, Hindu Mahasabha Constitution of Hindustan Free State, and Socialist Party, Draft Constitution of Indian Republic, 1948, after the breakaway from Congress).[22]

The Indians by their long association with the Britishers could not develop a strong liking for the American type. Hanson and Douglas remark:

> "Most delegates, however, shared the British prejudice against an American type Presidential system, with its rigid system of powers, and most looked to Britain as a model."[23]

As the Constitution started working the controversy went into the background but did not die down. In the beginning of 1975 before 25 June (the day on which Emergency was declared), the controversy again raised its ugly head. The Allahabad High Court decision declaring Indira Gandhi's election null and void had created a shocking stir in the country. It rocked the ruling party to its very foundation. There were suggestions from some members of the ruling party to have a limited dictatorship for 10 years. As a sequel thereto, Emergency was proclaimed on 25th of June, 1975 letting loose a reign of terror on the peace-loving people of India, especially in the northern belt. In the general elections of 1977 the poor, exploited and the harassed people of this country exhibited a fine sense of democratic revenge and made full use of the opportunity to punish the guilty men of the Emergency, dauntless of the latter's entrenched power. "The great tribute to our people is the last elections in which with all the authority vested in the ex-Prime Minister, the people rose in their wrath and indignation and threw her out with most of her henchmen and sycophants."[24]

Again, the old controversy on the Parliamentary or the Presidential type has been revived by those who feel that the Parliamentary type has failed. They advance the plea that the Parliamentary type could not prevent the reign of terror and the emergence of a totally subservient Parliament. They perhaps tend to forget that it was not the Parliamentary Government that had created all the trouble. It was rather the provision of emergency that opened the gates of hell, and this provision was borrowed from the Weimar Constitution of Germany that led the Germans towards Fascism, and not from the Constitution of Britain that has led the Britishers towards more and more of democracy.

Prime Minister in India—A Historical Background

Before Emergency there were some doubts lurking in the mind of every Indian that democracy had not taken deep roots in the Indian soil and that it was just a 'top-dressing soil'. But after the general elections of 1977 all those doubts have vanished. The elections have proved beyond doubt that the people have politically grown up to give right decisions at the right moment, that the money power is lessening and the pressure tactics are enervating. M. C. Chagla states:

> "We have had free and fair elections which have evoked the admiration of the whole world, and in these elections, our people, on the whole mostly illiterate, have shown a practical and shrewd

> common sense and have known how to separate wheat from the chaff."[25]

Mr. Chagla ascribes the successful working of the Parliamentary Government to the unitary character of the Indian polity born of the existence of one single powerful party, *i.e.*, the Indian National Congress:

> "Britain is a small and united country with a strong central government. The Prime Minister is much more powerful than the President.... In India we have had the parliamentary form of government since independence. It is important to remember that Congress as a monolithic body ruled the country. Almost all the states had Congress Chief Ministers and their appointment was really made in Delhi. Even members of the legislative were selected in the capital. Federalism was observed more in the breach than the observance. For all practical purposes India was a unitary government."[26]

Nevertheless, he feels that with the onset of Janata Party the unitary character of Indian polity is in danger and as an offset he pleads a change for the better. He, therefore, suggests an alternative in the form of Presidential government.

> "With the adoption of the Presidential system, the scramble for office will also go, because a seat in the Legislature will not lead to the Cabinet. The party system will become considerably modified and we will have the legislators attending to legislation and matters of policy rather than indulging in abuses and in throwing microphones at each other.... Therefore, the Presidential system will undoubtedly lead to better administration and less infighting among the parties and a less indecent scramble for tickets."[27]

On the other hand, Shri V. M. Tarkunde has his objections to the Presidential system. "If you want a more efficient and dynamic government, even if the government be less democratic and be always prone to convert itself into a dictatorship, you may vote in favour of the Presidential system. I will not. I believe in the wisdom of the old saying, which had become popular in the days of the British rule, that a good government is no substitute for self-government....once elected and installed in office, the President (under the Presidential type) is answerable to no one during his term of four or five years. He can be removed only by the cumbrous and impracticable method of impeachment....The Cabinet system, despite its defects, provides for a relatively greater answerability of those in power. The Cabinet must retain the confidence of the legislature, not so the President.... The American Presidency has been rightly described by some writers as "elected kingship". Democracy is very different from kingship, elected or otherwise... In addition to motive, an Indian President would have a better opportunity to establish a dictatorial regime....He would also be aided by the surviving cultural tradition which prefers *Ram Rajya* to *Swarajya* benevolent dictatorship to democracy.... Living through a further period of political instability is the price we must pay in order to keep alive the prospect of freedom."[28]

This controversy will go on as long as the instability is there to cause us anxiety. After the resignation of Morarjibhai Desai as Prime Minister on July 15, 1979, the controversy has again raised its head as no party in the Lok Sabha commands absolute majority to form a stable government. "In the light of the recent political developments and the consequent instability at the centre, a careful look is needed into the question whether the Westminster model is suitable to India....we may perhaps come to the conclusion that a Presidential system based on the French model would give greater stability to our country and make the Government more effective."[29] The general proclivity, however, goes in favour of the Parliamentary type and this settles the matter for the time being. After the General Elections of 1980 and with the Congress (I) returning to power the controversy was again sought to be raised but the effort was abandoned soon in face of the strong opposition by the press and the public.

Under the Hindu kings or emperors, there was always to be found a very important minister who could be called the first minister or the Prime Minister. In Sanskrit he was called *Maha Mantri.* During the Mughal period the highest repository of the king's conscience and confidence was titled *Wazir-i-azam.* During the British period there was only a Governor-General or a Viceroy who was an autocrat but not an emperor as he was appointed by the King of England for a fixed term. He was invariably an Englishman and was assisted by a Council in administering the country. The Council was also composed of all Englishmen. It was only later and that too under duress from Indian side that some Indians were also nominated thereon. This Council was called the 'Viceroy's Executive Council' and in no way his Council of Ministers, hence there was no Prime Minister and no Parliament.

The British Government under The Cabinet Mission Plan had authorised the Governor-General in India to establish an interim Government with the representatives of the political parties as early as possible. On July 22, 1946 Lord Wavell, the then Governor-General, communicated to the Congress and the Muslim League a new proposal for the formation of the National Government consisting of 14 members, 6 representing Congress and 5 representing Muslim League. The Congress accepted the proposal. Thus on August 24, 1946, J.L. Nehru was invited to form the Government. On September 2, 1946, the following persons formed the National Government: Shri

Jawaharlal Nehru, Sardar Vallabh Bhai Patel, Dr. Rajendra Prasad, Shri Asif Ali, Chakravarti Shri Rajagopalachari, Shri Sarat Chandra Bose, Mr. John Mathai, Sardar Baldev Singh, Sir Shaffat Ahmad, Shri Jagjivan Ram, Syed Ali Zaheer, Shri C.H. Bhabha.

On the 25th of October, 1946, five members of the National Government resigned to make room for the Muslim League members. Pandit Nehru was only the Vice-President of the Council of Ministers. There was, therefore, no Prime Minister in 1946. Pandit Nehru began to be called Prime Minister only after the 15th August, 1947, after India became a free country. It was only the Constitution of India which was enforced on the 26th of January, 1950, that gave him the legal right to be dubbed the Prime Minister of India.

REFERENCES

1. Nehru, J.L., *India's Quest*, Asia Publishing House, 1963, p. 16.
2. Nehru, J.L., Address of Welcome at Commonwealth Parliamentary Conference 1957 — A souvenir — India Branch Commonwealth Parliamentary Association, New Delhi.
3. Madhok, Balraj, *Murder of Democracy*, S.Chand & Co., 1973, p. 6.
4. Nehru, J.L., *India's Quest*, Asia Publishing House, p. 21.
5. *Ibid.*, p. 52.
6. Kulkarni, V.B., *My Country and My Rulers*, Jaico Press Pvt. Ltd., Bombay, 1977, p. 2.
7. Madhok, Balraj, *Murder of Democracy*, S. Chand & Co., 1973, p. 6.
8. Nehru, J.L., *India's Quest*, Asia Publishing House, 1963, p. 32.
9. Kulkarni, V.B. *op. cit.*, p. 1.
10. *Ibid.*, p. 2.
11. *Ibid.*, p. 4.
12. Bagehot, Walter, *The English Constitution*, Thomas Nelson & Sons, 1872, pp. 106-7.
13. *Ibid.*, p. 112.
14. *The Economist*, November 14, 1973.

15. Sharma, Siri Ram, *Parliamentary Government in India*, Central Book Depot, Allahabad, 1969, p. 7.
16. Rau, B.N., *Address to the Indian Council of World Affairs*, August 10, 1949.
17. Constituent Assembly Debates Official Report, Vol. VII, 4.11.48 to 8.1.49, pp. 962-963.
18. Mahajan, Vidya Dhar, *Constitutional History of India* (including the National Movement), S. Chand & Co., 1971, p. 151.
19. Mishra, R.N., *The President of the Indian Republic*—1964, p. 11.
20. Constituent Assembly Debates—November 4, 1948, p. 33.
21. Constituent Assembly Debates, Vol. VII, pp. 974 to 986 — December 10, 1948.
22. Austin, Granville, *The Indian Constitution—Corner Stone of a Nation*, Oxford University Press, 1972, p. 48.
23. Hanson & Douglas, *India's Democracy*, p. 96.
24. Chagla, M.C., Should we have Presidential form of Government? *The Illustrated Weekly of India*, 27 August, 1978.
25. *Ibid.*
26. *Ibid.*
27. *Ibid.*
28. Tarkunda, V.M., Objections to Presidential System, *The Illustrated Weekly of India*, August 27, 1978.
29. Palkivala, N.A., *The Hindustan Times*, August 18, 1979, p. 5.

2
The Prime Minister and the Party

Prime Minister's Relations with the Party

In a democracy we cannot think of a Prime Minister without any party at his back. Even dictators came to power in different countries with the help of the parties. Hitler captured power with the help of the Nazi Party in Germany. The Fascist Party in Italy catapulted Benito Mussolini to power nexus. In India it was the Indian National Congress that gave us three Prime Ministers, Pandit Jawaharlal Nehru, Lal Bahadur Shastri and Indira Gandhi. When the Congress Party became weaker and lost at the polls in 1977, Indira Gandhi had to resign the prime ministership, howsoever powerful she might appear to have become. The Janata Party carried on the crest of popular wave swept the polls in 1977 general elections. Out of this power game emerged the new Prime Minister, Morarjibhai Desai. We cannot conceive of Morarji as Prime Minister without the Janata Party at his back. The Prime Minister is fully conscious of this fact and is, therefore, always keenly anxious to have a firm hold over the party machine which is the prime source of his strength.

But the party has its own organisation and its own chairman. If the Prime Minister and the party President work in amity, there is no trouble; if they cannot go on together, the clash is bound to occur.

It is a well-known fact that the Parliamentary wing of every party elects its leader to lead it in Parliament. The leader of the majority party is usually invited by the Head of the State to form the government. The party President of the majority party has his hands on the lever of power and is the most important determining factor in the selection of the leader of the Parliamentary wing or, in other words, the selection of the Prime Minister.

Before Indian independence the Congress Party occupied a unique position in the national life. Most of the freedom-fighters subscribing to different political ideologies gathered under its banner to fight for national freedom. The common goal of national freedom kept them all united. It was not a political party. It was a national organisation, a national movement embracing within its ambit all the nationalist forces. It was only after independence that its character changed. But the people of India were slow to perceive the change. The people could not shake themselves off from the identification of the Congress with the nation. That is why the Congress Party dominated the political scene upto the first quarter of 1977.

After 15th August, 1947, Pandit Nehru became the first Prime Minister of India. The Congress presidency still carried a high status and the conflict for supremacy between the party President and the Prime Minister had been sparked off by Acharya J. B. Kripalani in 1946. "At the centre, the Prime Minister and the Congress President tended to regard each other at best with suspicion and at worst with outright hostility. Kripalani who succeeded Nehru in the Congress presidency when the latter became Prime Minister, tried to insist that political decisions should be made in consultation with the Working Committee, a body which he tried to insulate from governmental influence by limiting the number of ministers among its members to one-third of the total."[1] The Prime Minister of India, Pandit Jawaharlal Nehru was not only the leader of the majority party but also one of the national heroes who had successfully piloted the ship of Indian struggle to the port of freedom. He had a charisma of his own and was held in high esteem and affection by the people of India. He, therefore, forced Kripalani to resign the presidentship of the Indian National Congress.

> "The inevitable conflict between two heads, the head of the Government *i.e.* the Prime Minister and head of the party became quite evident. Kripalani's successor, Rajendra Prasad, though outwardly complacent, resented the dominance of the Government over the party and asked Patel for an early resolution of this continuing conflict."[2]

In theory the Congress Working Committee was the party's most important decision-making body but practically its status was being eroded. Under Nehru the Central Government initiated policy and implemented it. In this way the new class usurped the functions of the old Working Committee and set the influence of the party President on the wane. This accords with Milovam Djilas, analysis that as the new class grows stronger, the party grows weaker.

Prime Minister's Relations with the Party President

The clash between the Prime Minister and the Congress President again came to the fore when Babu Purushottam Dass Tandon was elected to the presidency. "In the latter months of 1951 Nehru forced a showdown by resigning from the Working Committee."[3]

The rift between Tandon and Nehru over the formation of Congress Working Committee led to serious quarrel. Tandon did not want to include Rafi and Kripalani. Nehru was angry. Rafi left the Congress but remained as Central Minister. He issued statements against the Congress President. Nehru was pressurised into calling for resignation of Rafi. Ajit Prasad Jain who had also resigned was asked to continue as Minister as he had issued no statements. The U. P. Congress passed a resolution urging upon Nehru to demand Ajit Prasad's resignation. Nehru himself resigned from the Congress Working Committee. As a sequel, the whole Congress Working Committee resigned.

Nehru's weapon of resignation did the job. Tandon seeing through the delicacy of the situation tendered his own resignation. At a special meeting of the All India Congress Committee in September 1951 Nehru was elected to succeed Tandon.

Until January 1955, Jawaharlal Nehru combined in himself the two posts of Prime Minister and Congress President keeping the party and the Government under his thumb. In itself this was unnecessary for since Patel's death it was clear that Nehru had no rival for supreme power. But Nehru made full use of these four years to create a Congress habit of mind which led the overwhelming bulk to look to the Prime Minister and not to the President of the Congress for political guidance. Thereafter, the Congress President was for all practical purposes a political non-entity. Nehru as Congress President was hailed as the saviour of the party in elections. "Nehru has proved an asset to the party in elections."[4] "Nehru was following a double standard while he himself occupied both the posts (Prime Ministership and Congress Presidency) he forbade the Congress Chief Ministers to hold office in the Pradesh Congress Committees. In 1953 he made the Congress pass a resolution for this purpose. He justified his ban on the ground that "the work of the Chief Ministers was, indeed, a very hard one and merger of two important positions would weaken both the offices....It had the effect of making the party nothing but a tool of his whims and fancies."[5] "His hold over the Congress was perhaps (1951-1964) greater than the Mahatma (1920-1947). He chose each successor President of the Congress Party (Dhebar, Indira Gandhi, Sanjiva Reddy, Sanjivayya and Kamaraj, all of them dancing to his tune)."[6] When Nehru was convinced that he had been accepted as the deity and that the Congress President had lost his fangs, he handed over the Presidency to Shri U. N. Dhebar.

Dhebar was Nehru's man and was content to remain a cypher. "From 1955 until Nehru's death the Congress President functioned as no more than a glorified office boy of the Union Government headed by the Prime Minister."[7] It also weakened the connection between the Congress Parliamentary Party and the Working Committee. It weakened the local or grass-roots level of the organisation. "Whatever Nehru wanted we did. When Nehru wanted C. B. Gupta to be appointed Chief Minister of Uttar Pradesh, we simply had to do it.[8] The subordination of the party boss to the political boss, *i.e.* the Prime Minister, created a stir in the party. Many active workers of the Congress like Vinoba Bhave turned their faces away from the Government.

Indeed, in his book *The Congress Party of India* (Gandhi *vs.* Syndicate) Stanley Kochanek assumed that the conflict had been decided, and that the Prime Minister had, at least in normal times, become the '*de facto*' leader of both party and government.

Dhebar's tenure as President was coming to an end. Nijalingappa was tipped as the likely successor. But Nehru had very subtly floated the idea that Indira Gandhi could be the most suitable candidate for the Presidency. Nehru wanted to avoid any further clash with the Congress Presidency. He, therefore, wanted Indira to occupy the Presidency knowing it fully well that there could be no question of conflict between father and daughter. "She only knew vaguely how far her father had floated the idea which seemed, to the public, to emanate from three stalwarts of the Congress."[9] When he returned to Delhi after his last visit to Dehradun, Uma Shankar Dixit, another "retainer" of the Nehrus, had gone to meet Nehru. One of the points Nehru mentioned to Dixit that evening was about his daughter. "Indu can take decisions. Help her." Kamaraj, the king-maker, is said to have confided to political colleagues and journalists close to him that Nehru had told him, "After me Indira."[10]

Dhebar called an unscheduled meeting of the Working Committee at which Lal Bahadur Shastri, in the presence of Kamaraj, Pant and Nehru, suggested that Mrs. Gandhi should be asked to accept the Congress Presidentship.

Durga Das, the eminent journalist, in his book *India from Curzon to Nehru and After* records :

"Pant, unaware of the background moves, was surprised by Shastri's proposal and said, "But Indiraji is not keeping good health. She must first..." Before he could complete the sentence, Mr. Nehru agitatedly interrupted to say, "There is nothing wrong with Indu's health. She will feel better once she has work to keep herself busy." That ended the argument and attention was next turned to the tricky question of communicating the decision to Nijalingappa. Nehru requested Pant to convey the message to Nijalingappa. Pant in turn entrusted the job to Kamaraj. Kamaraj in his turn suggested that in the circumstances, it would be better if Nijalingappa, Sanjiva Reddy and he issued a joint statement proposing Mrs. Gandhi. He then flew to Madras where the three met and issued the statement.

All this amply shows that Nehru was gravely concerned with the future of his only daughter, who was also a widow with two sons. That was the only way to help her enter the political life of the country. The elevation of his daughter to the Presidency ensured for him a smooth sailing. Nehru, therefore, killed two birds with one stone when he manoeuvred to secure her Congress Presidency. He had had bitter experiences with Acharya Kripalani, Babu P. D. Tandon and was eagerly desirous of leaving no scope for the recrudescence of any such ugly situation. There could be no noticeable difference between Nehru as Prime Minister and Indira as President. The Presidency had come back to Nehrus and all was right.

All suspicions between the Prime Minister and the Congress President were set at rest. There could arise differences of opinion between them but no serious clashes. There was, as a matter of fact, mutual affection and sympathy, an inborn filial desire to get on together. The decisions which she easily secured from her father might have been delayed or could have led to serious rifts if there had been some one else in place of Indira Gandhi.

She firmly declared that "as Congress President I intend to fight the communists (in Kerala) and to throw them out." When she found that Nehru vacillated, she told him plainly that the Prime Minister of India ought to pay heed to the directives of the Congress Party.

Acharya Kripalani in 1946 also wanted the Prime Minister to heed the directives of the party. Nehru and Patel resented this attitude and gave a tough fight to the Acharya resulting in the resignation of the latter. But this time no such awkwardness arose. On the contrary, the Congress President got what she wanted.

> "When Mrs. Gandhi could make no headway with her father, she turned to Pandit Pant, the Home Minister. She won him over to her side by detailing the state of violence which gripped Kerala....Nehru could not withstand the pressure brought on him by his daughter and his closest confidant. On August 1, 1959, the Communist Government was dismissed."[11]

Similarly, on the question of bifurcation of Bombay into Gujarat and Maharashtra she persuaded her father to agree to the vivisection. Her father yielded and the state of Bombay was divided. It was quite clear that the Prime Ministership and Congress Presidency had become family affairs resulting in collaboration and joint ventures. The dictatorial tendency of the Nehrus could brook no second position at any cost.

> "Thanks to Nehru's style of leadership, internal democracy in the Congress Party was already being eroded and clean and healthy contest for leadership was not possible in those circumstances."[12]
>
> "He reduced the position of the Congress President to an appendage and never relaxed his hold over the Congress Party."[13]

Nehru even shut his eyes to the unprincipled politics of Indira as the Congress President. "That Indira as Congress President should authorize an alliance with the Muslim League was regarded as the ultimate in compromised principles. It shocked many, even those who were apprehensive of another communist victory in Kerala."[14]

Evidently Nehru wanted a docile President who could easily reconcile himself or herself to position number two. After Dhebar his daughter was expected to perform the secondary role very well. Upto this point it was all right. But Nehru had a deeper motive to help Indira become President of the Congress. Indira was everything to him, his daughter as well as his son. He was grooming her to succeed him. "Desai was deprived even of his place in the cabinet later in 1963 through the implementation of the controversial Kamaraj plan. The plan was and is still regarded by some as a Machiavellian device by which the Prime Minister eliminated from the government all those who could have had any claim to succeeding him, and thus secured the post for his daughter."[15]

A docile President was certainly in the interest of Nehru's running of administration but in no way in the interest of the nation. "A powerful Congress President was necessary to supplement his authority and where necessary balance it."[16]

Durga Das wrote in his weekly diary in *The Hindustan Times* in June 1957 that "If Mr. Nehru is consciously building up anyone he is building up his daughter." "Durga Das says in his memoirs, published in London in 1969, that he had sensed this when Dhebar nominated her to the Working Committee two years earlier and her elevation to the Presidency of the party confirmed his suspicions."[17]

Nehru, of course, vehemently denied these insinuations and described them as the most fantastic kind of motive hunting on the part of his opponents. "He did not use the camouflage of the Kamaraj plan, he argued, for his mass support gave him the strength to discard any minister, however senior, from the government should he have wished to do so."[18] He further argued that if he had been anxious to strengthen Indira's chances of becoming Prime Minister he should have tried to win them over. He made no such attempt. But the facts speak otherwise. Nehru knew in his heart that he could not have done it as three of the five members of the Syndicate — Ghosh, Reddy and Patil — were anathema to him.

Some say Kamaraj plan was a clever device of punishment. "Nehru punished all those who had raised their hands against him when he was busy installing Kamaraj as Congress President or when he was teetering from the blow in NEFA."[19] Jagjivan Ram, S. K. Patil, Desai and many other central and chief ministers were thrown out of office on the plea of activising the Congress. This cleansing operation came to be known as the Kamaraj plan because he (Kamaraj) was the author. "Desai's comment was that Nehru had removed through the Kamaraj plan all possible successors from the path of his daughter, Indira Gandhi. Nehru was trying to do for Indira in 1963 what his father, Moti Lal, had done for him in 1929, passing on to him the highest office then open to an Indian nationalist, the Congress Presidency."[20] "The Kamarajaed men were not selected by chance. Indeed, there is ample evidence that the multiple perspectives which influence the making of Indian cabinets, at the centre and in the states, operated in the reverse process of purge. Geographical equity is apparent.

Morarji is from Gujarat, Jagjivan Ram from Bihar, Shastri from Uttar Pradesh, Patil from Maharashtra, Gopala Reddy from Andhra and Shrimali from Rajasthan. Ideology played a major part."[21] "Many others echoed the same thought, but never in public because of fear of Nehru."[22]

Since Kamaraj was installed as Congress President by Nehru, he accepted the secondary role in the beginning. On the 8th August, 1963, the Working Committee adopted Kamaraj plan in general terms. Nehru took the lead the following day by seeking permission to resign but as in 1954 and 1958, his colleagues proclaimed his indispensability as Head of the government. Kamaraj told the delegates that he had informed Nehru he would withdraw the proposal if Panditji insisted on resigning S.K. Patil, the Bombay city party leader, echoed the same sentiment by "hailing Nehru as leader of leaders, who must remain there (as Prime Minister) till the country gets out of all difficulties."[23]

Later on, after the Chinese invasion Nehru became weaker and weaker providing enough scope for Kamaraj to grow in stature. "A combination of circumstances had propelled Kamaraj, the Congress President, into a position of invidious prominence."[24]

Mr. Shastri who had been turned out under the Kamaraj plan from the Cabinet, was invited by Nehru after some time to join the Cabinet again. Nehru had to yield to the pressure exercised on him. "According to some sources, the ailing Prime Minister had been bullied by the 'Syndicate' into restoring Shastri to the Cabinet against his own inclinations."[25]

Party Choosing the Prime Minister

After the death of Nehru, Kamaraj played a very prominent part in the selection of the Prime Minister. He met many M.Ps. and Chief Ministers and declared that all had favoured Lal Bahadur Shastri as the most suitable candidate for the post of the Prime Minister. Morarjibhai severely criticized the consensus method used by Kamaraj. He even accused Kamaraj of manipulations to deprive him of what was rightfully his. Kamaraj shot into prominence as a king-maker. The Syndicate gave full support to Kamaraj in selecting Lal Bahadur Shastri. They wanted to regain the powers of the Congress Presidency which Nehru had so forcefully grabbed. They thought Lal Bahadur Shastri, a small, short, fragile and humble man, would remain under their thumb if they selected him. They were glad that the docile-looking man would be prepared to play the second fiddle. But their gladness was short-lived. Soon after becoming Prime Minister Shastri began to assert himself. He pushed the Syndicate to the wall and made them realise that Prime Minister was the Prime Minister and that he was bound to remain so. The primacy of the Prime Minister was established once more.

Shastri's death gave them a new hope. "Shastri's death at Tashkent once again roused the hopes of the party leaders, now collectively called the Syndicate, of regaining their hold over the administration, to install their own pliable instrument at the top. They had burnt their fingers once, had miscalculated the pliability of Shastri, burdening themselves with a Prime Minister who, though physically short, showed immense political maturity and strength, had virtually pushed them to the wall forcing them to content themselves with a secondary role."[26]

Gulzari Lal Nanda the acting Prime Minister again revived his hope that the patronage which he had earned because of his pliability would help him to reach the highest office. This hope got the fillip from his belief that men in the party had successively found themselves pushed into the background by two domineering, dynamic prime ministers. "In this reckoning, he failed to note that even the party leaders, however much their own self-interest demanded the installation of a docile man as Prime Minister, would not go in for one with no individual appeal of his own."[27]

After Lal Bahadur comes Indira Gandhi. Indira could not have become the Prime Minister but for the most active and enthusiastic support of Kamaraj the then Congress President. The Syndicate selected her as the most submissive and pliable a candidate, the darling niece of the uncles. The uncles did not know what they were doing. This time they committed the grievous blunder of their life by selecting a woman who had Nehru's blood in her veins minus the Nehru's cultured brain. "She being the daughter of her father, could not think of sharing power with others. She was in search of an opportunity."[28]

Anyhow, she was docile in the beginning as she was not free to do as she liked. She could not exercise full freedom in the making of her first Cabinet. Mrs. Gandhi was particularly keen to remove Nanda from the crucial Home Ministry....She intended instead to give the Home portfolio to Swaran Singh, while herself taking over the latter's External Affairs. Although she stuck to her own plans till the eleventh hour, Nanda was adamant in his desire to retain Home and Kamaraj was at his back. Gandhi gave way and told Nanda he could retain Home portfolio. Nijalingappa said that "her attitude would be one of democratic approach to national problems and that collective leadership would prevail."[29]

Indira Gandhi was conscious of her helplessness. Even states did not listen to her advice. When the United Left Front of opposition parties in West Bengal threatened to hold a general strike on March 10 to protest against the Government's food policy and to demand the release of arrested opposition leaders, Mrs. Gandhi visited Calcutta and advised the Congress Chief Minister of West Bengal to release the arrested leaders and to adopt a conciliatory approach. Her advice was quite good but the local Congress leadership paid no heed to it. As a result, violent rioting broke out in Calcutta on a scale that necessitated army intervention. At last the local leaders realised the wisdom of her advice to adopt the conciliatory method, but now it was too late. Lot of destruction and damage was already done.

Gradually, she began to muster strength to fight all those who stood in her way. She made up her mind on devaluation of rupee. "According to Asoka Mehta, she was even prepared, in the event of opposition from her colleagues, to re-shuffle the Cabinet and had already seen the President in this connection. Taken unawares and unable to fourmulate any coherent alternatives, Mrs. Gandhi's colleagues bowed to her wishes and to the persuasive arguments of her economic advisers."[30]

Kamaraj was upset when he learnt of the Prime Minister's decision. He took steps to call for a meeting of the Congress Working Committee to discuss the decision before it was officially announced. Indira was determined to assert her independence.

Kamaraj on his part was adamant on a showdown. He wanted to punish her and her advisers. He declared that the proposal would be debated freely on July 6 when the Congress Parliamentary Party was scheduled to meet. Criticism of devaluation had become synonymous with criticism of the Prime Minister who was openly attacked for not consulting the organisational leadership. Criticism of devaluation was almost unanimous and the Government was clearly on the defensive. Mrs. Gandhi kept silent throwing the onus of explanation on Chaudhary and Asoka Mehta. Not a single Cabinet colleague or Chief Minister came to their aid. According to *Link*, 'The Working Committee' discussion reflected popular feeling on devaluation in clear terms than any opposition rally of protest could have done. While Asoka Mehta was deputed by her to placate Morarji Desai, she took it upon herself to woo the Congress left.

She wanted to drop G.L. Nanda from her Cabinet but

Kamaraj and other members of the Syndicate did not allow her to do so. The Anti-Cow-slaughter agitation gave her the opportunity for which she had been waiting for long. One lakh naked sadhus marched on Parliament to press their demand for banning cow-slaughter. They became unruly and indulged in violence. It was November 1966. Indira lost no time in demanding resignation from Nanda who obliged her. Indira herself took over the Home portfolio on November 9. Later the same night she called to her residence Finance Minister Chaudhary and Commerce Minister Manu Bhai Shah to tell them to their astonishment that she had decided to drop them from the Cabinet. President Radhakrishnan, however, advised her to consult the party leaders.

The leaders when consulted showed their resentment at her bold action. They strongly opposed her intention to drop Chaudhary and Manu Bhai Shah. They equally vehemently opposed her suggestion to give Home to Chavan. As a compromise she appointed Chavan as Home Minister and abandoned her proposal to drop Chaudhary and Manu Bhai. By her action she indicated to the party leaders that she would do what she liked, at the same time she implied that she wanted to avoid confrontation but she would not mind to resort to it if the circumstances warranted.

Mrs. Gandhi possessed an uncanny sense of timeliness. She knew that time had not come for open clashes. In 1967 general elections she wanted Menon to fight election from North Bombay. But S. K. Patil (Bombay Congress Boss) and Morarji Desai were opposed to Menon's candidature and as a sequel thereto Menon's party nomination was rejected. Kamaraj on being persuaded by Indira took the initiative to have the matter referred back to the Central Election Committee. Mrs. Gandhi remained silent at the meeting in order to avoid crossing swords with the Syndicate. Menon was angry at the Prime Minister's weak stand and as a protest seceded from the Congress.

Indira emerged stronger after the ordeal of 1967 general elections. This time she kept her own counsel. In marked contrast to the formation of her first Cabinet in January 1966 she did not consult, at all, the Congress leadership including Kamaraj. She showed the list of her proposed Cabinet to Kamaraj a shortwhile before it was to be submitted to the President. On his (Kamaraj's) queries he was told abruptly that the changes were intended to avoid complications. The only one who enjoyed her confidence was Y. B. Chavan. The composition of the new Cabinet mirrored her increased independence. The general elections also highlighted weakness of the Syndicate as some of the stalwarts were rejected at the polls.

Slowly and slowly Mrs. Gandhi was preparing for the showdown with the Congress President. Dr. Zakir Hussain's candidature for the Presidency of India provided the opportunity. Kamaraj opposed Hussain's candidature. She countered Kamaraj's opposition by entering into negotiation with the Opposition. The Opposition's candidate for the Union Presidency was Subba Rao. She offered to sponsor Subba Rao for the Vice-Presidency if the Opposition supported Dr. Zakir Hussain for the presidency. But Kamaraj being anxious to avoid an open clash with her readjusted his tactics. While withdrawing his opposition to Hussain's candidature he insisted that there must be no deal with the Opposition.

She wanted Kamaraj to relinquish Congress Presidency when the latter's tenure was over. Kamaraj was, however, keen to continue for another term. She vehemently opposed his continuance and had her way. She was for G. L. Nanda to succeed Kamaraj. Now the tussle between the Right and the Left groups in the Congress started. The Right Wing sponsored S. K. Patil as rival contender for the post. As a compromise Mrs. Gandhi had to accept Nijalingappa, a somewhat slow-witted conservative and one of the original members of the Syndicate.

Mrs. Gandhi was not happy with Nijalingappa as the latter acted as uncle to her, and insisted on P.M.'s carrying out the directives from the Congress President. The battle for supremacy became inevitable. With the death of Dr. Zakir Hussain the Union Presidency became vacant. The Syndicate proposed the name of Sanjiva Reddy at a meeting of the Congress Working Committee. She did not like Sanjiva Reddy for some personal reasons. She had some fears that Sanjiva Reddy on becoming the President of India would dismiss her and her Cabinet. Dr. V. V. Giri, meanwhile, resigned as Vice-President and announced his candidature for Presidency. Indira Gandhi decided to support Giri.

On 16 July, 1969 she fired the first shot. "As a dramatic sequence Indira Gandhi as Prime Minister relieved Morarji Desai of the Finance portfolio."[31] She had not forgotten Desai's stand on Bank Nationalisation. "As long as I am the Finance Minister this cannot be implemented. If Prime Minister wants to do it, she will have to change her Finance Minister."[32] On 13 August, 1969, she sought the right of free vote for the Congress members of Parliament and assemblies in the impending Presidential election. On August 17, 1969 Indira Gandhi said that she had asked for a free vote in the Presidential election to avoid a serious split in the party.

On August 18, 1969, Indira sent a letter to all the Congress members of Parliament stating that "the Congress Party had been going through a period of agony during the past few weeks, when senior colleagues in the party had taken different stands. The difference arose not because of any struggle for power, nor as a result of clash of personalities, but because of basic differences on policy which had existed for some....The Prime Minister must have pre-eminent position....I told the leaders that I will fight back."[33] When the Syndicate reminded her of discipline, she retorted, "the Syndicate leaders were talking in terms of discipline in a narrow-minded sense."[34]

Acharya Kripalani severely criticised Indira's stand on conscience vote or free vote. He contended that there could be no conscience voting if political parties were to survive and charged that the Prime Minister had launched on "an adventurist political career," in making a plea for free vote. H. V. Kamath, PSP leader, said that there would be chaos and dictatorship in the country if political parties functioned without discipline. She was aware of the contradiction in her stand. "She was the architect of the 'free vote' and play of 'conscience' if it served her own interests, on the other hand, she was not prepared to extend the same principle to Parliament."[35]

V. V. Giri won the election and became the President of India. The Congress was split. The majority of the Congressmen rallied round the banner of Indira's socialism. The Syndicate came badly mauled out of the battlefield of political tactics. Indira Congress became the real Congress. The king-makers were severely battered. Like the Moghuls she liquidated all those who had helped her in elevation to Prime Ministership. The primacy of the Prime Minister was established once again. After the Bangladesh victory an article in the *Sunday Times* (U. K.) described her the most powerful woman in the world. *Sunday Times Magazine* published a four-page profile of Mrs. Gandhi under the heading "Most Powerful Woman in the World". Phillips Norman, who wrote the feature, said, "Like Joan of Arc who was her heroine, she overcame womanhood to win a great victory and afterwards became woman once more in dignity. She is stronger than Nehru was. Two-thirds majority commanded by her Congress Party in Parliament makes her supreme and silken autocrat. Her enemies no less than her admirers liken her to Trimurti. She is *Brahma*, the creator of the new India; *Vishnu*, the preserver of its democracy; and *Shiva*, the destroyer as she destroyed the army of Pakistan."[36] "She plays politics by the customary rules and, when necessary, makes rules of her own. She foisted Dev Kant Barooah on the Congress *gaddi*. He was a third-rate politician entrusted with the responsibilities of a second-rate politician. He coined a new slogan '*Indira is India. India is Indira.*' All this reflected the stronghold of the Prime Minister on the party machine. The Congress President was now virtually, so to say, in the pocket of the Prime Minister. "The power struggle of 1969 immeasurably weakened the institutions and Mrs. Gandhi instead of strengthening them after victory, accelerated their decay."[37] "Mrs. Margaret Alva a Congress member of the Rajya Sabha, who was a member of the Parliamentary Congress Election Campaign Committee, said she had protested to the Congress President against having to seek out Mr. R. K. Dhawan, Mrs. Gandhi's P.A., every time any election posters were needed. Dhawan evidently controlled the whole operation of the printing of posters and assigned the work to a few printers of his choice. He also controlled the election purse-strings. Any candidate wanting more than the minimum election expense quota laid down by the party had to approach Dhawan. Mrs. Alva offered to resign on the issue but was restrained from doing so by Mr. Barooah. She was among Mrs. Gandhi's friends who was kept away from No. 1, Safdarjang Road by Dhawan."[38]

To win popular acclaim Mrs. Gandhi raised an attractive slogan for the masses, '*Gharibi Hatao*' (Remove Poverty). She took steps to nationalise Banking Business and terminate privy purses to rajas and maharajas.

Now the P. M. was the monarch of all she surveyed. The taste of power smelt pleasantly sweet in her mouth. Indira looked higher and became more and more ambitious. "In the process of removing potential power contenders and weakening their base, Mrs. Gandhi hit at the roots of the already inadequate and weakly embedded institutionalization of political process. Nehru's strongest point was that he was an institution builder. The weakest point of Mrs. Gandhi is that she has totally ignored them. Though Nehru left many gaps and gave inadequate nourishment to these institutions, nevertheless they withstand the pressures of the political power struggle after his death."[39] She did not resign in response to the verdict passed by the Allahabad High Court declaring her election from Rae Bareili null and void. To suppress Opposition and save her position she declared Emergency in the country and got laws enacted removing the effects of the verdict of the Allahabad High Court. She arrested all those who appeared to be hostile to her; even the men of her own party like Chandra Shekhar, Ram Dhan, Mohan Dharia etc. She tempered with the Constitution and through 42nd amendment changed the basic features of the Constitution. The independence of the Judiciary was highly diluted. Through a reign of terror she got her will imposed on her party and the Parliament. The Prime Minister emerged on the national horizon in the garb of a dictator. The party President was totally eclipsed.

The general elections of 1977 ended Indira's dictatorial regime. A new party known as Janata Party—a conglomerate of four parties—replaced the Congress. The former organisations like Congress (O), Jan Sangh, B.L.D. and the socialists came together but failed to merge themselves into a unity. There was no Janata Party, rather there were Janata parties. They had of course, restored Democracy but they had failed to furnish a true alternative to the Congress. The unchallenged supremacy of the Prime Minister had been exploded. The President of the Janata Party had created a power equation. He could not be called a figure who like the moon borrowed his light from the sun. The then Prime Minister Morarjibhai Desai tried to establish his supremacy by dismissing Charan Singh and Raj Narain from his Cabinet. But under strong pressure from the party he had to take back Charan Singh as a No. 2 man in the Cabinet. He adopted the same tactics which Nehru had adopted after the death of Pandit Pant. Nehru had appointed two Deputy Prime Ministers. Similarly Morarji Desai had also appointed two Deputy Prime Ministers, Shri Charan Singh and Shri Jagjivan Ram.

It is now quite obvious that the struggle for supremacy between the Prime Minister and the party President has not been finally settled. It is going on. It is a game of hide and seek and depends upon the personality of the incumbents and the circumstances prevailing at a time. Nehru because of his status as a national hero and his personal charisma dominated the scene as long as he lived. Lal Bahadur Shastri because of his brave role in the Indo-Pak war rose high in stature. Mrs. Gàndhi because of her chivalrous part during Bangladesh war and by the adoption of some radical measures rose to dizzy heights. In the power struggle between the Prime Minister and the party President the latter has in the end to yield. The struggle is still going on and will go on unless and until there is some considerable change in the party structure. If we adopt the British Conservative System, the struggle can end. In Britain the leader of the Conservative Parliamentary Party is the solely acknowledged leader of the party. It is he who nominates the chairman of the Conservative Party who in his turn knows his secondary position and plays willingly and silently the secondary role. On the other hand, the National Executive of the Labour Party is a powerful body and the Prime Minister cannot act always like the ring master of the circus. Anyhow, the tendency of the Prime Minister to control the Party is always there. 'A Prime Minister, whether Conservative or Labour, effectively controls his party and is not restrained by it, despite the differences in the formal constitutions of the parties.[40]

After the election of 1980, the Prime Minister has virtually become the party herself. Like her father, she is occupying both the offices. She is the Prime Minister as well as the President of the Congress (I). She is the maker and the master of the party. She has full control over the party and shows no intention to relax her grip. She has once again established the supremacy of the Prime Minister, and is determined to maintain it at any cost. Like her father she wants to develop in her party men the habit of looking towards the Prime Minister and not to the Congress President for the solution of problems which confront them. Giri Lal Jain writing in *The Times of India* about Indira Gandhi's hold over the party remarks: "She is the party. Even the prodigals recognise that her popularity alone keeps it in power."[41]

REFERENCES

1. Hanson, A.H., *India's Democracy*, Vikas Publishing House, p. 70.
2. Pandey, B.N., *Nehru*, Macmillan, London 1976, p. 300.
3. Moraes, Frank, *Sunlight and Shadow*, Jaico Publishing House, 1964, p. 65.
4. Moraes, Frank, *Nehru: Sunlight and Shadow*, p. 65.
5. Jain, P.K., *The Glorious Revolution in India*, p.13.(Gitanjali Prakashan, New Delhi 1978).
6. *Ibid.*, p.15.
7. Rafeek Ahmad, Y., A report on the office of the Indian Prime Minister under U.G.C. Fellowship Scheme, Mysore University, 1964, p. 20.
8. Brecher, Michael, *The Succession in India*, Oxford University Press, London, 1964.
9. Murthy, R.K., *The Cult of the Individual—A Study of Indira Gandhi*, Sterling Publishers, New Delhi, 1977, p. 1.
10. Malaviya, H.D., in an 'interview to Janardhan Thakur author of All the Prime Minister's Men,' p. 18.
11. Murthy, R.K., *The Cult of the Individual*, p. 1.
12. Bhargava, G.S., *Morarjibhai—Prime Minister of India*, Indian Book Co., Delhi, 1977, p. 20.
13. Munshi, K.M., Indian Constitutional Documents, Vol. I—Pilgrimage to Freedom (1902 to 1950), Bharatiya Vidya Bhawan, Bombay, 1967, p. 277.
14. Bhatia, Krishan, *Indira—A Biography*, Young Asia Publications, New Delhi, 1975, p. 150.
15. *Ibid.*, p. 161.
16. Bhargava, G.S., *After Nehru India's New Image*. 1966,

p. 108.
17. Quoted by Trevor Drieberg in his book *Indira Gandhi — A Profile in Courage*, Vikas Publications, Delhi, 1972, p. 38.
18. Bhatia, Krishan, *Indira—A Biography*, Young Asia Publications, New Delhi, 1975, p. 161.
19. Das, B.C., *The President of India*, S. Chand & Co., New Delhi, 1977, p. 244.
20. Brecher, Michael, *The Succession in India , A Study in Decision-Making*, 1967, p. 14.
21. Das, B.C., *The President of India*, 1977, p. 244.
22. Brecher, Michael, *The Succession in India*—1967, p. 12.
23. *Ibid.*, p. 14.
24. Moraes, Frank, *Sunlight and Shadow*, pp. 191-5.
25. Masani, Zareer, *Indira Gandhi—A Biography*, Hamish Hamilton, London, 1975, p. 125.
26. Murthy, R.K., *The Cult of the Individual — A Study of Indira Gandhi*, Sterling Publishers, New Delhi, 1977, p. 37.
27. *Ibid.*, p. 38.
28. Jain, P.K., *The Glorious Revolution in India*, p. 35.
29. Nijalingappa in Introduction to *The Split*, 1970, by Atulya Ghose.
30. Masani, Zareer, *Indira Gandhi — A Biography*, Hamish Hamilton, London, 1975, p. 160.
31. Ghose, Sankar, *Changing India*, Allied Publishers, 1978, p. 141.
32. *The Hindu*, Madras, 14th September, 1969.
33. Ghose, Sankar, *Changing India*, p. 149.
34. Mrs. Gandhi's speech at Lucknow on September 7, 1969.
35. Jain, P.K., *The Glorious Revolution in India*, p. 98.
36. *Sunday Times*, U.K., March 12, 1973.
37. *Everyman's* (weekly), January 19, 1975, p. 9.
38. Kalhan, Promilla, *Black Wednesday — Power Politics*, Emergency and Elections, p. 39.
39. *Everyman's* (weekly) January 19, 1975, p. 9.
40. King, Anthony (Ed.), *The British Prime Minister*. 1969, p. 170.
41. Jain, Giri Lal, "Choosing Chief Ministers" *The Times of India*. Fabruary 18, 1982, p. 8.

3
Prime Minister and Parliament

The Prime Minister and the Parliament

The modern Prime Minister in every Parliamentary democracy is a baby of Parliament. So is the Indian Prime Minister. The leader of the majority party in the Indian Parliament is invited by the President to form a government of his own. After the general elections of 1977 the Janata Party won a clear-cut majority. The Janata Parliamentary party elected Morarji Desai as their leader. The President of India invited Morarji Desai to form a government. Morarji gave a list of his ministers to the President who gave approval to the list. In this way Morarji Desai became the Prime Minister of India replacing Indira Gandhi who was defeated in her constituency of Rae Bareli.

The Prime Minister as leader of the House having a majority of the members at his back wields immense powers. Along with the Speaker he controls the procedure of the House, frames daily programme of the house; controls introduction and passage of Bills. He is the mainspring of the legislation which he arranges adroitly to run the administration. At the time of voting his whips run about to bring in the Parliament hall all the M.Ps. of his party to see that the Bill introduced by his government is passed. If the Bill is not passed, the repercussions for him can be disastrous. He may have to resign. He, therefore, sees to it that strict discipline is enforced in the ranks of his party. He knows it that without the support of his M.Ps. he cannot secure the legislation of his choice; cannot have a firm grip on the administration and the foreign policy.

There are two very important things which have sparked off controversies, *e.g.* (1) can he summon Parliament as and when he likes, (2) can he dissolve the Parliament as and when he desires. Constitutionally, the power to summon and dissolve Parliament belongs to the President. Now the question arises whether the President can summon and dissolve the Parliament on his own or on the advice of the Prime Minister. Ordinarily, it is said that the President shall summon the Parliament as and when he is advised by the Prime Minister. The thing is not as simple as it appears to be. Is the President to summon Parliament only when the Prime Minister wishes? This question creates some implications demanding serious consideration. What should the President do when the Prime Minister because of serious defections in the ruling party does not want to face Parliament? He disregards the advice of the President and demand of the opposition to resign. Such like situation has not arisen at the centre so far but who knows, in future it may. However, we have example of such a situation in West Bengal. "The Chief Minister Ajoy Mukherji refused to summon the legislature in spite of the repeated advice of the Governor."[1]

The important point was whether the Governor could summon the Legislative Assembly without the advice of the Chief Minister or not. On this point conflicting views have been expressed by eminent jurists, politicians, Members of Parliament and State Legislatures, the Home Ministry, the Law Ministry and the Governors. "The Law Ministry is of the view that the Governor has no powers to summon the State Legislature against the wishes of the Chief Minister."[2] Even some of the Governors agreed with this view at the Governors' Conference[3] (held in New Delhi in November 1967, presided over by the President). "This is also the opinion of N. Sanjiva Reddy, former Speaker (now President of India) of the House of the

People."[4]

B. Gopala Reddy the Governor of U. P.—"disagreeing with the contention of opposition leader Charan Singh that he had discretionary powers to resummon the State Assembly, the Governor has informed the President that in his view he (Governor) could act only on the Chief Minister's advice about the summoning or prorogation of the House."[5]

Now we come to the opposite views which support summoning of legislature without the advice of the Chief Minister. K. Santhanam, "I think the Governor will also be entitled to call a session if he thinks that the Ministry is trying to evade its responsibility under the Constitution."[6]

This is also the opinion of L. M. Singhvi. "If and when there is a reason to believe that the Chief Minister and the Council of Ministers do not command the support of a clear majority in the Legislative Assembly, the Governor can, in his discretion, take steps to ascertain the position. Notwithstanding any difference of opinion with the Chief Minister and the Council of Ministers, the Governor is entitled to summon the House, to meet at such time and place as he thinks fit and he can justifiably treat this as a matter in which he is required to act in his discretion under the Constitution."[7]

"Mr. G. S. Pathak the Ex-Governor of Mysore, former Law Minister of the Union Government, agrees with this view that the Governor can summon the legislature without consulting the Chief Minister."[8]

Dharam Vira, the Governor of West Bengal, dismissed the Ministry when his advice of summoning the State Legislature immediately was not accepted by Ajoy Mukherji, the then Chief Minister.

Prime Minister as Leader of the House

What should the President do when the same situation as it arose in West Bengal raises its ugly head at the centre too? Obviously, if there are doubts about the majority of the Prime Minister in the House of the People and if he does not want to face it on one pretext or the other, the President has the power to summon Parliament without the advice of the Prime Minister. Evidently, the Prime Minister who has lost the confidence of the House forfeits his right to rule over the country, particularly when the opposition claiming a majority is keen to form the Government as was the case in West Bengal. We may quote the judgement of the Punjab and Haryana High Court which held "the power under article 356 was independent of the executive power of the Union referred in Articles 53, 73 and 77 of the Constitution."[9]

If the President can exercise the powers given to him by Article 356 independently of his Ministers, then there is a reasonable ground to conclude that the powers given to him by Article 85 can be exercised independently. This article empowers the President to:

(1) summon each House of Parliament from time to time;
(2) prorogue the Houses, or either House;
(3) dissolve the House of the People.

Here we may point out an interesting incident which occurred in West Bengal. It may recur at the centre in the same manner in future. The President has to address the first opening of Parliament after general elections or the first session of Parliament at the beginning of every year. The address that he reads is prepared by the Prime Minister. Is the President supposed to read the address *in toto* or he can skip over the portion he finds objectionable?

The West Bengal Cabinet inserted a paragraph in the Governor's address, which not only cast a reflection on the judiciary but also amounted to Governor's humiliation. 'The Governor, Dharam Vira, therefore, asked the Chief Minister to delete the objectionable paragraph from the address,'[10] 'but the Chief Minister did not agree to that.'[11] 'This left the Governor with no alternative except to skip over the objectionable paras while reading his address.'[12]

'This action of the Governor was supported by Prakasa, the former Governor of Maharashtra.'[13] Govinda Menon, the Law Minister of India, also said that "there was no provision that he should read the text prepared by the Cabinet." "He further said that the Governor was not merely a mouthpiece of the Council of Ministers. He had also to defend and preserve the Constitution."[14]

"Asoka Sen, the former Law Minister, Government of India and a well-known jurist, and Y. B. Chavan the then Home Minister agreed with this view."[15]

Like the speech from the throne in England, the Presidential address is prepared by the Cabinet. Like the King or Queen the President can also make suggestions for certain changes in the draft of his address. In England, however, suggestions of the King or Queen are not accepted, he or she has, therefore, no alternative but to read it as it is. But whatever she reads, responsibility would be that of the Cabinet for in England it is believed, "the King can do no wrong." Every official document signed by the King is countersigned by the Minister concerned. This is not the case in India. Here we follow no maxim, "The President can do no wrong." Constitutionally, the Ministers are not responsible for the advice which they tender to the President and the question whether any and, if so, what advice was tendered cannot be enquired into by any court [Article 74 (2)]. If on the advice of the Prime Minister, the President violates the Constitution, he may be impeached on that ground (Article 61).

The President of India, like the Governor of West Bengal can skip over the portion he finds exceptionable in the draft of address handed over to him by the Prime Minister.

Prime Minister and the Dissolution of the Lok Sabha

The next important point we are going to discuss is whether the President can dissolve Parliament without consulting the Prime Minister. At the centre no such eventuality has arisen so far where the Prime Minister asked for dissolution and the President refused. The President has so far maintained the convention of acting on the advice of the Prime Minister in this regard. Indira Gandhi's first request for dissolution was made on December 27, 1970, more than a year before Parliament's term was to end. The President conceded her request and issued a communique the same evening. Her second request for dissolution was also granted in 1972. Again, her third request for dissolution in 1977 was also accepted by the President.

The fifth, Prime Minister Charan Singh's request for dissolution of the House along with his resignation on August 20, 1979 had been accepted by the President in consonance with old convention. But this time President's action had been severely condemned in certain quarters because of the peculiar situation arising out of the fall of Janata Government when Prime Minister Morarji Desai resigned on July 15, 1979 fearing defeat of his government in view of the defections from Janata Party after the introduction of no-confidence motion by Y. B. Chavan, Leader of the Opposition in Lok Sabha. Charan Singh resigned as Deputy Prime Minister on July 16, 1979 and formed a new party Janata (Secular) under the chairmanship of Raj Narain. The defections from Janata Party reduced its strength to 204 in the House of 538 members. The President invited Y. B. Chavan to explore the possibility of forming an alternative government, on Chavan's failure he called upon Morarji Desai, leader of the Janata Parliamentary Party, and Charan Singh, leader of Janata (S), to prove the majority as claimed by both of them. Ironically the two lists submitted by them contained 40 names in common.

Each list contained 279 names whereas the effective membership of the House was 538. 28 members of leftist parties CPI(M), RSP and Forward Bloc had declared a neutral stance. The real strength, therefore, came to 510. On scrutiny by the President it was found that Charan's list contained more genuine names. Charan Singh was, therefore, called to form the government with the support of Congress (S) and Congress (I) subject to vote of confidence by the House for his list also did not claim absolute majority of the House (only 264 members). The Parliament was called in session for the purpose. The 20th of August, 1979 was fixed for debate on the vote of confidence. Since Congress (Indira) withdrew support to Charan Singh government, Charan Singh resigned fearing defeat on the floor, and recommended a mid-term poll. The President accordingly dissolved the Parliament ordering elections in December 1979 and, at the same time, asking Charan Singh to continue to work as Prime Minister till the elections were over. The President's action has been criticised on the following grounds:

(a) Charan Singh had never enjoyed the support of the majority in Parliament,
(b) He never dared face the Parliament;
(c) He is just a nominee of the President in the shape of a Caretaker Prime Minister;
(d) The President should have invited Jagjivan Ram, leader of the largest single party (Janata) in the Parliament; and
(e) There was no ostensible reason for dissolution as Jagjivan Ram was claiming that he was in a position to form government. The President should have given chance to Jagjivan Ram to complete the process he started with Y. B. Chavan.

Is it necessary that a valid and ostensible reason to dissolve Parliament should exist? "There was no ostensible cause for dissolution of the Lok Sabha in

1970. The Government, even though it was a minority government, had never been defeated and had been carrying on with the support of the Communists in the opposition."[16]

It has, therefore, become imperative to ascertain the real constitutional position in this respect.

Speaking in the Lok Sabha on December 10,1969, late Shri P. Govinda Menon, the then Union Law Minister, said that the President had the power to dissolve the Lok Sabha, but on the binding effect of the Prime Minister's advice to the President to dissolve the Lok Sabha he remarked, "the Constitution was silent on the question and that it was a matter of political convention".[17]

Speaking in the Constituent Assembly on December 30,1948, the Chairman of the Drafting Committee Shri B.R. Ambedkar said that "under a Parliamentary system of government, there are only two prerogatives which the King or the Head of the State may exercise: one is the appointment of the Prime Minister and the other is Dissolution of Parliament."[18]

"It is well accepted in all Parliamentary systems of government that the Prime Minister can choose the time of dissolution of Parliament for holding a general election purely on the basis of the possible political advantage from a personal or party level. Mr. Wilson did so earlier this year on the basis of opinion polls in his favour, though the step was proved to be a miscalculation".[19] Sir Anthony Eden in 1955 and Wilson in 1970 advised the Queen to dissolve the House of Commons a year ahead of its tenure when there was no need for a general election [20]

Now we take the opposite side that the President cannot refuse dissolution if asked for by the Prime Minister. "If the President acts contrary to ministerial advice he may provoke a chain reaction the end of which might well be either the President's impeachment or a formal amendment of the Constitution clipping his wings for good."[21]

The opinion in England whether the King can dissolve the Parliament without consulting the Prime Minister is divided. One view is that the decision must rest with the Crown and this view is supported by Asquith, Churchill, Keith, Keir. "The King retains for the benefit of his people discretion in the matter of dissolution".[22]

But the right of the Prime Minister to advise to dissolve has been recognised. Bonar Law: "What advice on this matter should be given to the Sovereign is a question not for the Cabinet but for the Prime Minister.[23] Robert Blake in his biography of Bonar Law: "I think whatever happens, the responsibility of a dissolution must rest with the Prime Minister."[24]

Holdane: "The only Minister who can properly give advice as to a dissolution of Parliament is the Prime Minister."[25] In 1950 and 1951 Mr. Attlee consulted a few senior colleagues but clearly made up his mind about the dissolutions which terminated his two administrations.

It is said that King George V temporarily refused a dissolution to Asquith in 1910. Asquith himself on December 18,1923 enunciated the doctrine that it would be 'subversive of constitutional theory' to contend that the King was bound to grant a dissolution when advised to do so by the Prime Minister.[26]

Similar views have been expressed by Sir Ivor Jennings.[27] Anson is also of the view that the Crown may refuse dissolution if it is improperly requested. For example, when a Ministry after suffering defeat in the House of Commons and being placed in a minority at the ensuing elections, requests for a dissolution again the King may refuse.[28] "This is so because the right of dissolution is not a right of repeated dissolution."[29]

Churchill stated categorically in the debate on the Education Bill 1944, that although advice to dissolve comes from the Prime Minister, it is only advice, and may, in exceptional circumstances, be disregarded. "This is one of the exceptional occasions when the prerogative of the Crown comes into play and where in doubtful circumstances the Crown would refer to other advisers. It has been done on several occasions."[30]

Sir John Simon was of the opinion that the King has no choice but to accept the advice for dissolution. In England, though the dissolution of Parliament at any time is a prerogative of the Crown, yet since 1784, the Crown has never refused to accept the advice of the Cabinet in such matters. Since 1918, it has been established in England that it is the Prime Minister who on his own account has the sole right to advise dissolution.[31]

Prof. Laski argues that the King has no discretion whatever in this matter. "The King's public acts must be of an automatic character; he must, in public view, accept the advice of his ministers."[32] In view of the automatic acceptance of dissolution on the advice of the Ministry in 1961 it can be said that the controversy has been settled in favour of Laski's viewpoint.

Summing up the discussion on the right of the King to refuse dissolution, Prof. Keith says,"It appears that there is some divergence of views among the authorities on the question whether the King can refuse a dissolution to a Prime Minister who asks for it. The better opinion is that the power still exists but that it could be properly exercised only in exceptional circumstances."[33]

What those exceptional circumstances can be, Stannard gives one specific instance. The contingency for refusal was there if Mr. Chamberlain had advised a dissolution in May 1940, when Germans were crossing the Albert Canal.[34] Theoretically, the Crown still retains the power to refuse dissolution provided it can get a suitable and stable alternative Ministry from the House without a recourse to dissolution.

The knowledge of practice on the subject prevailing in other countries will help us greatly in understanding the real position with regard to the right of the Prime

Minister to secure dissolution from the President.

According to French Constitution, the President might dissolve the Lower House with the consent of the Senate. Taking advantage of this provision President MacMohan in 1877 forced the resignation of a Ministry that had the confidence of the Lower House, and with the concurrence of the Senate dissolved the House.

"President Millerand took a strong line against Mr. Briand in 1922 and forced him to resign. But his subsequent conduct offended the newly elected House so that both the Houses passed a vote of no-confidence in him and he had to resign."[35]

Whenever the Head of the State is either a President or a Governor-General, as is the case in the Commonwealth countries, he is likely to exercise this power more independently because even if his action is not supported by the electorate, ordinarily consequences for him may not be so catastrophic as they can be for the British Monarch. It was perhaps because of this reason that Lord Bying, Governor-General of Canada in 1925, refused Mackenzie King's request for a dissolution on the ground that the leader of the opposition was in a position to form and maintain an administration without dissolution....He called upon the leader of the opposition Meighan to form a Government being under the impression that such a government would be able to secure a working majority in the House of Commons. But Meighan, who then framed the new acting ministry, failed to get a majority and so the Governor-General had to dissolve the House. But at the Imperial Conference it was stated that the authority of the Governor-General in connection with dissolution was only such as the royal person enjoyed in the United Kingdom, which meant that Lord Bying had exceeded his authority.[36]

"Sir Patrick Duncan, Governor-General of the Union of South Africa, refused to grant a dissolution to General Hartzog in 1939. He called upon General Smuts to form a Government after the resignation of Hartzog and the

General was successful in forming the Government."[37]

"Under Weimar Republic in Germany, Von Schleicher asked President Von Hindenburg to dissolve legislature but his request was refused. There was nothing for the Chancellor to do but to resign. He was followed by Adolf Hitler who in 1932 asked for the dissolution of the Reichstag and got it."[38]

The Constitution of Eire requires the Irish President to act on the advice of Ministers on all matters [Art 13(9)-(11) of the Constitution of Eire of 1937] but at the same time gives him absolute discretionary power (contrary to the Irish rule) to refuse to dissolve Dail Eireann [Article 13(2)] on the advice of a Taoiseach who has ceased to retain the support of a majority in Dail Eireann.

Riddell in the Canadian Constitution observes, "He (Governor-General) must avoid becoming a party man, he must not grant a dissolution to enable a political party to continue in office."[39]

After a long discussion we come to the conclusion that the Prime Minister in consultation with the Cabinet has the sole right to advise dissolution of Parliament. The Head of the State may grant or may not grant the request. Ordinarily, he concedes to the request but in cases where he feels that he can secure an alternative government within the same legislature, he may refuse to grant dissolution.

Similarly, in India the President ordinarily grants the request made by the Prime Minister to have the Parliament dissolved. Smt. Indira Gandhi's request to the President for the dissolution of Parliament was granted thrice, first in 1970, second in 1972 after the Bangladesh War and third in January 1977. The first two elections did her a lot of good but the last one proved to be a calamity for her party. It was a miscalculated move. Prime Minister may choose the most appropriate time for dissolution but the electorate may upset the well-designed calculations of the political prophets. We may recall Churchill's defeat in 1945 and Attlee's narrow victory in 1950.

So far there has been no occasion when the President felt compelled to reject the request for dissolution. However, at the state level the instances of refusals are there. Rajpramukh of Travancore-Cochin did not grant dissolution to P.S.P. Chief Minister Pattom Thanu Pillay, when a vote of lack of confidence was passed against his government in February, 1955.

In Punjab when Chief Minister Gurnam Singh resigned, he advised the Governor to dissolve the Punjab legislature but the advice was rejected and an alternative ministry by Lachhman Singh Gill was installed. [40]

In the absence of any precedent of refusal at the centre, we shall have to imagine in keeping with the constitutional position as to what can happen in future. The Indian Constitution contains no specific provision defining the circumstances under which the President can grant or refuse a dissolution, it is open to him to refuse a dissolution when asked for by a defeated party leader whose party is in minority in Parliament or when the leader of the opposition is in a position to form an alternative government to run the administration with stability. "The power of dissolution is said to be a power of the electorate. It is an appeal from the legal sovereign to the political sovereign to secure mandate from the electorate. His role (President's or Governor's) is that of an umpire who has to see that the game is played not only according to rule but in the correct spirit.[41]

REFERENCES

1. *The Times of India*, November 16, 1967, p. 1.
2. *The Times of India*, November 12, 1967, p. 1.
3. *The Statesman*, November 11, 1967, p. 1.
4. *The Sunday Standard*, April 7, 1968, p. 1.
5. *The Hindustan Times*, September 12, 1968, p. 8.
6. *The Statesman*, New Delhi, November 11, 1967, p. 8.
7. Siwath, J.R., *The Indian Presidency*, Haryana Prakashan,

Delhi, 1971, p. 80.
8. *The Statesman*, New Delhi, November 11, 1967, p. 8.
9. *The Tribune* March 2, 1968, p. 8.
10. *Patriot*, March 7,1969, p. 1.
11. *The Indian Express*, March, 6, 1969, p. 1.
12. *Patriot*, March 7, 1969, p. 1.
13. *The Indian Express*, March 10, 1969, p. 3.
14. *The Indian Express*, March 12, 1969, p. 2.
15. *The Hindustan Times*, March 11, 1969, p. 6.
16. Madhok, Balraj, *Murder of Democracy*, p. 103.
17. Lok Sabha Debates, December 10, 1969.
18. C.A. *Debates*, Vol. VII (December 30, 1948), p. 1158.
19. Rangachari, K., Seminar on Constitutional Questions relating to the Power of Dissolution of Lok Sabha, December 1970, The Institute of Constitutional Studies, New Delhi.
20. Bharadwaj, K.K., in Seminar on Constitutional Question relating to dissolution.
21. Jain, H.M., *The Union Executive*, p. 67.
22. Keith, A.B., *The King and the Imperial Crown*, 1936, p. 140.
23. Balfour told the House in November 1918, mentioned by Robert Blake in his Bonar Law's Biography.
24. *Ibid.*, p. 52.
25. Balfour told the House in November 1918, mentioned by Robert Blake in his Bonar Law's Biography.
26. Nicolson, Harold, *King George the Fifth*, p. 116.
27. Jennings, Sir Ivor, *Cabinet Government*, 1959, pp. 111-12.
28. Anson, *The Law and Custom of the Constitution*, 5th edition, 1922, pp. 325-330.
29. Laski, Harold J., *Parliamentary Government in England*, 6th edition 1959, p. 409-12.
30. Quoted in Keith's *British Cabinet System*, 1952, p. 301.
31. Jennings, Ivor, *Cabinet Government*, 1959, p. 419.
32. Laski, H.J., *Parliamentary Government in England*, 1938, p. 430.
33. Keith, A.B., *The British Cabinet System*, 1952, p. 302.
34. Stannard, H., *The Two Constitutions*, 1950, p. 17.
35. Munshi, K.M., Quoted in *Indian Constitutional Documents*, Vol. I, 1967, p. 261.
36. Zink, H., *Modern Governments*, 1959, p. 673.
37. Siwach, Quoted in the *Indian Presidency*, 1971, p. 92.
38. Heneman, H.J., *The Growth of Executive Power in Germany*, 1st ed., 1934, p. 1177.
39. Riddell, W.R., *The Canadian Constitution in Form and Fact*, 1923, pp. 34-35.
40. *The Tribune*, November 26, 1967, p. 1.
41. Mishra, R.N., *The President of Indian Republic*, 1964, p. 85.

4
The Prime Minister and the Council of Ministers

Formation of the Council of Ministers

It is strange to note here that procedure for the appointment of the Prime Minister has not been precisely spelt out. It is not a case of oversight or an unintended omission. It was decided to introduce this element of vagueness in the Constitution after a prolonged debate on its pros and cons and on the various alternatives in the Constituent Assembly and its Committees. Thus in the Constituent Assembly and the Union Constitution Committee (UCC) at least two alternative fromulae for the appointment of the Prime Minister and other Ministers were proposed and considered.

These were as follows:

1. It should be explicitly provided in the Constitution that the Prime Minister shall be the person commanding a majority in the Lower House of Parliament. He will then name the other Ministers.
2. The Prime Minister as also the other Ministers should be elected by the Lower House of Parliament, by single transferable vote, in accordance with the proportional representation system.

These proposals were, however, eventually rejected by

the Constituent Assembly in favour of the provisions of Articles 74 and 75.

The second proposal regarding the election of the Prime Minister and other Ministers by the proportional representation system would have invariably produced weak and divided Cabinets and would have encouraged from the start narrow localism, opportunism and the politics of defection.

As far as other Ministers are concerned, the written provisions of the Constitution are clearer than those relating to the appointment of the Prime Minister. Even then these are an insufficient guide to actual practice. There have been Ministers who virtually appointed themselves, as, for example, Sardar Patel and Maulana Azad.

As long as Mahatma Gandhi was alive—the interim government and the first post-independence Cabinet in 1947 were formed in his life time—his advice played an important part in Cabinet making.

Since we follow the British pattern, we shall have to act as the Britishers do. Accordingly, a person commanding a majority in the Lower House of Parliament is to be invited to form the government of his choice with the approval of the President. In England since 1923 (Baldwin was appointed instead of Lord Curzon) the Prime Minister has been selected from the Lower House. In 1963, after the resignation of Harold Macmillan, the Queen appointed Earl of Hume, member of the House of Lords, as the Prime Minister. But just after his appointment Earl of Hume resigned his seat in the House of Lords, contested a seat in the House of Commons and became its member, strengthening thereby the already established convention that the Prime Minister should invariably belong to the Lower House.

"In India, however, there is no such convention. Both in the Centre and the States, the Prime Minister and the Chief Ministers have come from the Upper House[1]". In the first general elections of 1952, Morarji Desai, after his defeat at the polls, was made a member of the Upper House of the State Legislature (Bombay) and was appointed as the Chief Minister of Bombay. Likewise, C.B. Gupta, in the general elections of 1957, was elected to the Upper House of the State Legislature (U.P.) and was then appointed as the Chief Minister of Uttar Pradesh. There is only one such example at the Centre. Indira Gandhi after the death of Shastri was appointed as the Prime Minister when she was sitting in the Rajya Sabha. Hence, a member of the Rajya Sabha, elected or nominated, can be appointed as the Prime Minister of India. In the State of Madras (now Tamil Nadu) in 1952, C. Rajagopalachari was first nominated as member of the Upper House of the State Legislature and then appointed as the Chief Minister of Madras.

The matter becomes quite simple when a single individual commands majority in Parliament. The difficulty arises when no single individual claims majority. Such a situation prevailed in England in 1923, when Prime Minister Bonar Law resigned. "The Conservative Party which had a majority in the House of Commons was ready to support both Lord Curzon and Baldwin. King George V exercised his discretion and appointed Baldwin as Prime Minister."[2] Similarly, in January 1957, Anthony Eden resigned on the grounds of ill-health. It was universally expected that R.A. Butler who acted as the Prime Minister during his absence would be appointed but Macmillan was appointed instead by the Queen. Again, in 1963 after the resignation of Harold Macmillan, the Queen appointed Earl of Hume as Prime Minister against the expectation of the public.

Such an eventuality arose in India at the Centre in July 1979. Morarjibhai, Prime Minister of India, resigned as a sequel to large scale defection in his Janata Party. Shri Y.B. Chavan, leader of the opposition and mover of no-confidence motion against Morarji government, was called in by the President to explore the possibilities of forming an alternative government within a week. On Chavan's failure to do so, the President asked Morarji and Charan Singh to submit the list of their supporters in Parliament to substantiate their claim to majority. Both the lists submitted by them contained 40 names in common. On scrutiny the President discovered that the list by Charan Singh had more genuine names though still short of majority. He, therefore, asked Charan Singh to form the government subject to facing the Parliament soon to seek vote of confidence from the Lok Sabha. Accordingly the Lok Sabha met and Charan Singh was to face it on August 20, 1979. But Congress (I) having a following of 70 members withdrew its support. Charan Singh had a following of 95 members of his own party and the support of 75 members of Congress (Swaran Singh). Evidently, in the House of 538 members, Charan Singh had no chance to stand. Before meeting the House he resigned and advised the President to dissolve Parliament for fresh elections. The President after careful study accepted the Prime Minister's advice, dissolved the Lok Sabha and ordered general elections in December 1979.

The President has been severely criticised for accepting the advice of a Prime Minister (Charan Singh) who had no majority in Parliament and could not dare face it. It is said that he should have called Jagjivan Ram, leader of Janata Parliamentary Party, the largest single party (204 members) in the House. On this point there has been a controversy in the past too. On August 20, 1979, Charan Singh resigned without facing the Lower House. He was, therefore, asked by the President to continue to work till the general elections in December 1979. According to late M. C. Mahajan, the President is to "choose a person who in his opinion can form a stable government and then leave him to face the legislature. He is not bound to invite the leader of the largest party."[3] "A. K. Sarkar another Chief Justice of India and H. M. Seervai, the Advocate General of Maharashtra, also agree with this view."[4]

The then Governor of Madras, Sri Prakasa, did not accept the above view. In 1952 the Congress emerged as the largest party securing 155 seats against the combined strength of the opposition 166. But the Governor called Rajaji, leader of the largest party, to form the government. Rajaji was not even elected, he was just nominated.

Similarly, in February 1967, Dr. Sampurnanand, the then Governor of Rajasthan, refused to invite Maharawal Lakshman Singh, the leader of the United Front having a majority in the Legislative Assembly. The Governor declared, "I had left the reported views of the 15 independent MLAs out of reckoning as they had no policy and no party or group.[5] He invited Sukhadia, the leader of the Congress Party, to form the government. The Congress had a strength of 88 out of 183.

Unfortunately, the practice of inviting the leader of the largest group has not been consistently followed in India. When mid-term elections were held in Kerala on March 4, 1965, though the Communist Party was the largest leading a group of 40 out of 133, yet its leader was not invited to form the government. The example set by the Governor of Kerala reminds us of President, Ebert of Germany under Weimar Constitution. "After the Reichstag elections of May 1924 the German National People's Party clamoured for the right to form the new government (because it was the largest). Ebert refused to accept their point of view."[6] The action of Ebert like the Governor of Kerala was contrary to the customs which govern the formation of British and French Cabinet. The possibility of the Indian Presidents following the same course of action at the Centre cannot be called something unconstitutional.

There can be certain situations when the leader of the largest group may not be invited to form the government. "This may have to be done when all the other groups combine to form a common United Front before the election and when such a United Front has a majority in the House of the People."[7] At the state level such a United Front was formed in Kerala during the election of February 1967. Though the different groups fought under their own banners, the non-Congress parties gave themselves a second name of United Front. This was accepted by the Governor even if they were splinter groups, and when they jointly elected their leader, he was invited to form the government regardless of what group was actually the largest after the elections. A similar United Front was formed by the non-Congress parties in West Bengal in 1968 when the mid-term poll was held there. Late Mehr Chand Mahajan, ex-Chief Justice, was of the opinion that "if the party in power fails to obtain a majority, its leader should not be invited to form a government even if it is the largest."[8] Setalvad also agrees with this view.[9] But A. K. Sarkar, ex-Chief Justice, does not agree to this interpretation. The fact that it held power before the polls should not disqualify the largest single party.

No consistent stand was followed in this regard. "In Bihar, the leader of the Congress party, which had a following of 145 out of 318 was invited to form the government."[10] In West Bengal, on the other hand the Congress which was the largest party having a strength of 127 out of 280 was bypassed and the United Front (formed after the elections) was invited. Ordinarily, the claim of the largest party to form the government should not be ignored unless its leader declines the offer, as happened in Punjab where Gian Singh Rarewala, Congress (after elections, February 1967—48 out of 104), had refused to form the government. This course of action was followed by the Governor of U. P. (Biswanath Das)[11] and 'Rajasthan Governor Sampurnanand'.[12] They did it after ascertaining the position of the independents. Such a position has been termed as dangerous by some of the statesmen. The duty of the Governor is not to assess the situation but to invite the leader of the largest party and inquire if he can form the government. Mehtab is of the opinion that "If it is left to the Governor in the case of states or to the President in the case of Centre, if any party is in a position to form the government then the democracy is a guided one."[13] K. Santhanam concurred with Mehtab.

"K. Subba Rao, the former Chief Justice of India, held the similar view when he said that the President should call upon the leader of the majority party to form the ministry and if there is no majority he should call upon the leader of a coalition."[14]

After this discussion we conclude that ordinarily a person having a majority in the legislature should be invited to form the government. Secondly, he should be preferably from the Lower House.

A Prime Minister can be chosen by consensus. Kamaraj selected Lal Bahadur Shastri in this way. He consulted most of the Chief Ministers and very important members of Parliament and declared that all agreed on Lal Bahadur Shastri. In this connection Kamaraj did not follow the British example set by Harold Macmillan in 1963. "Kamaraj did not consult all the M.Ps. He consulted barely 250 — less than half the members."[15]

Harold Macmillan in 1963 had used the similar procedure to pick his successor. "In Britain 90 percent of the M.Ps. were interviewed personally—not by just a single interested individual but by as many as five party whips and leaders. And the remaining 10 percent were asked to communicate their preferences by the telegraph or telephone."[16] In India a powerful person of all-India importance played a very significant role in selecting the Indian Prime Minister. Subsequent approval by the majority party of the Parliament was no more than a formality. Kamaraj, the most powerful Congress President, had the opportunity to select two Prime Ministers—Lal Bahadur Shastri and Indira Gandhi. After the death of Nehru he selected Lal Bahadur Shastri. After the death of Shastri, Kamaraj got the second opportunity to select a new Prime Minister. His eyes fell on Indira Gandhi this time. He was not happy with Shastri for his independent stance. He, therefore, thought of supporting someone more flexible and less experienced in statecraft and political management. Among the central figures of the Congress Party Indira Gandhi was the only person who could fulfil these qualifications. As a woman she was expected to be more accommodating and adaptable. She had never commanded an organised following of her own. "Thus she could be relied upon to play second fiddle to the syndicate all the time."[17]

The drama to select Janata Prime Minister after the defeat of Indira Gandhi in the general elections of 1977 is a pointer to the same direction. Morarji Desai could not have become Prime Minister but for the word of J. P. Narain in his favour.

The Jana Sangh had decided to favour Jagjivan Ram. Their reason was that the election of a Harijan as the Prime Minister would have given the Janata Party a "bright new image".[18] Besides, C. F. D. had a following of minorities and so-called progressive elements (Socialists and Chandra Shekhar group). By supporting Ram, Jana Sangh wanted to gain popularity with the Muslims. Some critics of the Jana Sangh were of the view that Jana Sangh's support for Jagjivan Ram had stemmed from an ulterior motive. They preferred Ram because he had no large following of his own and such a Prime Minister would be easier to control.

The supporters of Morarji Desai could see little chance for him to succeed in the case of contest. The masterminds behind Desai were the Sarvodaya leaders and the old political manipulator from Uttar Pradesh Chandra Bhan Gupta. Raj Narain was helping Gupta in his manoeuvres.

After the election, the Sarvodaya leaders held a meeting of their own to know J.P.'s mind to back the right candidate. Siddhraj Dhadda, President of the Sarva Sewa Sangh, rushed to Patna to return with the news that J.P. was for Morarji Desai. This important bit of information had been conveyed quietly to Desai to ingratiate himself with the rising star.

Jagjivan Ram and Bahuguna were insisting on election—the democratic way. They were told that an election at that stage would create dissensions in the Party. After a long discussion "Ram and Bahuguna finally agreed to a via media—a consensus in the usual Congress style."[19] Let J. P. meet the M.Ps. one by one to ascertain their views and then declare the unanimous result. J. P. agreed to this to the disappointment of Sarvodaya leaders. They requested J. P. to take the help of Acharya Kripalani in taking the consensus. J. P. agreed. So, in the evening of 23 March, 1977, Secretary of the Gandhi Peace Foundation, Radhakrishna, announced to newsmen on behalf of J. P. the process that would be followed the next morning. The two old men J. B. and J. P. would sit at two separate tables, and the M.Ps. would file past them one by one, giving them their choice on a little chit of paper.

"The supporters of Morarji knew they had lost the battle. It would be merely a farce next morning; the outcome was already clear."[20] Late in the night when it was calm, four Sarvodaya men—Radhakrishna, Siddhraj Dhadda, Narain Desai and Govind Rao Deshpande assembled at the Gandhi Peace Foundation. It was all very unfair, they agreed J. P. would be declaring the name and it would be accepted as J. P.'s choice but the case might be otherwise.

The four Sarvodaya leaders drove to Ram's house in search of Chandra Shekhar. A big meeting was going on inside. All the supporters of Ram, George Fernandes, Nandini Satpathy and H. N. Bahuguna were busy like a bee. The visitors sent a word to Chandra Shekhar, who was one of the closest men to J. P. but he did not admire Morarji Desai and did not see anything wrong in the procedure that had been adopted.

All the four then drove to Morarji Desai's; after that

to L. K. Advani who told them that Jana Sangh group was in favour of Ram because they had been informed that this was J.P.'s choice. Radhakrishna told him that on the contrary J.P. was all for Morarji Desai. At five in the morning they were active again. Radhakrishna and Narain Desai went to Morarji and Govind Rao and Siddhraj Dhadda to Nanaji Deshmukh.

From Nanaji's residence both of them went to Biju Patnaik. Patnaik told Radhakrishna and Narain Desai that Charan Singh had threatened to withdraw from the Janta if Jagjivan Ram was selected for leadership.

At Rajghat they talked to Atal Bihari Vajpayee. He said he had no idea that J.P. was for Morarji Desai.

The crowd of M.Ps. that had left at night was collecting again in the morning at the Gandhi Peace Foundation. The time for the formal election of the leader in the Central Hall of Parliament was fixed at 12 noon. Suspense was rising.

On the advice of J.B. Kripalani, the four of them requested the M.Ps. to drop the procedure already agreed. C.B. Gupta and Raj Narain had by then played their trump-card. C.B. Gupta deputed Raj Narian to the Willingdon Hospital to work on Charan. "Jagjivan Ram is going to become the Prime Minister", Raj Narain announced this to the sick man. Raj Narain dropped another bomb. Babuji, of course, will be the Prime Minister in name only. The real Prime Minister will be your friend Bahuguna.

The trick worked. Charan Singh hated Bahuguna, one of his biggest enemies in U.P. politics. "I would prefer to go back to jail than work under these people", he fumed. Raj Narain was ready with the solution, "you had better convey your feeling to Jayaprakashji fast, or it would be too late."

The moment Raj Narain returned with the letter from Charan Singh, C.B. Gupta called the M.Ps. into a formal meeting with himself in the chair. Raj Narain quickly got up to read out Charan Singh's letter. Immediately thereafter he proposed that instead of the unnecessary process of consensus, the two leaders J.P. and Kripalani should be authorised to name the leader. The resolution was promptly seconded. Several members shouted in protest. Jagjivan Ram got wind of the new development and quietly drove away. In this way the procedure favouring Ram was scuttled and the decks were cleared for the reception of Morarji as leader of the Janata Parliamentary Party.

Now it is quite clear that all the Prime Ministers of India were selected by the most powerful personalities of the time, Nehru by Gandhi, Shastri and Indira by Kamaraj, Morarji Desai by J.P.

One thing particularly needs mentions here. Almost all the Prime Ministers have come from Hindi hinterland—the most dominating region in Indian politics. "After the death of Shastri some of the syndicate members floated the idea to Kamaraj that he should himself become the Prime Minister. Kamaraj at once rejected the idea on the ground that he knew none of the two all-India languages, namely, Hindi and English."[21]

Another interesting fact comes to limelight. During the post-independence period of 32 years all the Prime Ministers except Morarji hailed from U.P. Even Desai could not have realised his long-cherished dream of Prime Ministership without the support of U.P. group. "Even in the election of Mr. Desai U.P. played a decisive role."[22] We have already known how Raj Narain got a letter from Charan Singh (who was under treatment at Willingdon Hospital) that he would never accept Jagjivan Ram as leader. The letter when produced before J.P. had its desired effect.The Janata Paliamentary Party hardly ever mattered.

What should be the qualities of the Prime Minister? Ordinarily, no qualities have been prescribed in the Constitution for the Prime Minister. However, the qualities which a Prime Minister is expected to possess can be cited as under: He must possess pep of leadership. He should be a charming speaker to drive home his point of view. He should be patient and hardworking. He must have his fingers upon the pulse of the people and should be in the know of public opinion obtaining during a particular period. He must be an expert in the art of propaganda and a good psychologist. He must have an impressive personality so as to inspire loyalty amongst his colleagues and confidence among the people. He should be fair-minded, considerate, persuasive, easily accessible and confidential. He should not only be honest but also appear to be honest. He should rise above immediate and petty gains, nepotism and favouritism.

Sajal Basu lists simplicity as one of the qualities. Indira Gandhi lacked in this quality and this was one of the causes of her failures. "Years lived in luxury mostly at Government expense, she cannot adjust herself to modest living."[23]

Robert Blake enumerates qualities of the Prime Minister as follows: "Courage, tenacity, determination, firm nerves, and clarity of mind, a certain toughness of the skin and a certain insensitivity, or at least the lack of great sensitivity. Nor should a Prime Minister be worried too much by scruples and doubts. And if tact and the power to manage men are there too, so much the better."[24]

These are generally the qualities which go to the making of a leader and Prime Minister is certainly a leader, a great leader of the great Indian nation. Many people had certain reservations about Shri Lal Bahadur Shastri, when he became Prime Minister of India. Within a year he won the status of a national hero. It will be interesting to note what Michael Brecher has to say about him: "It was this combination of qualities—humility, patience, respect for conflicting viewpoints, sensivity to powerful emotional currents, along with subtlety and quiet firmness that Shastri brought to the awesome task of succeeding Jawaharlal Nehru."[25]

Dismissal of Ministers by the Prime Minister

The formation of the Council of Ministers poses a ticklish problem for the Prime Minister. Under Article 75 ministers are appointed by the President on the advice of the Prime Minister and they hold office during the pleasure of the President, which in reality means so long as they enjoy the confidence of the Prime Minister. "This right of the Prime Minister is undisputed."[26] In 1946 when the first Indian government was formed under the leadership of Jawaharlal Nehru, he was not free to choose his ministers. "The task of forming the Interim Government was given to a special Parliamentary Committee comprising Jawaharlal Nehru, Sardar Patel, Maulana Azad and Rajendra Prasad. The Viceroy still presided over the meetings of the Cabinet. Sardar Baldev Singh was included in it at the instance of the British Viceroy".[27] Patel virtually appointed himself and was adamant on retaining Home even in the Interim Government. Suffice it to say that like Patel and Azad, Prasad (Rajendra Prasad) too was a "must" for the Cabinet, whatever the likes and dislikes of the Prime Minister.[28] As long as Nehru and Patel were alive, Nehru's freedom of choice of his ministers was substantially limited.

The differences between Nehru and Patel reached a critical stage, again, in January 1948, following Gandhi's historic fast undertaken to bring about a change of heart in the Sardar.[29] During his five years of office Patel threatened to resign as many as four times — a resignation a year on an average. Yet Nehru was never able to accept his resignation and to relieve him of his office. "Moreover Patel's resignations also testify to Patel's superior political tactics *vis-a-vis* Nehru, for he never addressed his resignation to the Prime Minister."[30]

Nehru had rather to take in N.V. Gadgil who was a Patelite. While forming a Council of Ministers a Prime Minister has to take into account certain factors like geography, religion, race, experience and influence in the party. He sees to it that different areas of the country get representation, the North, the South, the East and the West. These considerations obliged Nehru at times to draw into his Cabinet persons whom he positively disliked, like K.M. Munshi. 'But all kinds of considerations,' he believed, 'have to be borne in mind in making a Cabinet.'[31]

"Motivated more by consideration for stability than for reform in 1953, Nehru pressed two Chief Ministers— G.B. Pant of Uttar Pradesh and Morarji Desai of Bombay— both right wingers to join the Union Cabinet." ...."As a result of Nehru's preference for continuity and stability in the Government, the face of his Cabinet remained almost unaltered."[32] He also sees to it that persons belonging to different religions enter his Council. "C.H. Bhabha was included in the team by Pandit Nehru following a decision by the Congress High Command to give representation in the Government to the affluent and influential Parsi community of India."[33] Some of the Ministers from the previous Council who get elected again are retaken on the basis of the experience they have already gained. Some of the important personalities in the party who have a following of their own must enter the Council of Ministers. We have already mentioned that Sardar Patel, Maulana Azad (and after Patel, Pandit Pant) virtually appointed themselves and could not be ignored at any cost. The merit of a person may also win him entry into the Council. Krishna Menon was inducted into the Cabinet by Nehru who was impressed by the intellectual calibre of the former. Krishna Menon while in London, both before and after independence, had done commendable service to promote the interests of the Indian nation. First he served as Indian High Commissioner in London. Later on, Nehru brought him to Delhi and appointed him Defence Minister of India.

"The Prime Minister must concentrate on the doctrine

of horses for courses, not only in using the specialist knowledge of individual ministers but also in reflecting the changing priorities of national and international relationships. Horses for courses includes the great and unteachable quality of being able to handle the House of Commons."[34]

The ministerial appointments should reflect a real rapport with the party nationally, and above all the country. The Prime Minister is there because people want him to be there.

The Prime Minister's personal likes also play an important role. Nehru appointed Pandit Govind Vallabh Pant who was Chief Minister of U.P. as the Home Minister of India because he regarded Pant as one of his most trusted friends. Similarly, Mrs. Gandhi brought Bansi Lal from Haryana, to appoint him as the Defence Minister of India, Lal Bahadur Shastri brought in Indira Gandhi as the Minister of Information and Broadcasting motivated by his affection for the Nehru family.

"The case of the backward classes also demands attention. Jagjivan Ram representing scheduled castes always gets a seat in every bandwagon of the Cabinet. The compulsion of times requires experts in the Cabinet. We can refer to the names of Shri Gopalaswami Iyengar as Defence Minister and Shri C.D. Deshmukh as Finance Minister. Two of the former Finance Ministers, Sir Shanmukham Chetty and Sir John Mathai, were also men of administrative experience."[35] A reference may also be made to experts in British Cabinet such as Lord Cherwell, Lord Ismay, Lord Woolten and Sir Arthur Salter.

"Allocation of portfolios is a chess problem for the Prime Minister. He has to distinguish between claims and counter-claims. One interesting fact comes to light about No. 4 position in the Cabinet. Indira Gandhi after joining the Central Cabinet of Lal Bahadur Shastri with the portfolio of Information and Broadcasting was ranked fourth in the order of precedence. After the death of

Shastri she rose to be the Prime Minister of India. Lal Bahadur Shastri, before he became Prime Minister, ranked number 4 in Nehru's Cabinet." [36] Some say that No. 4 is a lucky omen. Anyhow, it is just a coincidence and cannot be accepted as a rule.

The Prime Minister prepares the list of his colleagues and submits it to the President who usually gives his approval. In case the President is interested in the inclusion of someone of his liking in the Cabinet, he can suggest the name to Prime Minister who may or may not accept his request because the will of the Prime Minister is the ultimate deciding factor. "The President may press the claims of certain persons for inclusion in the council to a point, he may require the exclusion of certain other persons. But he may succeed only if he can convince the Prime Minister."[37]

"The Prime Minister is quite free in the selection of his ministers. He is not fettered, for example, in the sense that an Australian Labour Prime Minister is, under the unworkable system adopted in his country under the guise of democracy."[38] Their 'caucus' (Parliamentary Labour Party) elects the members of the Cabinet, and the Prime Minister has 'to assign to a team he has not selected, the various ministerial portfolios.'

Clement Attlee, the Labour British Prime Minister, believes in full freedom to the Prime Minister for the selection of his colleagues. "I don't believe in that at all. You must have confidence in the man incharge. If he has not got that confidence, he is not fit to be Prime Minister." [39]

"Like Nehru's, Mrs. Gandhi's Cabinet has been entirely her own handiwork. She has fully exercised her authority as Prime Minister to choose her ministerial colleagues."[40] "Shastri prepared the list of ministers without consulting any of his colleagues."[41] "I have not consulted a single person in so far as the formation of my Cabinet was concerned."[42]

Cabinet's Collective Responsibility and the Prime Minister

Every Prime Minister expects his Cabinet to work as a team under his captaincy, on the principle of collective responsibility. Free and full discussion in the Cabinet is allowed. Once a decision is arrived at, it must be accepted by every member of the Cabinet. Every member must own the child of which he may not be the father. Outside, in the Parliament as well as in the public every member will defend the decision with full force. No criticism of any kind in public is permitted. The Younger Pitt, Prime Minister of Britain, tried to enforce this principle strictly. "The Younger Pitt in 1792 dismissed his Lord Chancellor for publicly dissociating himself from Pitt's creation of the sinking fund."[43]

Mr. Raj Narain, the Health Minister, and Mr. Charan Singh, the Home Minister, issued statements in 1978 against their own government (Janata Government) for not taking speedy action against Indira Gandhi for her excesses in Emergency. The Cabinet authorised the Prime Minister, Desai, "to take appropriate action against Mr. Charan Singh and Mr. Raj Narain for having violated the principle of collective responsibility."[44] We should know what Morarji Desai has to say about the concept of collective responsibility.

"He (Morarji) pointed out that the normal democratic procedure was that on all policy issues the Prime Minister should consult his or her Cabinet colleagues. If the majority disagreed with the decision of the Prime Minister, the latter should abide by the majority opinion or give up his or her position."[45]

Evidently, the Cabinet must work democratically *i.e.* deciding issues by majority and implementing them unanimously.

With every decision of the Cabinet shown to have been accepted unanimously, and with every minister defending the proposal though he might have voted against it at the Cabinet meeting, it is incumbent on the Prime Minister to defend his colleagues as and when the situation may demand. "The Prime Minister has to take a decision on the spur of the moment to appease the Parliament by his handling of the matter."[46]

When a food minister was vainly trying to assure the House that it need not feel concerned over the fertilizers, the Prime Minister sensed the feeling in the House more accurately and promised an immediate enquiry. When a law minister antagonised the House by bringing the Representation of the People Bill at the fag-end of one Parliamentary session and hinted at further legislation by the President during the recess, the Prime Minister once again defended his colleague by promising legislation by Parliament as soon as possible, if necessary, by a longer session.

It will be interesting to know Krishna Menon's remarks on collective responsibility. "Whether in England or here the term 'collective responsibility' covers many sins and also excludes many virtues. Collective responsibility as such does not exist today. It's not even that for the sins of one ministry the whole Cabinet would resign, if it were so, the resignation of certain members would not have taken place. Collective responsibility regarding decisions on action which, concerning a ministry, don't necessarily come before Cabinet becomes a farce. They would come here if the Prime Minister thought it was necessary or if the minister thought it was necessary and no doubt any member could raise it. But you must appreciate the fact that while in certain circumstances, through the consent of the Prime Minister, one minister may call for the papers of another ministry, this is not usually done. First of all, each man has his own troubles. Secondly, he does not want to antagonise his colleagues or create difficulties. So collective responsibility, in the sense that a decision once made is everybody's, is very rarely a myth, certainly in the Indian Cabinet. Even today one Cabinet member speaks almost like a Swatantra Party man, another member speaks very much more, with the emphasis of Gandhi's philosophy, a third one speaks, perhaps, with a socialist point of view, and so on."[47]

Menon's portrait of collective responsibility is unclear. The simple fact that the decision once taken must be accepted by all and defended publicly when necessary has been unnecessarily mystified. The Cabinet like a team must swim or sink together. Once a decision is taken, it must be defended by all. If the Parliament does not approve of a Bill put forth by them, all of them should go taking it as a lack of confidence in them. It does not mean supervision of all by all. Calling of files from any ministry is the job of the Prime Minister and not of a minister. In the words of Dr. B. R. Ambedkar, "Collective responsibility can be achieved only through the instrumentality of the Prime Minister."[48]

There have been instances in which a particular minister was sacrificed by the Prime Minister even though he was not at fault and his action was approved by the Cabinet. In December 1935 Sir Samuel Hoare (later Lord Templewood) was foreign secretary of Britain. Mussolini, dictator of Italy, had invaded Abyssinia but was meeting with only limited success. Britain and France did not want the balance of power to be upset. To keep Mussolini away from Hitler, both Britain and France were prepared to make generous concessions to Italy. Hoare was instructed to visit Premier Laval to come to an amicable settlement with France and Italy. The cession of certain parts of Abyssinia to Italy was agreed upon. The pact was made in draft form and sent to London for the approval of the Cabinet. The news of the pact leaked out to French press and so on to London, leading to a tremendous uproar. Undoubtedly, the opposition to the pact was widespread and bitter. At first the Cabinet supported the pact, approved it but sensing the mood of the House of Commons and the public they changed their stand. The Prime Minister Baldwin finding his government in jeopardy changed his mind and decided to repudiate the pact. Neville Chamberlain was deputed to ask Hoare to dissociate himself from the pact in the House. When Hoare refused, they deserted him.

After the Chinese invasion in 1962, a bitter and serious attack was mounted by a majority of the M.Ps. on the then Defence Minister Shri V. K. Menon for the debacle in NEFA. Nehru first tried to defend Menon but sensing the danger to his government he deserted Menon. Menon had not pursued an independent policy. What he did was in accordance with the policy as laid down by the Cabinet. As a matter of fact all the members of the Cabinet were responsible for the debacle. The Cabinet should have resigned as a whole. To save his Cabinet Nehru asked Menon to go.

The Prime Minister, like a deity, governs the birth and death of his ministers. Like power over appointments his power of dismissals is also without restraint.

"In Britain the right to dismiss was so well established that while Salisbury was reconstructing his Cabinet after Lord Randolph Churchill's resignation, Northcote learned only from the newspaper that he was no longer foreign secretary."[49]

"In 1903 Balfour, an easy-going Prime Minister, unhesitatingly dismissed a number of his colleagues as a result of a complicated imbroglio."[50]

"The Prime Minister has also the power to dismiss ministers. The only limitation on this power is the prudential one: he must avoid provoking effective revolt."[51]

In 1938 Chamberlain dismissed the Secretary of State for Air, Lord Swington, although the latter had the confidence of the Cabinet and was evidently a successful administrator. Hore Belisha, who had been active and efficient till late in 1939, was asked to resign on January 4, 1940 as the British Prime Minister had found there was an acute resentment among the senior British officers against the Secretary for War.

The Prime Minister Macmillan decided in 1962 to

overhaul his Cabinet to give it a new and fresh look. With one stroke he dropped seven ministers at a time. "Instead of a reshuffle it was dubbed a purge by the Press and nicknamed 'the night of the long knives'."[52] 'I was kicked out as though I was an office boy caught with a half-crown from the petty cash', one minister was reported as saying. Another was said to have called it 'the most brutal humiliation of my life'. Mr. Selwyn Llyod, writing in a *Sunday Telegraph* article following 23 January, reflected soberly: "No one likes to be asked to give up high office. It is even more unpleasant to be asked to do so at short notice. It would be humbling for me to pretend to feel otherwise."

"Lord Attlee has said that an important quality in a premier is the capacity to dismiss inadequate ministers."[53] Attlee once called a minister and told him to resign. On being asked the reason of removal, Attlee replied, "Because I don't think you measure upto the job."[54] "In a softer mood, his formula was, "well you've had a good innings. Time to go back to the pavilion and put up your bat."[55]

On the question of Britain's entry into the European market Mr Wilson told his Cabinet colleagues not to go "beyond the terms of his November statement and that while they could contribute to the great debate on the question of Britain's membership, ministers who wanted to campaign against the Cabinet decision to explore the conditions available within the treaty of Rome setting up the community would have to resign."[56]

"In his draft Introduction to the new Edition of Bagehot's classic, the English Constitution, Mr. Crossman, after 18 years in politics, included a sentence that the British Prime Minister can liquidate the political career of one of his colleagues as effectively as any of the leaders of the Soviet Union can remove rivals. His publishers protested and he removed the observation. In 1967 after three years in the Cabinet, the only thing he regretted about his introduction was the omission."[57]

Role of the Cabinet whose Leader is the Prime Minister

As a matter of fact, the phrase 'A minister holds office during the pleasure of the King' has come to mean 'Pleasure of the Prime Minister'. Similarly, in India the same phrase 'A minister holds office 'during the pleasure of the President', in substance means 'pleasure of the Prime Minister'. Thus the constitutional right of the Prime Minister to reshuffle the Union Cabinet or the portfolios of individual ministers, whenever he or she considers necessary, is legally and constitutionally indisputable. "This is actually the prerogative of the Prime Minister."[58]

At an important conference attended by several central ministers, the Governor of East Punjab, the ministers of East Punjab Government, Nehru felt that the action taken by a department of the Central Government in stopping supply of water to West Punjab canals was not right and he was anxious to see the wrong remedied. The Minister-in-charge N. C. Gadgil, however, persisted with his arguments in support of the action he had already taken. Suddenly the Prime Minister who was presiding flared up, "Mr. Gadgil, if you disagree, I want your resignation here and now."[59]

Rajagopalachari, then Home Minister, immediately saw the embarrassing situation and asked all others to withdraw. He apparently remonstrated with success, for when all went back to the conference room, the discussions were resumed in a calm atmosphere as if nothing had happened.

"After the election of 1952, Nehru dropped out all Patelites — Gadgil, Munshi, Diwakar and Santhanam."[60] He also planned to axe Baldev Singh and Jagjivan Ram who were suspected to have hobnobbed with Patel and his group at one time or another. However, Jagivan Ram was ultimately retained at the instance of President Rajendra Prasad.

"Shrimali (Minister of State for Education) was

dropped by Nehru as part of the Kamaraj plan as he was not prepared to allot the sums for Dhirendra Brahmachari's Yoga Ashram."[61] Mrs. Gandhi was personally interested in Brahmachari and wanted to help him. According to Shrimali, Dr. K. C. Saiydain himself was sent by Nehru to persuade Shrimali, but the latter stuck to his guns on the ground that the Yoga Ashram did not deserve support because money given to it had not been properly accounted for.

It was not the style of Nehru to dismiss his ministers. He would usually request the minister concerned to resign and go, and none is known to have ever declined. Nehru rarely dismissed a minister, and all those who resigned owing to differences with Nehru were non-Congressmen.[62]

"After the Chinese invasion, and as early as October 22, 1962 many Congress M.Ps. led by veteran Congress leaders like U.N. Dhebar (former party President) and Mahavir Tyagi (a former Union Minister) and H. K. Mahtab (deputy leader of the Parliamentary Party) openly organised the offensive against Krishna Menon."[63] "At the same time, Lal Bahadur Shastri, Party chief whip Satyanarain Sinha and Morarji Desai persuaded Nehru to drop Menon in the interest of the nation and the party."[64] Indira, worried about her father and anxious to ward off any possible damage to him, rushed to Vice-President Dr. Zakir Hussain to request him to tell Nehru that Menon's sacrifice would quieten the storm.

"Nehru is reported to have told Chavan about that time that they (Party) want Menon's blood, 'if I agree, tomorrow they will ask for my blood'."[65]

With great hesitation Nehru asked Menon to resign and the latter obliged him. Nehru accepted Menon's resignation from the Congress on 8 November, 1962, it was the greatest setback for Nehru which weighed him down.

Lal Bahadur Shastri was not happy with T. T. Krishnamachari, the Finance Minister, who enjoyed the confidence of Kamaraj, the king-maker. He took no time in dismissing Krishnamachari and inducting his own nominee. "While making this change, he did not consult the party, not even Mrs. Gandhi."[66]

Mrs. Indira Gandhi removed Humayun Kabir and Asoka Sen as she was not pleased with their performances. Indira Gandhi wanted to expel Nanda and she got the opportunity in 1966. It was reported that many a party man had been carrying talks to the Prime Minister to the effect that Nanda was strengthening his hands through intelligence activities against his colleagues and by secretly sympathizing with the communal Rashtriya Swayam Sevak Sangh and the *Sadhus* in a bid for the Prime Ministership, for his astrologers had predicted a third term for him. So Mrs. Gandhi was keen on Nanda's ouster. The Anti-cow slaughter demonstration by *Sadhus* turned violent and the blame was laid on Nanda's door. Nanda put in his resignation on November 18, 1966 which was readily accepted.

The Bangalore meeting of the Congress Working Committee proved to be the precursor of a great political storm. Mrs. Gandhi presented to the Committee her note on economic policy. The old leadership consisting largely of the Syndicate and Deputy Prime Minister Morarji Desai accepted her note on economic policy but in retaliation, as it were, they imposed upon her their own nominee Sanjiva Reddy for the Presidentship of the Indian Republic.

Coming back to Delhi, on 16 July, 1969, she peremptorily relieved Morarji of the Finance portfolio. Morarji Desai in turn submitted his own resignation on 19 July 1969 which was promptly accepted.

Her next step was to remove from her Cabinet all those ministers who had not remained loyal to her during her struggle with the Syndicate. She had supported V. V. Giri's candidature for Presidentship against Sanjiva Reddy put up by the Syndicate. As a result the Congress was split in 1969.

Mrs. Gandhi's Cabinet reorganisation in June 1970 effected the following changes. Jagjivan Ram was shifted from Communication to Defence; Fakhruddin from Industrial Development to Food and Agriculture; Chavan from Home to Finance; Dinesh Singh from External Affairs to Industrial Development; Swaran Singh from Defence to Foreign Affairs. "These wide-ranging changes were invariably interpreted in the Indian and foreign press as a demonstration of Prime Minister's growing grip over the party and the government."[67]

In the mid-term poll of 1971, Indira won with a record majority, 350 seats out of 520 in the Lok Sabha. On 18 March, 1971 she was unanimously elected leader of the Congress Parliamentary Party. She announced her new Council of Ministers on March 19, 1971, dropping seven full-fledged Cabinet Ministers and appointing five new ones (dropping Baliram Bhagat, Dinesh Singh, Gulzari Lal Nanda, D. Sanjivayya, V. K. R. V. Rao, Triguna Sen and K. Raghuramaiah). She spared Jagjivan Ram and Fakhruddin in view of the loyalty they had displayed towards her during her struggle with the Syndicate.

In 1978, Prime Minister Morarji Desai nurtured a serious divergence of opinion with Home Minister Charan Singh and Health Minister Raj Narain over action in Emergency cases against Smt. Indira Gandhi. The Prime Minister demanded resignations from both of them and they obliged.

A minister has to resign if he develops serious differences with the Prime Minister. In 1950, Shyama Prasad Mukherjee resigned as he did not agree to the Nehru-Liaqat Ali pact. Shri John Mathai resigned in 1950. He told the newspaper reporters in June 1950 that he had resigned from the Congress because of differences of opinion on fundamental principles of public policy between him and the Prime Minister. "The three non-Congress Ministers Dr. Mathai, Dr. Ambedkar and

Dr. Deshmukh had not only differed on policy matters but were very critical of the dominant role played by the Prime Minister, Shri Nehru, in watering down the principles of Cabinet functioning. This gave rise to clash of personalities culminating in their resignation."[68] In 1954, V. V. Giri resigned as he could not agree to the modification of the Award given by the Appellate Labour Tribunal in the Bank's case. In 1966, Mahavir Tyagi resigned in protest against the signing of the Indo-Pak agreement known as Tashkent Declaration. In 1967, M. C. Chagla resigned following the adoption of regional language as the medium of instruction at all levels. In 1969, Asoka Mehta resigned as the Government took a pro-Soviet stand on the Czechoslovak crisis.

Prime Minister may or may not accept resignation. Pandit Nehru had not accepted the resignation of Shri Deshmukh because he was satisfied that though Shri Deshmukh was technically responsible for the leakage of budget proposals, it did not justify his leaving office.

Indira Gandhi accepted the resignation of Morarji Desai on 19 July, 1969 when she felt she could not get on smoothly with him any longer after her clash with the Syndicate.

Morarji Desai accepted the resignation of Charan Singh and Raj Narain in 1978 when serious rift arose between them over action against Indira Gandhi in Emergency excesses.

A resignation is, sometimes, used as a weapon to get work done. Sardar Patel resigned four times during his tenure of four years to drive his point home and to get things done the way he wanted, though all his resignations were addressed to Gandhiji and not the Prime Minister Nehru. Patel threatened resignation in 1948 over his differences with Nehru on the question of the settlement of the Meo immigrants from Pakistan.

Nehru also used the threat of resignation as an instrument to force the reluctant Party, Parliament or Cabinet into submission.

The Janata ministers also resort to this method to get concessions from the Prime Minister. L. K. Advani, minister for communications, threatened to resign when Charan Singh was asked to quit. George Fernandes had threatened to resign if the railway workers were not granted bonus.

The strength and effectiveness of a resignation depends upon the personality of the tenderer and the conviction of the Prime Minister as to the seriousness of a resignation. "Resignation is the metaphorical 'ultimate deterrent' of ministerial infighting and, like the nuclear deterrent, its real effectiveness may be said to lie in its potentiality rather than its use."[69]

It was the threat of resignation which enabled Llyod George to win substantial policy concessions from Asquith and the Cabinet, including the appointment of the 'Shell Committee' (to deal with the Shell Shortage on the Western Front) and reorganisation of the war office in 1915, and the introduction of full-scale conscription in 1916. Bonar Law, according to Beaverbrook's account did much by threat of resignation to secure the evacuation of Galliopoli in 1915. Aneurin Bevan by the same means ensured the introduction of legislation to nationalise the steel industry in 1946. Lord Cherwell scotched the treasury move to make sterling convertible in 1952, and J. R. Bevins prevented the dropping of his Television Bill in 1963.

"Resignation is a matter of strategy and persuasion as well as honour and dissociation."[70]

Prime Minister as leader of the Cabinet exercises immense prowers embracing all aspects of state life. He has complete control over agenda. If the Prime Minister dislikes a particular item, however important it may be, he can safely and cunningly place that item at the bottom of the agenda in the hope and expectation that there will be no time left to deal with it adequately. In other words, it is the Prime Minister who decides which matter is to be discussed in the Cabinet meeting.

'Who will speak and how long at the meeting', this is also decided by the Prime Minister. "Sir Winston Churchill usually had so much to say that no one else had much chance to speak."[71] "Mr. Attlee is generally thought to have been the model chairman."[72] He managed to prevent discussion from dragging on. He would have the papers circulated to each minister before the meeting and the ministers were expected to have digested this information thoroughly, and to be able to say yes or no to a suggested course of action without having to make long speeches. It was very unlikely that a minister was able to uncover new information or fresh arguments. "Llyod George had it that a minister who spoke for more than five minutes was a bore."[73] It is easy to imagine the Prime Minister saying something like this : "Well gentlemen, you have read the relevant papers, you know the arguments. I don't suppose you have any more to say, so I assume that you are in agreement with such and such a course of action." A minister might not be able to interrupt and demand to speak unless he was willing to risk the wrath of the Prime Minister.

Usually, it is thought that at the Cabinet meeting the matter under discussion is decided after taking account of the opinions of individual ministers. No such thing happens. "The Prime Minister will himself sense whether most of the Cabinet are in favour or not."[74] In a moment of grave crisis when the Cabinet is sharply divided, the Prime Minister may use some method. In 1931 when the Labour Cabinet under Ramsay Macdonald was passionately seized of the economic crisis, the Prime Minister had to take a count of the hands. So feverish was the excitement that in their memoirs ministers have given contradictory accounts of the voting. Michael Brecher says about Shastri Cabinet, "Decisions continue to be by consensus, there is never a vote."[75]

The Prime Minister can abruptly end a meeting if he feels that the meeting is not serving the purpose for which it was called. On June 29, 1927, Neville

Chamberlain wanted to discuss the dispute over the House of Lords. It was not on the agenda and though he did try to bring it up at the end of the listed business, Baldwin rose and walked out of the room, thus ending the Cabinet.[76]

Bonar law was not in favour of long discussions. Being a businessman he was set in his ways. He prepared a business like agenda, believed in quick, on the spot decisions within the shortest possible time. "Sooner than let discussions or controversy be raised, he would cut things short by suggesting a Committee."[77]

No Cabinet can meet unless the Prime Minister calls the meeting. "The sole right of the Prime Minister to call a Cabinet was established by Gladstone and Disraeli."[78] Disraeli on two occasions—over the annexation of Fiji and over the Bulgarian atrocities—simply ignored requests by some of his colleagues to hold a Cabinet. The extreme position was reached in 1894 when Gladstone went on a holiday to Biarritz and forbade any meeting of the Cabinet in his absence."[79]

All these studies show how powerful the Prime Minister is : "The Prime Minister is said to dominate his Cabinet through his power to appoint and dismiss its members, to control its operations and even to bypass it altogether by the use of Cabinet Committees and informal conversations with individual ministers."[80] Foreign Secretary Lord Hume revealed in 1962 that every Cabinet Minister is in a sense the Prime Minister's agent.

The Prime Minister has to maintain respectable distance from his colleagues as he cannot be free with them. Some of the Prime Ministers have looked outward for guidance and advice. "Macdonald did not delight in the company of his colleagues."[81] Baldwin once told Dawson, Editor of *The Times*, "It is easier for me to talk these matters over with you than with any of my colleagues."[82] Llyod George believed "there can be no friendship between the five top men in a Cabinet."[83] There are instances of even the Prime Minister's ignoring or bypassing the Cabinet. During Shastri's tenure as Prime Minister Kashmir Leader Sheikh Mohd. Abdulla applied for passport to make pilgrimage to Mecca. Only two members of the Cabinet were favourably disposed, all others believed that it was a political mission to seek support abroad for an independent Kashmir. Some senior ministers raised serious objections. The Prime Minister listened quietly and then said, "I think that a passport should be granted and I have asked Swaran Singh to do so."[84]

In 1877, during the Russo-Turkish War, Disreali persuaded the Cabinet to issue an ultimatum to Russia, threatening war in the event of a second Russian campaign against Turkey in the spring of the following year. His Cabinet kept silent. "Disraeli sent a secret emissary to inform the Czar that the Cabinet was entirely united in its determination to go to war, if there was a second campaign. The other ministers including the foreign secretary were kept in ignorance of this demarche.[85]

"The British military misadventure in Egypt over the nationalization of the Suez Canal in 1956 was the unshared responsibility of the tory Sir Anthony Eden, later Lord Avon."[86] He himself took the decision and prepared the plan for Anglo-French attack on Port Said without Cabinet consultation.

The fate and future of Tibet was of crucial importance for India's security. The Chinese broke all their promises and invaded Tibet. After consolidating their position in Tibet they grabbed thousands of miles on Indian land when the Indians protested, they invaded India and humiliated her. "K.M. Munshi and N.V. Gadgil were neither flatterers nor mentally ill-equipped persons and yet on the question of Tibet their well-considered point of view was brushed aside."[87]

Indira Gandhi believed in forming a caucus of her own. When she became Minister for Information and Broadcasting for the first time, she encouraged a group of leftists around her, known as "Back-benchers' club". It included I.K. Gujral, Asoka Mehta, Dinesh Singh, Chandra Shekhar and Nandini Satpathy. Never able to trust anybody for long, she kept changing her set of advisers, until in the end she found the sort of people who suited her temperament and style the best — a set of fawning wheeler-dealers."[88]

Mrs. Gandhi's decision to devalue rupee in January 1976 was reported to be taken on the advice of three persons, collectively called 'Kitchen Cabinet'. (Food Minister C. Subramaniam, Planning Minister Asoka Mehta and Commerce Minister Dinesh Singh).

Prime Ministers sometimes look to their personal friends for reliable advice. "Chamberlain kept closely in touch with Geoffrey Dawson, Editor of *The Times*. Churchill sought advice from the Oxford physicist, Lord Cherwell (and later brought him into the government in a special statistical office). Macmillan had a close confidant in John Wyndham."[89]

Indira Gandhi declared Emergency at the night of June 25, 1975 without consulting her Cabinet. Some of the Ministers were surprised to hear of the news on B.B.C. Early in the morning the Cabinet was called in a hurry and presented with a *fait-accompli*. They had no option but to ratify her decision.

Some of the well-meaning friends had been urging Indira Gandhi to take back Emergency and declare elections but she would not listen. "Some of us (Chandrajit Yadav) had been trying to persuade her to hold the elections soon after the Chandigarh session. She took a unilateral decision in March 1977. Neither the Cabinet nor the Chief Ministers were ever consulted." Mrs. Gandhi set up her own secretariat which emerged in due course of time as a rival focus to the Cabinet secretariat and lent her immense strength; "As a result of its vicious role, the Cabinet and even its senior members began to lose importance. The coterie advising the Prime Minister, with no constitutional basis became an all powerful instrument of the executive."[90] "Her successful shuffling and reshuffling of her team made her by far superior to each of her Cabinet colleagues."[91]

The tendency in the Prime Minister to bypass the Cabinet whenever he feels like doing so, raises its head like the hood of a cobra again and again. "Morarji waxed indignant on the breach of joint responsibility of the Cabinet by the former Home Minister, Charan Singh who had made his public statement on the 'pack of impotent men' facing Mrs. Gandhi. Charan Singh retorted by asking the Prime Minister whether he had adhered to the principle of joint responsibility by unilaterally announcing the decision to enforce complete prohibition throughout the country within four years without consulting the Cabinet. He also cited half a dozen similar decisions by Morarji which had not been put up before the Cabinet at all. These include his announcement on abolishing untouchability in five years (a sheer bravado) on abjuring nuclear explosions for peaceful purposes and on the merger of Sikkim."[92]

It appears that there is always a bitter struggle going on between the democrat and the autocrat in every Prime Minister. The autocrat in him sometimes emerges so powerful that the contradictions come up on the surface. Mr. Desai who was accused of autocracy by Charan Singh had publicly declared himself to be a firm democrat. Mr. Desai had told a foreign journalist at the time of his assumption of office of the Prime Minister, "Every minister will be free. The policy will be laid down by the Cabinet. Our collective opinion will be there for evolving policies. I will give my advice if there is anything to be corrected. The minister will take my advice, I would take theirs. The Cabinet will work like a family. I am not going to force my policy on any one."[93] Thus the Prime Minister controls his party, Parliament, the Cabinet and the Civil Service, He also controls to a great extent the succession to his position. Lord Woolton also accepts the omnicompetence of the Prime Minister. "Prime Ministers are oft to be autocratic in the disposal of their ministers, and I can see no other way by which the practice could operate."[94] Why is it that Prime Ministers have become so powerful ? The reason can be sought in the changing pattern of values. The members of Parliament now find no scope to make their mark on the floor of the House. They are, therefore, becoming more and more eager to give loyal service to the Prime Minister and not to cause any nuisance either to him or the chief whip. "Promotion seems to depend on knuckling under the Prime Minister's decisions....His will becomes an Act of Parliament."[95] "Most of those men (M.Ps.) who intend to spend a portion of their life in politics want office. They want office, perhaps, because of a desire for success and fame but many want office because this is the only way they achieve the purpose for which they entered politics."[96]

The Prime Minister's power of patronage wins him a large number of followers. His mere remark that he will help is taken as a word of honour by his followers. Every Prime Minister is gathering more and more powers in his hands. The two world wars left immense powers in his hands which he can use at will. Taking stock of all these things, it is being openly said that a sort of Prime Ministerial government has evolved in course of time. "There is thus no Parliamentary or Cabinet government in England but Prime Ministerial government. The collective responsibility of the Council of Ministers has now given place to their collective obedience to the imperious will of the Prime Minister who exercises powers on a scale not matched even by the American President."[97] Similar is the case in India.

"The 'efficient secret' of the Indian Constitution is, therefore, prime ministerial absolutism which is sought to be justified by calling attention to the existence of emasculated free institutions."[98]

If this is a fact, we cannot accept the doctrine of *primus inter pares*. A person who exercises tremendous powers over his colleagues, his partymen and Parliament, cannot be called 'first among equals'. He should be veritably called "first above equals". "The Prime Minister is more than first among equals. He is unequal."[99]

The Cabinet has been belittled over the last 15 years. Some commentators have relegated it from the 'efficient' to the 'dignified' part of the British Constitution. "They have discarded 'Cabinet Government' along with Parliamentary Government as apt descriptions of the nature of British Central Government in favour of 'Party Government'. 'Prime Ministerial Government' or more subtly, Government by Prime Minister in Cabinet."[100] Even those who evade these titles and depict dicision-making at the top a complex affair find that the Cabinet has become so fragmented and diluted that it can be scarcely called an institution. It has virtually disintegrated into inner Cabinets, partial Cabinets, Cabinet Committees, ministerial meetings. etc. The real decisions take place in these small bodies, "the Cabinet simply ratifies."[101] Mr. Crossman also points to the decline of the Cabinet and the rising star *i.e.* the Prime Minister. "Each of these executives, moreover, owes his allegiance not to the Cabinet collectively but the Prime Minister who gave him job, and who may well have dictated the policy he must adopt. In so far as ministers felt themselves to be agents of the Premier, the British Cabinet has now come to resemble the American Cabinet.[102]

In India after the death of Sardar Patel, Nehru became the undisputed leader of the Cabinet and the party. Even the senior ministers who had a base of their own used to look to Nehru's mood before they opened their mouths. It was virtually a one man show, the so-called Prime Ministerial government.

During Emergency from June 1975 to April 1977. Indira ruled like a despotic queen. Her ministers were so docile that it was said jocularly that there was only one man (Indira) in the Cabinet while all others were women. In order to have unlimited power in her hands she heavily diluted the Cabinet, emasculated the judiciary, domesticated the party and tempered with the Constitution to deshape it beyond recognition to suit her own purpose. Undoubtedly, she had proved that hers was the Prime Ministerial Government. "In practice, the Prime Minister stands on a superior footing and speaks with a dominant voice. His pre-eminence is an established fact."[103] He may be as T.T. Krishnamachari said humorously "an autocrat if the party that elects him and the Parliament to which he is responsible are both inactive."[104] He may also be described as "manager-in-chief of the Government's business."[105] It is the holder who lends prestige and strength to the office and not the office to him. "The office of the Prime Minister is what its holder chooses and is able to make of it."[106] "The Parliamentary democracy has now collapsed at Westminster....The basic defect in the British system of government is the supra-presidential powers of the Prime Minister."[107]

Writing about the forty-second amendment in the Indian Constitution M.C. Kagzi says, "Implicit in this amendment is the objective of making the Prime Minister, who is the head of the Council of Ministers, the real executive."[108] Prof. Dastur of Bombay University without mincing words states clearly, "The provision like this one moved the country towards a Prime Ministerial Government."[109]

All these sweeping statements about the Prime Ministerial Government cannot be taken at their face value. There is some grain of truth in them, but not the whole truth. The Prime Minister has admittedly become very powerful, but certainly not omnipotent. "He is the undoubted master of the government but he is not the government itself."[110] Harold Wilson has described the task of the Prime Minister as "conducting an orchestra and not playing the instrument himself."

It is very risky for the Prime Minister to ride rough shod over his colleagues. He gives due consideration to their views. "To become and remain Prime Minister a man must carry these major colleagues, who are his rivals, with him. He can dictate to them, but must cooperate, consult and negotiate with them and even at times defer to them."[111] Some of his colleagues are equally powerful and he cannot ignore them. Nehru could never ignore Patel, Azad or Pant. "The Prime Minister is only as strong as his colleagues let him be. Without their support he falls."[112]

Indira Gandhi tried to behave like a dictator. But look, what was the result ? She was no more even as an MP. after the election of 1977. "A Prime Minister who habitually ignored the Cabinet, who behaved as if Prime Ministerial Government were a reality — such a Prime Minister could rapidly come to grief."[113] "Mr. Macmillan's purge in 1962 is generally believed to have weakened him. Macmillan, as a sequel, was less dominant in his new Cabinet."[114]

Some commentator believed that all the seven ministers fired by Macmillan in 1962 were light-weights. Macmillan could not touch the heavyweights.

Nehru thought of many a time to dismiss Patel but could not do so. "Towards the close of 1947 Nehru reportedly toyed with the ideas of dismissing Patel but he was apparently unable to implement them."[115] Not to speak of Patel, Nehru could not even expel N.V. Gadgil— a Patelite. Gadgil used his influence many a time to get a decision changed by Nehru. "Quite apart from Patel, Nehru had also to swallow his pride as Prime Minister *vis-a-vis* another Cabinet colleague — a Patelite — N.V. Gadgil on several occasions during 1947-52."[116] At the close of 1947 Gadgil opposed Nehru's decision to send Mirza Ismail out as an ambassador and Nehru had to cancel the appointment. in 1950, Gadgil took exception to the last two paragraphs of draft, Nehru-Liaqat Agreement, which provided for the reservation of seats to the Indian Muslims in the legislatures and Government services. Gadgil's main objection was that these proposals were a negation of the basic secular philosophy of the

Congress and as such "a betrayal of the last forty years of history. This enraged Nehru. But when the Cabinet met the next day, the last two paragraphs were omitted. Again on 11 September, 1950, a meeting in Nehru's office was attended by Gadgil, C. Rajagopalachari and the then Governor of Punjab. Following a heated argument on the subject under consideration, namely, river water (supply of water to Pakistan), Nehru demanded resignation from Gadgil. Gadgil retorted appropriately. The same afternoon Nehru invited Gadgil to tea and apologised to him.

The Prime Minister who tries to overrule the decisions of his Cabinet for a long time, is digging a grave of his own. "Prime Minister who sought to overrule such decision, he would not last long."[117] Harold Macmillan has been amply praised as a successful administrator but this does not mean he could impose his own will on his Cabinet. Only a mad man would try to do so. Lord Hill has recorded of him, "if he found himself in a minority he accepted the fact with grace and humour."[118]

Cabinet as an institution still stands. Sometimes, it may be overshadowed, or out of deference for the Prime Minister, it may bend itself but it cannot be broken. "The normal, regular and natural procedure is for the cabinet to discuss and decide great issues and emergencies such as the application to join the common market; the sale of arms to South Africa; the Arab-Israeli War; the Russian occupation of Czechoslovakia."[119] Churchill, the war-time hero Prime Minister of Britain who exercised immense powers during war and acted despotically, avoided the authoritarian way and instead consulted the Cabinet on all important issues to involve them maximally in the decision-making process. During August 1941 discussions between Churchill and Roosevelt over the Atlantic Charter were concluded in Newfoundland. "President could sign on his own authority, but Churchill felt obliged to refer the matter to Cabinet in London."[120]

A wise Prime Minister who voluntarily submits

himself to reasonable limitations, never gets any moment to repent. "A sensible Prime Minister is always counting noses in Cabinet."[121]

Pandit Nehru whose style of working was dubbed by his critics as autocratic one, preferred to work under self-limitations and never went beyond the breaking point. "When the Constituent Assembly was to meet, Jawaharlal selected Gopalaswami Aiyengar for its presidentship. But the opinion of the Congress members was so overwhelmingly in favour of Rajendra Prasad that Jawaharlal submitted to the inevitable.[122] in 1949 began the search for the President of India as the Constitution was to come into force on January 26, 1950: "As soon as it came to be known that Jawaharlal was backing Rajaji against Rajendra Prasad, there was an uproar among Congress members of the Assembly.....Nehru offered Rajendra Prasad the chairmanship of the Planning Commission, Rajendra Prasad declined. By the end of 1949 Nehru asked him to accept the Presidentship of the Congress, Rajendra Prasad turned down the offer.....There was a stormy debate at the party meetings over the draft resolution. Sardar Patel came with the proposal that the President of the Constituent Assembly should be the first President of the Republic."[123] Dr. Rajendra Prasad was overwhelmingly elected to be the first President of India. Nehru, again submitted to the inevitable with sportsmanship. "Cabinets have obstructed Prime Ministers. Sir Winston Churchill was reluctant but had to withdraw from the Suez Canal Zone in 1954."[124]

During Indira's regime when the Syndicate sponsored the candidature of Sanjiva Reddy for Presidentship, Indira did not submit. She did not relent and split the Congress party. In this way she ignited a long struggle with the old guard culminating in her downfall as well as her party's. "The Cabinet is no university seminar; it is a meeting where divisive matters are settled."[125] "The Cabinet is now the political Crown of Britain, its supreme directive."[126] Let me quote from Macmillan's memoirs to show that the Prime Minister who fired seven ministers at a stretch in 1962 was no dictator. He says that "he submitted for Cabinet decision the major policy questions—about Europe, Cyprus, Oman, Syria, Lebanon, Jordan and Nyasaland—and frequently asked each member for his views, even on subjects far removed from his departments' interests. Sessions were no formalities. Discussions were lengthy, and when agreement could not be reached, the meetings were adjourned. He was frequently apprehensive whether a particular measure would win Cabinet acceptance; he never took it for granted."[127]

Mr. Wilson also depended upon his Cabinet for important decisions. As a matter of fact, no Prime Minister would like to go it all alone. He would prefer to share his burden with some of his colleagues, some of whom have the capability to sit on his chair. "He (Wilson) was punctilious that the Cabinet should take the crucial decisions, which it did after long wrangling, considerable soul-searching, reservations of position and even resignations. The Cabinet took the initial economic decisions of the Labour Government in 1964 including import surcharges and the refusal to devalue. It settled policy on Rhodesia and South East Asia; it resolved to stay East of Suez and later to withdraw; it decided not to lift the ban on the sale of arms to South Africa, and to apply to join the European Economic Community after six to seven meetings devoted to that one subject. It fixed policy on the immigrations of Kenyan Asians, the invasion of Anguilla and the Arab-Israeli War. It decided to exclude C.S. gas from a treaty banning chemical and biological weapons. It agreed in 1968, after a marathon set of meetings, on a cut in the rate of growth of public expenditure including an increase in health service charges and the deferment of the raising of the school leaving age....Cabinet government was, therefore, a reality."[128] "The development of the Committee system has lessened the importance and power of the Prime Minister."[129] The creator of the government has to depend on committees where the issues are thrashed threadbare to arrive at the truth.

His power over civil service is also very limited. "His approval is necessary for the appointment of permanent secretaries but the element of power should not be over-emphasized."[130]

A Prime Minister is constantly under pulls from different directions. The road before him does not lie through roses, at every step he faces thorns which make him bleed, sometimes putting him on a high note of circumspection. "The Prime Minister is limited by lack of time and lack of staff, by the experience of a Cabinet with far greater legal authority than his own, by the presence of colleagues with wills, responsibilities and spheres of authority of their own, by the demands and pressures emanating from civil service, interest groups, Parliament, party and public."[131]

Prime Ministers have on a number of occasions been overruled by Cabinets both before and since the ascent of the Prime Minister to pre-eminence. Sometimes, they have been driven from office by their own partymen. "In may 1940 Neville Chamberlain was forced to resign after a division in the House in which forty one of his conservative supporters voted against him, and some sixty abstained. Chamberlain's majority was still eighty one and in normal times this would probably have been enough to keep him in office. But this was a war time crisis when national unity was necessary....so, without any party meetings, Churchill replaced Chamberlain."[132]

Mr. Macmillan was under such severe attack from within his own party in 1963 that he felt obliged to resign.

The sustained opposition in his party in July 1965 compelled Alec Douglas Hume to resign.

"On March 16, 1976 Mr. Wilson announced his resignation as opposition to him within the party mounted. Mr. James Callaghan replaced him on April 5, 1976."[133] The constant wranglings and rifts in Morarji Desai's Cabinet culminated in his resignation in July, 1979. His Deputy Prime Minister Chaudhari Charan Singh left the party (Janata Party) with his followers. His second Deputy Prime Minister, Babu Jigjivan Ram also threatened to leave the party. The large-scale defections in his party made him see the writing on the wall that he would not be able to defeat the no-confidence motion against his government introduced in the House by Y.B. Chavan, the leader of the opposition. As a result, he felt obliged to resign before the Parliament met.

Hence the concept of Prime Ministerial Government is a myth. It has failed to stand the test we have applied to it. A Prime Minister who often disregards his Cabinet, makes his position susceptible to inner intrigues and conspiracies. Those Prime Ministers who make a habit of standing on the collective wisdom of their Cabinet, find in due course of time that they acquired legs of steel, while those who try to stand on their own, discover later on that they are standing on props of clay. "Cabinet is a democracy, not an aristocracy....My own conclusion is that the predominantly academic verdict of overriding Prime Ministerial power is wrong."[134] It will not be out of place to quote Richard Crossman who lays emphasis not on authoritarianism but on the dominating role about which there can be no two opinions. "Do you see what I mean by Prime Ministerial Government. It does not mean that he is a dictator, it does not mean he can tell his ministers what to do in their departments. But it does mean that in the battle of White Hall this man in the Centre, this Chairman, this man without a department, can exert, when he is successful, a dominating personal control."[135] The Prime Minister must dominate otherwise he will just look like a minister. "This is not something new. Prime Minister dominated even before the Prime Minister's position as party leader was an important factor in the rise of his status and power....As early as

1882, *The Times* wrote of Gladstone that in the eyes of the opposition as indeed of the country he is the government and he is the liberal party."[136]

Even Nehru who was accused of dictatorial behaviour gave more weightage to the Cabinet than to the Prime Ministership. "As I conceive it, the Prime Minister's role is, and should be, an important role. He is not only a figurehead but a person who should be more responsible than any one else for the general trend of policy and for the coordination of the work of various Government departments. The final authority necessary is the Cabinet itself. But in the type of democratic set-up we have adopted, the Prime Minister is supposed to play an outstanding role."[137] Krishna Menon also did not believe in the Prime Minister's omnicompetence. A Prime Minister would neglect his Cabinet at his own risk. "The fact that a matter is not referred to Cabinet cannot for outside purposes be regarded as depriving it of sanctity because, if the Prime Minister did not refer a matter to Cabinet, it is his own decision, and his own funeral if anything goes wrong."[138]

REFERENCES

1. Siwach, J.R., *The Indian Presidency*, p. 140.
2. Jennings, Sir Ivor, *Cabinet Government*, 1st edition, 1959, p. 23.
3. *The Indian Express*, March 25, 1968, p. 6.
4. *Ibid.*, March 26, 1968, p. 6.
5. *The Statesman*, March 5, 1967, p. 1.
6. Heneman, H.J., *The Growth of Executive Power in Germany*, 1st edition, 1934, p. 133.
7. Siwach, J.R., *The Indian Presidency*, p. 144.
8. *The Indian Express*, March 25, 1968, p. 6.
9. *Ibid.*
10. *The Statesman*, March 6, 1967, p. 1.
11. *Ibid.*, March 13, 1967, p. 1.
12. *Ibid.*, March 5, 1967, p. 1
13. Mehtab, Hare Krishna, *The Tribune*, March 27, 1965.

14. Siwach, J.R., *The Indian Presidency*, p. 145.
15. *Times of India* (New Delhi), 2 June, 1964 and *Hindustan Times* (New Delhi), 2 June, 1964.
16. Bhargava, G.S., *After Nehru*, 1966, p. 51.
17. Gangal, S.C., *Prime Minister and the Cabinet in India*, Navachetan Prakashan, Varanasi, 1972, pp. 30-31.
18. Thakur, Janardan, *All the Janata Men*, Vikas Publishing House, New Delhi, 1978, p. 23.
19. Thakur, Janardan, *All the Janata Men*, Vikas Publishing House, New Delhi, 1978, p. 24.
20. *Ibid.*
21. Gangal, S.C., *Prime Minister and the Cabinet in India*, 1972, p. 31.
22. Sharma, Radhey Shyam, *Who After Morarji?* Pankaj Publications, New Delhi, 1978, p. 13.
23. Basu, Sajal, *Underground Literature during Indian Emergency*, Minerva Associates (Publications), Calcutta, 1978, pp. 20-21.
24. Robert Blake, *The Office of the Prime Minister*, Oxford University Press, 1975, p. 19.
25. Brecher, Michael, *The Succession in India : A Study in Decision Making*, Oxford University Press, London, 1967, p. 93.
26. Maulana Azad, *India Wins Freedom*, Orient Longmans, p. 168.
27. Gangal, S.C., *The Prime Minister and the Cabinet*, p. 47.
28. Jatkar, S.D., *Journal of Constitutional and Parliamentary Studies*, Vol. III, No. 1, January-March, 1969.
29. Pyare Lal, *Mahatma Gandhi*, Vol. I, p. 489.
30. In October 1946, the threat of resignation was only verbally given out. In January 1947 and again in January 1948, Patel's resignation offers were addressed to Gandhi. And in summer 1948, it was addressed to the then Party President, Rajendra Prasad.
31. Nehru to Mrs. Pandit, 2 May 1950 MPP (Mrs. Pandit's Papers).
32. Pandey, B.N., *Nehru*, p. 346.
33. Maulana Azad, *India Wins Freedom*, p. 163.
34. Wilson, Harold, *Governance of Britain*, Weidenfield & Nicolson, 1976, p. 30.
35. Mahajan, V.D., *The Constitutional History of India*, p. 156.
36. *The Hindu*, July 3, 1964.
37. Bannerji, A.C., *A Survey of Indian Constitution*, A Mukherji & Co., Calcutta, p. 115.
38. Wilson, Harold, *Governance of Britain*, p. 28.

39. *Ibid.*
40. *The Hindustan Standard*, Calcutta, March 15, 1967.
41. Das, B.C., *The President of India*, S. Chand & Co., New Delhi, 1977, p. 254.
42. Mankekar, D.R., *Lal Bahadur Shastri*, Popular Prakashan, Bombay, 1964-65, p. 139.
43. Wilson, Harold, *The Governance of Britain*, p. 72.
44. Aggarwal, Chandra Prakash, *Indra Gandhi and (Then and Now) Janata*, Hindustan Exporters, Chandausi, 1978, p. 11.
45. Working Committee Meeting, July 21, (before Congress split) in 1969.
46. Sharma, Siri Ram, *Parliamentary Government in India*, 1969, p. 62.
47. Brecher, Michael, *The Succession in India*, 1967, p. 111.
48. *The Indian Journal of Political Science*, July-September-December 1966, p. 19.
49. Walker, Patrick Gordon, *The Cabinet*, Jonathan Cape, London, 1970, pp. 82-83.
50. Blake, Robert, *The Office of Prime Minister*, p. 37.
51. Madgwick, P.G., *Introduction to British Politics*, Hutchinson Educational Ltd., London, 1971, p. 44.
52. Herman, Valentine, (ed.), *Cabinet Studies*, Macmillan Press, London, p. 174.
53. King, Anthony (ed.), *The British Prime Minister*, 1969, p. 13.
54. *Ibid.*
55. Wilson, Harold, *The Governance of Britain*, p. 34,
56. *The Times*, 17th and 20th February, 1967.
57. Mackintosh, John P., *The British Cabinet*, 1968, p. 437.
58. Dash, S.C., *The Constitution of India : A Comparative Study*, pp. 325-356.
59. Dutt, Subimal, *With Nehru in the Foreign Office*, Minerva Associates, Calcutta, p. 283.
60. Gangal, S.C., *Prime Minister and the Cabinet*, 1972, p. 51.
61. Kalhan, Promilla, *Black Wednesday, Power Politics, Emergency and Elections*, Sterling Publishers, New Delhi, 1977, p. 19.
62. Das, B.C., *The President of India*, 1977, p. 347.
63. Nayar, K., *Between the Lines*, Paperback edition, p. 177.
64. Durga Das, *India from Curzon to Nehru and After*, 1969, p. 365.
65. *Ibid.*, 364.
66. Murthi, R.K., *Cult of the Individual*, p. 36.
67. Gangal, S.C., *Prime Minister and the Cabinet in India*, p. 76.
68. Jatkar, S.D., *Journal of Constitutional and Parliamentary*

Studies, Vol. III, No. 1, January-March, 1969.
69. Alderman, R.K. and Cross, J.A., *The Tactics of Resignation*, Routledge and Kegan Paul, New York, 1967, p. 57.
70. Herman, Valentine and Alt, James E., *Cabinet Studies*, p. 87.
71. Benemy, F.W.G., *The Elected Monarch*, p. 79.
72. *Ibid.*
73. *Ibid.*, p. 79.
74. *Ibid.*, p. 80.
75. Brecher, Michael, *The Succession in India*, p. 109.
76. King, Anthony (ed.), *The British Prime Minister*, p. 21.
77. Benemy, F.W.G., *The Elected Monarch*, p. 168.
78. Walker, Patrick Gordon, *The Cabinet*, p. 80.
79. *Ibid.*
80. King, Anthony (ed.), *The British Prime Minister*, 1969, p. 170.
81. Madgwick, P.J., *Introduction to British Politics*, Hutichinson Educational Ltd., London, 1971.
82. Baldwin to Dawson, Editor of *The Times* quoted in Lord Hutchinson - Vansittart, The Mist Procession, 1958, p. 354.
83. Llyod George, quoted in Thomas Jones, p. 52.
84. Brecher, Michael, *The Succession in India—A Study in Decision Making*, 1967, p. 108.
85. Blake, Robert, *The Office of the Prime Minister*, 1975, p. 52.
86. Kulkarni, V.B., *My Country and My Rulers*, 1977, p. 125.
87. *Ibid.*, p. 131.
88. Thakur, Janardan, *All the Prime Minister's Men*, 1978, p. 19.
89. Kalhan, Promilla, *Black Wednesday — Power Politics, Emergency and Elections*, 1977.
90. Sikri, S.L. *Our Developing Consitution Trends, Issues and Problems*, S. Nagin & Co., 1978, p. 41.
91. *Ibid.*
92. *The Blitz*, Independence Day Special, August 12, 1978.
93. *The Tribune*, April, 25, 1977.
94. King, Anthony (ed.), *The British Prime Minister*, 1969, p. 12.
95. Jones, G.W., *The Modernization of British Government*, edited by William Thornhill, Pitman Publishing Pvt., Australia, 1975, p. 170.
96. *Ibid.*, p. 11.
97. Kulkarni, V.B., *My Country and My Rulers*, p. 62.
98. *Ibid.*, p. 64.
99. Haines, Joe, *The Politics of Power*, Jonathan Cape, London, 1977, p. 8.
100. Jones, G.W., *The Modernization of British Government*, edited by William Thornhill, Pitman Publishing Pvt., Australia, 1975, p. 31.

101. *Ibid.*
102. Wilson, Harold, *The Governance of Britain*, 1976, p. 4.
103. Das, Sukumar, The Office of Our Prime Minister, *The Indian Journal of Political Science*, July-Sep-Dec, 1966, p. 19.
104. Constituent Assembly Debates of November 25, 1949, pp. 956-57.
105. Carter, Herz and Runney, *The Government of Great Britain*, 1958, p. 185.
106. Earl of Oxford and Asquith, *Fifty Years of British Parliament*, p. 207.
107. Humphary and Berkeley, *The Power of the Prime Minister*, 1968, p. 118.
108. Kagzi, M.C., *The June Emergency and Consitutional Amendment*, p. 90.
109. Sikri, S.L., *Our Developing Constitution, Trends, Issues and Problems*, S. Nagin and Co., Jullundur, 1978, p. 83.
110. Kulkarni, V.B., *My Country and My Rulers*, 1977, p. 125.
111. King, Anthony (ed.), *The British Prime Minister*, p. 189.
112. *Ibid.*, p. 179.
113. Walker, Patrick Gordon, *The Cabinet*, 1970, p. 95.
114. *Ibid.*
115. Gangal, S.C., *The Prime Minister and the Cabinet in India*. Navachetana Prakashan, Varanasi, 1972, p. 49.
116. *Ibid.*, p. 50.
117. Wilson, Harold, *The Governance of Britain*, p. 9.
118. Lord Hill, *Both Sides of the Hill*, 1964, p. 235.
119. Walker, Patrick Gordon, *The Cabinet*, p. 96.
120. *Ibid.*
121. Neustadt, Richard E., *The British Prime Minister*, edited by Anthony King, p. 147.
122. Munshi, K.M., *Indian Constitutional Document—Pilgrimage to Freedom*, p. 277.
123. *Ibid.*, pp. 278 to 281.
124. Jones, G.W., *Modernization of British Government*, edited by W. Thornhill, 1975, p. 34.
125. *Ibid.*, p. 32.
126. *Ibid.*
127. Quoted from Macmillan's memoirs in *The Modernization of British Government*, edited by William Thornhill, p. 33.
128. Jones, G.W., *Modernization of British Government*, p. 33.
129. Madgwick, P.J., *Introduction to British Politics*, 1971, p. 54.
130. *Ibid.*, p. 60.
131. King, Anthony, (ed.) *The British Prime Minister*, 1969, Introduction p. IVX.

132. Walker, Patrick Gordon, *The Cabinet*, p. 94.
133. Jewell, R.E.C., *Outlines of Public Administration*, Charles Knight and Co., London, 1976, p. 31.
134. Wilson, Harold, *The Governance of Britain*, p. 8.
135. Crossman, Richard, *Inside View*, p. 67.
136. Walker, Patrick Gordon, *The Cabinet*, p. 86.
137. Nehru's note to Gandhi, 6 January, 1948, Patel's Correspondence, Vol. 6, pp. 17-21.
138. Brecher, Michael, *Succession in India : A Study in Decision-Making*, Oxford University Press, 1966, p. 109.

5
The Prime Minister and the President

Election of the President and the Prime Minister

India after independence decided to do away with all the monarchs who had treacherously played the role of reactionaries in aiding and abetting the Britishers, in lieu of protection, in the political crimes which the Englishmen committed in order to prolong their stranglehold over India in the interest of Britain. The monarchy was the most maligned and hated institution which no one defended except the kings and their stooges. The nation was, therefore, fully determined to embark on an experimental career in launching the republic. India like Ireland, Burma, Ghana and Pakistan chose to have a President as head of the state.

The constitutions of different countries were consulted by the drafting committee to explore the way in which the President was to be selected.

Ireland provides for election of its President by direct vote of the people through the system of proportional representation by means of single transferable vote. The Constitution of the Fourth French Republic provided that the President of the Republic would be elected by the Parliament. In Burma the president was elected by both chambers of Parliament in joint session by secret ballot. Instead, the Constituent Assembly of India selected a method which "was unique, brilliant in its originality, simple in its design, democratic in its details, and inexpensive in its operation."[1]

Different propositions to elect the President were

mooted in the Constituent Assembly. Pandit Nehru was opposed to direct election of the President by the people. He said, "when the members of the Assembly themselves are being elected by the votes of millions where is the necessity for electing the President by adult franchise."[2]

The size of the electorate acted as a bar to agreeing to the direct election. Dr. Ambedkar told the Constituent assembly that "the size of the electorate forbids our adopting adult suffrage in the matter of election of the President....I would have understood the argument in favour of direct election because of the principle that wherever a person is endowed with enormous powers, it is only natural that the choice of such a person should be made directly by the people. A President directly elected by the people would vie with Parliament in the exercise of power. He would refuse to act as the constitutional head. He would prefer rule to reign. Nehru told the Assembly that "if we had the President elected on adult franchise and did not give him any real powers, it might become a little anomalous."[3]

Both Nehru and Ambedkar lost much of the ground of their argument when they declared later that election by the electoral college was tantamount to direct election on adult franchise. K.M. Munshi employed the same argument in support of his thesis that the President is in no way handicapped from speaking in the name of the people as against his ministers who represent only the majority party in Parliament.[4]

B.N. Rau in his memorandum had suggested reference of "election of the President by the two Houses of the Union Parliament, to the Committee set up in pursuance of a resolution passed by the Constituent Assembly on 30th April, 1947, to report on the main principles of the Union Constitution."[5]

K.T. Shah was the lone champion of the Presidential system of Government modelled on the United States system. "He suggested through an amendment to Article

41 that the Chief Executive and Head of the State in the Union of India shall be called the President of India."[6]

Shri Alladi Krishnaswami Ayyar opposed K.T. Shah on the ground that an infant democracy could not afford to take the "risk of a perpetual cleavage, feud or conflict or threatened conflict."[7]

After full discussion it was decided that Parliamentary type of government best suited the Indian conditions. Since Presidential system of government was rejected, direct election by the citizens of India was not provided. As the President was to head the Indian federation, it was thought proper that he should be elected by the elected members of Parliament as well as of the State Legislatures.

The President of India has been invested with immense powers as enumerated in the Constitution. But the Parliamentary type of government agreed upon by our forefathers reminded the President again and again that he must not use those powers himself but only on the request of the Prime Minister. But such a functionary cannot altogether forget that he wields a lot of powers given to him by the Constitution. He, therefore, tries to assert himself from time to time to imply that he cannot abandon hissing even though he may have lost the fangs. No head of state can ever tolerate too much interference by the Prime Minister whom he appoints; the germs of this tussle between the Head of the State and the Head of the government could be discerned even before the Constitution was ceremoniously launched.

Rajaji, the first Indian Governor-General of India, resented the subtle suggestions put to him from time to time by some ministers. He did not mind consulting the appropriate ministers on certain relevant points that were raised in the draft addresses sent in advance. "Accommodating as he was in many matters, Rajaji, however, strongly opposed other people's attempts to influence his judgement, or encroach on the inherent powers of his office which till then suffered no revision or restriction."[8]

One evening Bimanesh Chatterji was discussing with Rajaji his plans for visiting Tiruvannamalai, a pilgrim spot in South India. Rajaji remarked, "the Prime Minister seems to think that this tour is not only not necessary, but ill-timed. However, I am already committed to it, and a large number of people are looking forward to my visit there. You can therefore go ahead with the plan....If I accept every piece of advice that comes in my direction, then this may as well be wound up."[9]

Prime Minister's President

The crux of the problem: what is the degree of relationship between the President and the Prime Minister? Is President bound to accept every advice of the Prime Minister? Before we delve deep into the question we must recall 42nd amendment of the Constitution which made it binding upon the President to accept every advice of the Council of Ministers.

Mr. Jatti, Acting President, was compelled to accept the advice of Janata Prime Minister to dissolve nine State Assemblies under this clause. Immediately after the general elections of March 1977, the Janata Party took the reins of government in their hands at the Centre and found to their dismay that their writ could not run throughout India as long as the nine states were being ruled by Congress ministries. Such States were Punjab, Himachal, Haryana, Rajasthan, Madhya Pradesh, Uttar Pradesh, Bihar, Orissa and Bengal. The Janata Government in order to have fresh elections in these states sent on 22nd April, 1977 a formal declaration to Mr. Jatti, for his signatures. That very evening Shri Morarji, Prime Minister, met Mr. Jatti, Acting President, on a short notice, to inform him that the Government wanted to dissolve the assemblies of the nine states. The Acting President expressed his inability to accept the advice of the Government. Hot words were exchanged between Jatti and Charan Singh and the former threatened to resign. The Prime Minister sent a letter to Jatti by the Cabinet Secretary making three points. First, he reaffirmed the Government viewpoint that the President was bound by the advice of his Council of Ministers as per 42nd amendment. In case he was not able to act accordingly, he shouid honourably resign. Secondly, he impliedly referred to Mr. Jatti's inability to sign on the ground of sentiments in regard to the Congress party and reminded him that the President was expected to be above party. Thirdly, Mr. Desai told Jatti to let him have his final reply by 8 p.m. so that, if necessary, he could go on the air that night and take the nation into confidence.

Mr. Jatti asked the Cabinet Secretary to see him at 7.30 p.m. by which time he decided to sign the proclamation and not to precipitate the crisis.

The 42nd amendment has been modified by 44th amendment. The President can now send back any Bill to the Council of Ministers for reconsideration and if the Council of Ministers dittoes its previous decision, the President will have to give his consent. Nevertheless, the question of how far the President can go to accept the advice of the Prime Minister is of academic interest. In this connection it is pointed out that the Council of Ministers is there to aid and advise the President. Literally, it means the Council of Ministers can only help and give advice. It is for the President to accept the advice or not. The President will make decisions. Oddly enough, if the President is to make decisions, the ministers cannot be held responsible to Parliament for the decision of the President. In Parliamentary type of government such an anomalous situation is untenable. Then what is the real meaning of aid and advice"? This poses a question which demands discussion. "Aid and advice" as a constitutional phraseology was invented under the Constitution of Canada, that is the British North America Act, 1867, Section II of the Act provides for a council to aid and advise in the Government of Canada."[10] From the British North America Act this phrase was incorporated into Sections 9 and 50 of the Government of India Act, 1935 which provided for a Council of Ministers to aid and advise respectively the Governor-General of British India and the Governors of the British Indian provinces.

"Aid and advice", it is said, "Is a technical expression which has since acquired a definite meaning in Constitutional Law and whenever that expression was used, what was intended was that the 'aid and advice' shall be followed by the dignitary to whom that 'aid and advice' was given.[11]

The expression 'aid and advice' is nothing but the statutory form of the English convention by reason of which the King acts as a constitutional head, only on the advice of Ministers while all power is legally vested in himself.[12]

In a Parliamentary form of government it is the head of the state who aids and advises the Prime Minister in running the administration of the country. "The royal power in British politics is limited to the power of suggestion"[13] It has been observed rather in a smug way that the advice of ministers was not binding on the President because in "legislation, out of respect, out of courtesy, such a language was not used, and it was not said that this shall be binding on the President of India."[14]

The reason for not making the advice of the ministers binding on the President in letter of law is, in all probability, a respect not for the Presidency but for the personality of Dr. Ambedkar, who as Chairman of the Drafting Committee had a natural prejudice for retention of phrases coined by himself.

Aiding and Advising the President

Dr. Rajendra Prasad while presiding over the Constituent Assembly had pointed out that there was nothing in writing in the Constitution which made it binding on the President to accept the advice of his Council of Ministers. The dialogue between Dr. Prasad and Dr. Ambedkar is reproduced below:

Mr. President: There is another amendment which has been moved by Hukam Singh in which he says that the President may promulgate ordinances after consultation with his Council of Ministers.

Ambedkar: I am very grateful to you for reminding me about this. The point is that that amendment is unnecessary because the President could not and will not act except on the advice of the Ministers.

Mr. President : Where is the provision in the Draft Constitution which binds the President to act in accordance with the advice of the Ministers?

Ambedkar: I am sure that there is a provision and the provision is that there shall be a Council of Ministers to aid and advise the President in the exercise of his functions.

Mr. President : Since we are having this written Constitution, we must have that put clearly somewhere.

Ambedkar: Though I cannot point it out just now, I am sure there is a provision. I think there is provision that the President will be bound to accept the advice of the Ministers.

Some Honourable Members : Article 61(i)

Mr. President: It only lays down the duty of the Ministers, but it does not lay down the duty of the President to act in accordance with the advice given by the Ministers. It does not lay down that the President is bound to accept the advice. Is there any other provision in the Constitution? We will not be able even to impeach him, because he will not be acting in violation of the Constitution, if there is no provision.

Ambedkar: May I draw your attention to Article 61 which deals with the exercise of the President's functions. He cannot exercise any of his functions, unless he has got the advice 'in the exercise of his functions'. It is not merely 'to aid and advice'. 'In the exercise of his functions', those are the most important words.

Mr. President. I have my doubts if this word could bind the President. It only lays down that there shall be a Council of Ministers with the Prime Minister at the Head to aid and advise the President in the exercise of his functions. It does not say that the President will be bound to accept that advice.

Ambedkar: If he does not accept the advice of the existing Ministry, he shall have to find some other body of Ministers to advise him. He will never be able to act independently of the Ministers.

Mr. President : Is there any difficulty in providing somewhere that the President will be bound by the advice of the Ministers?

Ambedkar : We are doing that. If I may say so, there is a provision in the Instrument of Instructions.

Mr. President : I have considered that also.

Ambedkar. Paragraph 3 reads: In all matters within the scope of the executive power of the Union, the President shall in the exercise of the powers conferred on him, be guided by the advice of his Ministers. We propose to make some amendment to that.

Mr. President: You want to change that. As it is, it lays down that the President will be guided by the Ministers in the exercise of the executive powers of the Union and not in its legislative power.

Ambedkar: Article 61 follows almost literally various other constitutions and the Presidents have always understood that that language means that they must accept the advice. If there is any difficulty, it will certainly be remedied by suitable amendment.[15]

"The expression 'aid and advice' is only a

Constitutional euphemism.[16] The idea of the Instrument of Instructions was ultimately abandoned and the article was left as it was. The correct interpretation of the words 'aid and advice' is that while initiative to deal with all matters of policy will be with the Cabinet and the Prime Minister, the final decision shall be such that the President can give his assent with honour and self-respect.[17] "By not making 'aid and advice' binding on the President, the makers have let a big interrogation to the future."[18]

The decision bearing on Articles 73 and 74 in the case of Ram Jawaya Kapur and State of Punjab is given below:

> "The expression 'aid and advice' in Article 74 may apparently suggest that it is left to the President to accept the advice or ignore the same and thus the decision on all matters will be of the President himself. But on a true interpretation of the expression in the context of the relevant provisions of the Constitution, it becomes abundantly clear that the functions of Ministers or Council of Ministers are not merely giving advice; they can take decisions which must take effect."[19]

Article 78 does not imply that simply by their capacity to take decisions or make proposals, the Ministers became the repository of executive power. Since all executive actions under Article 77(i) will be deemed to have been taken in the name of the President, the Ministers while taking action or suggesting proposals will simply act as administrators on behalf of the President.

Is there any judicial remedy if the President does not accept the advice of his ministers? There is none. Article 74(2) states that the question whether any and if so what advice was tendered by Ministers to the President shall not be enquired into by any court.

Obviously, the courts cannot interfere in cases where the advice by the Council of Ministers was unaccepted by the President. If there is any remedy it may lie with the Parliament or with the threat for resignation by the Prime Minister. If the President is convinced that the Prime Minister is strong enough to create political crisis by resigning, he may yield.

Dr. Rajendra Prasad was always skeptical of the view that the President was bound to accept the advice of the Ministers. He asserted himself on certain topics about which he felt strongly. In 1951-52 just before general elections he sent a message to Parliament regarding his views on the Hindu Code Bill which was then before the House. His message said that personally he was opposed to the passing of the Bill but if adopted by Parliament he would give assent to it, however reluctant he might be.

Rajendra Prasad sent another letter to the Prime Minister on September 15, 1951 telling Nehru that Congress had never discussed the Bill, that the Constituent Assembly was not empowered to deal with such a measure. He further pointed out that the repercussions may affect the chances of the Congress at the next elections.[20] Jawaharlal Nehru sent his reply the same day. To strengthen his position he sought the opinion of two counsels Setalvad and Alladi Krishnaswami.

The Cabinet accommodated the views of Dr. Rajendra Prasad by postponing the legislation not so much because of his disapproval of the measure as the President, but because of his high status, as elder statesman of the ruling party.

Shortly after the elections, the main parts of the Bill were introduced in the New Parliament as separate Bill and finally passed in 1955. The Hindu Marriage Act and in 1956 the Hindu Succession Act, The Hindu Minority and Guardianship Act and the Hindu Adoption and Maintenance Act.

"The relationship between the President and the Prime Minister is unique in character and will mostly depend upon the personal equation existing between the two and the prevailing socio-political circumstances. The President and the Prime Minister balance each other and while President has normally to act on the advice tendered by his Council of Ministers, he may in certain circumstances refuse to accept that advice.[21] A few years later, while laying the foundation-stone of the Indian Law Institute at New Delhi on November 28, 1960, Rajendra Prasad again raised the question of studying in a scientific manner the scope of the powers and functions of the President: "In this connection it may be pointed out that there is no provision in the Constitution which in so many words lays down that the President shall be bound to act in accordance with the advice of his Council of Ministers.

Jawaharlal Nehru requested the then Principal of the Institute (B.K. Sinha who was also Chief Justice of India) not to circulate the speech and his wish was fulfilled. The liberty of speech was denied to the President of India—the fundamental right of freedom of speech guaranteed in the Constitution was grossly violated by the Prime Minister of India himself.

Every advice emanating from the Prime Minister cannot be always acceptable is substantiated from Som Nath Affair. After the fall of Junagadh, Sardar Patel as Deputy Prime Minister of India pledged the Government of India to the reconstruction of the historical shrine of Som Nath. The Cabinet with Nehru in the chair decided to reconstruct the temple at the government expense. Nehru was furious and approached Gandhiji to persuade Patel not to involve government in the affair. Gandhi suggested to Patel to collect sufficient funds from the public and Sardar agreed. K.M. Munshi was appointed by the Government of India as Chairman of the Advisory Committee on reconstruction. He prepared the trust deed and took steps for implementing the scheme. Jawaharlal many a time criticised Munshi in this connection. The latter pointed out to him in a long letter that everything was being done from the very beginning in accordance with the decision of the Cabinet taken under his guidance.

At the time of installation of the deity, Sardar Patel having passed away, K.M. Munshi approached Rajendra Prasad for inauguration ceremony. He requested Rajendra Prasad to accept the invitation only if he was prepared to come and not fail them.

When Nehru came to know of the affair he strongly protested against Prasad's performance of the opening ceremony. But Rajendra Prasad rejected Prime Minister's advice and attended the function.

On hearing the news of Sardar Patel's death (died on 15.12.1950) in Bombay, Jawaharlal issued a directive to the Ministers and the Secretaries forbidding them to go to Bombay to attend the funeral. N.V. Gadgil and Satyanarain Sinha defied the directive and attended the funeral. Jawaharlal also requested Dr. Rajendra Prasad not to go to Bombay, the President did not concede the request.

"Once they have given an advice, the Council of Ministers are rid of their responsibility and there is no political or judicial authority to compel the President not to do otherwise than in accordance with such advice."[22]

"Rajendra Prasad had expressed privately on a number of occasions that there would be an early collapse of the Congress. He had felt the need for the exercise of the President's powers in the interest of the stability of the nation."[23]

President Rajendra Prasad had been maintaining upto the last days of his Presidency that the President was under no obligation to say yes to what came from the Prime Minister. We have already discussed some of the episodes wherein the President disregarded the advice of the Prime Minister and acted on his own. We are going to narrate more, a couple of interesting incidents in this connection. Bimanesh Chatterji, Rajendra Prasad's secretary, was arranging President's Hyderabad tour. He was told by the States Minister, Mr. Iyengar, that in Hyderabad the President had better stay in camp rather than in Faluknama Palace where the visiting Governor-Generals used to stay. The luxuriously furnished palace set in the midst of beautiful surroundings had been specially built by the Nizam for the exclusive use of touring Viceroys. Bimanesh carried the Minister's message to the President who asked the former to go on with the arrangements. The same evening the Prime Minister called Bimanesh and exclaimed, "Listen, we must be reasonable! The P.W.D. Minister of Hyderabad was telling me that the stretch of road between the city and the Faluknama Palace is in a state of disrepair. Moreover, if the President were to stay at the palace then it would put the civil administration under unnecessary pressure to make the necessary security, transport and other coordinating arrangements. Therefore, you should explain the position in detail to the President and keep the States Minister posted with the final outcome."[24]

Next morning Bimanesh conveyed to the President all that the Prime Minister had said. He also told the President a huge sum would have to be spent for repairing the road for his visit. Raising his head from a file, the President said, "Whatever may be spent for the repair and reconstruction of the road will provide relief to a number of poor labourers of the State. So, where is the waste? You may go ahead with the proposed plan for my stay in the Faluknama Palace."[25]

One day the Prime Minister running into Bimanesh in a corridor of Rashtrapati Bhawan enquired of him, "What is happening? Is it really necessary for a battalion of people to accompany the President on his tour?" ....Puffing at his cigarette, the Prime Minister continued,

"There used to be a saying among British seamen, 'Join the Royal Navy and see the world' Now you seem to be subscribing to a new slogan: 'Join the President's staff and see India'. I am sure you must be aware of the reaction the President's circus creates in the various states".[26] Saying this the Prime Minister journeyed to the Président's study.

When the Prime Minister came out from the President's study, Bimanesh asked him whether the size of the tour party had been discussed. The Prime Minister raised his fist in the air and walked off.

On entering President's chamber Bimanesh found him flushed and breathing heavily. Suddenly the President spoke in a hoarse voice: "The President of a country does not go on tours with just a valet and a stenographer....The people who accompany me can do some contacting of the masses, which is not a small return. No changes need be made in my touring arrangements."[27]

President Eisenhower of America invited Dr. Prasad to visit America. Nehru did not want Prasad to go. Nehru's objection stemmed from his desire to vindicate his own right to decide these matters. Nehru used tact and wrote to Prasad, "So many of us have been to America, that it does not seem necessary for you to visit the U.S. immediately."[28] Dr. Rajendra Prasad replied laconically, "I will choose my own time." Actually he never chose. He did not want to surrender his right to decide these matters for himself.

Rajendra Prasad had not liked the Treaty with China in 1954, At the Governors' conference when China's intrusion into India was being discussed, Rajendra Prasad said that if India had not signed the Treaty of 1954 with China, China would not have intruded into India. "Mere mention of this subject sent Jawaharlal Nehru into an explosion."[29]

Nehru did not like Dr. Prasad's belief that the President of India possessed much more power under our Constitution than the British monarch could ever exercise under British Constitutional Law.

Because of this tussle a sort of hostility had developed between Nehru and Dr. Rajendra Prasad. "Durga Das once asked Pandit Govind Ballabh Pant why Nehru was so much against Rajen Babu. Pant reportedly replied that Nehru's courtiers had made him believe that Rajendra Prasad was a revivalist and that he might one day try to stage a *coup d'etat* with the help of the Rashtriya Swayam Sevak Sangh and the Jan Sangh."[30]

"In a period of rapid transition Dr. Rajendra Prasad neither reigned nor ruled, he acted not only as Head of the State, but as the voice of free India. He was our George Washington."[31]

President Radhakrishnan also did not believe that every kind of advice emanating from the Prime Minister was binding on him. Whenever he felt like doing so, he asserted himself like Rajendra Prasad though avoiding open clashes at the same time.

In 1962 following the Chinese aggression there was a rumour that a widespread dissatisfaction prevailed in the Congress party against the Prime Minister's handling of the whole situation. A sizeable section of the party wanted a change in leadership. This section also approached the President reminding him of his rights and duties under the Constitution pressing the President to 'act', and the President was reported to be in receptive mood. "Had the Chinese advance continued, anything might have happened."[32]

Dr. Radhakrishnan had shown lot of courage and statesmanship through his criticisms of the Government's policy. In his address to the first convocation of U.P. Agricultural University in November 1963, he attributed the stagnation of India's agriculture to administrative machinery. In his Republic Day broadcast to the nation in 1964, he cautioned the country against complacency about corruption. "It would be well to recognise," he said, "that tolerance of our society for weak, inefficient and unclean administration is not unlimited."

During Nehru's last days and Shastri's starting days Dr. Radhakrishnan rose in stature. "Nehru's successor was a person of scant learning and mediocre stature. Soon after Nehru's death, therefore, President Radhakrishnan began to emerge as the key figure on the political scene. In the last days of Nehru, with his authority diminished on account of physical illness and military debacle on the northern borders, the centre of gravity has begun to shift to the President.... Increasingly, Indian leaders are consulting the President, and Dr. Radhakrishnan is feeling the way toward a more significant role for himself as well as his office."

Dr. Radhakrishnan by his qualities of head and heart had endeared himself to the people of India so much so that Pandit Nehru was not happy with him. "His simple way of life, his readiness to meet anyone who sought interview and his unfailing courtesy towards his visitors, however unimportant in protocol-ridden Delhi, created the image of a President of the People. This was etched even strongly when he decided to hold periodical gatherings in the Mughal Gardens to receive petitions from aggrieved citizens."[33]

India's first President Dr. Rajendra Prasad died in retirement (1963) in Patna. In Delhi Nehru was preparing to leave on a tour for Rajasthan to collect money for the Prime Minister's National Relief Fund. On hearing the news of death, Nehru wrote to President Radhakrishnan that he would not be able to attend Rajendra Prasad's funeral adding by way of advice to the President with whom his relations were yet cordial, "I do not see any reason for you to go." Radhakrishnan replied, "No, I think I must go and attend the funeral. That respect is due to him and must be paid....I think you should give up your programme and come with me."[34]

President Giri never accepted the proposition that the President of India is a rubber stamp. "It is an erroneous impression in the minds of many sections of people that the President is a rubber stamp of the Prime Minister and the Cabinet, and that it is obligatory for him to affix his signatures to whatever is submitted to him by the Prime Minister. The Constitution gives a position of undisputed primacy to the office of the President and he should not do anything which would result in subtraction from responsible government."[35]

President Fakhruddin Ali Ahmad did not subscribe to the theory that the President was under compulsion to accept whatever was put before him by the Prime Minister. "Late Fakhruddin Ali Ahmad also felt that the President had certain reserve powers (flowing from his oath of office) and could dismiss a ministry and order a fresh poll."[36]

When Indira Gandhi felt, just before the elections of 1977, that the conditions were going out of control, she met the President to take over the administration with the help of the army. "It was alleged that he had been assigned the task of making the Army Chief of Staff, the Air and the Navy Chiefs to agree to take over the administration of the country for a limited period, suspend the Constitution and postpone the general elections which were only a month and a half away."[37] The President did not oblige her. He was shocked and got the third fatal heart attack.

President Sanjiva Reddy during his tour in the South repeatedly declared that he is not a mere Constitutional Head.

There occurred large-scale defections from the Janata party on the eve of the Monsoon Session of Parliament beginning on 9th July, 1979. The opposition to the Prime Minister (Morarji Desai) within the party mounted. Chandra Shekhar, President of the Janata Party, permitted the members not to fight Morarji's battle with regard to the corruption charges against his son Kantibhai. Y.B. Chavan, leader of the opposition, moved a no-confidence motion against the Janata Government, the Janata Executive Committee held emergency meeting on 14-15 July, 1979. Morarji was persuaded to resign, and he resigned on 15 July, 1979 from Prime Ministership. The President accepted his resignation and requested him to continue till the new government was formed.

Morarjibhai wanted to talk to the nation on 16th July, 1979 but the President asked him not to do so on the ground that caretaker Prime Minister had no right to address the nation. Consequently, the talk was cancelled.

In accordance with the constitutional practice the President asked Y.B. Chavan, leader of the opposition, to explore the possibility of forming a Government. Chavan failed. Morarjibhai, leader of the largest party (Janta), and Charan Singh, leader of Janata (S) were asked to prove which of them could command majority in the House. Morarji submitted a list of 280 followers whereas Charan Singh of 279. The total of both the lists (559) exceeded the exact number of the Lok Sabha (538). The President, after verification, was satisfied that Charan Singh's list contained more names but not majority of the House (264 names). He, therefore, called Charan Singh on 26th July, 1979 to form Government subject to seeking vote of confidence in the House very soon.

In all this drama the President did not consult his Council of Ministers. Whatever he did, he did on his own. How can we say that the President has no discretion and that he is always to go by the advice of his ministers? "In view of the Article 74(2), it is clear that there is no legal obligation on the part of the President to accept the advice. If he does, it is under a convention."[38]

Dr. K M. Munshi defends the thesis that the

President is not a figure-head. Even the framers of the Constitution did not envisage a powerless President. In support of his thesis he adduces the following arguments:

1. The President was not to be a figure-head; several members of the Constituent Assembly thought that the President was being given too much powers. Dr. Rajendra Prasad to Ambedkar, "Some people think that too much power has been given to the President." No responsible member of the Assembly stated that the President under the Constitution was to be powerless.
2. The Assembly considered the models of the British monarch and the French President. The former was found impracticable in the Indian context while the latter was ruled out.
3. The British convention according to which the monarch must act in accordance with the advice of his ministers has not been incorporated in the Constitution. "This seems to be a deliberate and not an incidental omission."[39]
4. The President is enjoined to act "in accordance with this Constitution."
5. The President is bound by his oath to 'faithfully' execute the office of the President and to preserve, protect and defend the Constitution.
6. The election procedure ensures that the President was not a creature of Parliament nor the nominee of the Party.
7. The President was made responsible to the people.
8. If powers of the President are passed on to the Prime Minister, character of quasi-federation will be totally destroyed.
9. His principal role was to "prevent a Parliamentary Government from becoming Parliamentary anarchy."[40]

We may add some other arguments given by J.R. Siwach (pp. 162 to 168) in his book, The Indian Presidency:

10. The President will ordinarily accept the advice of the Council of Ministers but he will always do so is not admitted.
11. The Constitution debars the Judiciary from examining what advice was given to the President. It implies that there is no legal bar on the President to act independently of his Cabinet.
12. The Governor-Generals of the dominions are not expected to follow the advice of their Council of Ministers blindly.
13. Certain discretionary powers have been given to the President by articles 347, 352, 356 and 360. In these articles the phrase "if the President is satisfied", according to the Privy Council means personal satisfaction.[41]

When to declare Emergency and when to revoke it depends on the personal satisfaction of the President. "When an Emergency is declared under Article 352, the normal Constitution is converted into a semi-dictatorship, is maintained only for the shortest possible time and is operated in the most restrained manner. It should also be his duty to revoke such proclamation as the Emergency is over."[42]

14. The President has also been given discretionary powers by Articles 126 and 223 for the appointment of the acting Chief Justices of the Supreme Court and High Courts in case of vacancy.

Article 74(i)—The word 'discretion' has not been unnecessarily used. It neither makes the advice binding nor prevents the President from exercising his individual judgement. "There is an area where he should discharge his duties in the exercise of his discretion"[43]

Let us try to ascertain which areas have scope for the President to act on his own.

1. Appointment of the Prime Minister—When none of the political parties had a clear majority in July 1979, after the fall of Janata Government, President Sanjiva Reddy used his discretion in calling Charan Singh to form a Government even though Charan Singh and Morarjibhai had each claimed a support of 279 members.
2. Summoning the session of Parliament.
3. Assenting to Bills or withholding assent therefrom, or sending them back for reconsideration.
4. Summoning a joint sitting of both Houses under Article 108.
5. Giving assent to the Bills reserved by the Governor under Article 201.
6. Sending messages to Parliament under Article 86.
7. Seeking an advisory opinion of the Supreme Court under Article 143.
8. Nominating members to Lok Sabha and Rajya Sabha under Articles 80 and 81.
9. Appointing members of the Union Public Service Commission under Article 316.
10. Appointment of Attorney-General under Article 76 (5)
11. Appointment of the Election Commission under Article 324 (2).
12. The President may issue such directions to any state as he considers necessary or proper for providing adequate facilities for instructions in mother tongue at the primary stage of education to children belonging to linguistic minority groups under Article 350A.

"Dr. Prasad had authorized alternative Hindi numerals under the proviso of clause (2) of Article 343".[44] However, after the end of fifteen years on January 26, 1965, when Hindi was to replace English as the official language, unless the Parliament provided otherwise, this authorization came to an end. His successor Dr. Radhakrishnan did not issue any fresh order for the use of Devnagari numerals.

13. Appointment of the Governors under Article 155.
14. Appointment of Comptroller and Auditor General under Article 76.

There are certain more matters where the President may exercise his individual judgement after consulting a body other than the Council of Ministers:

1. Giving a decision on the disqualification of members, after consulting the Election Commission.
2. Giving grants from the Union to certain states under Article 275 after consulting the Finance Commission.
3. Making rules of procedure, for a joint sitting of both the Houses after consulting the Speaker and the Chairman of the Rajya Sabha [Article 118 (3)].
4. Appointing judges for the High Courts and the Supreme Court after consulting the Chief Justice of India.
5. Consulting Attorney-General of India on legal matters.
6. Consulting Supreme Court on Constitutional matters.
7. Consulting the Governor of a state to specify Scheduled Castes under Article 341 and Scheduled Tribes under Article 342.
8. Issuing directions in accordance with the whole

or any part of the report of the Committee of Parliament on Official Language.

9. Recommendation of the Commission constituted under clause (1) of Article 344 and report of the Committees constituted under clause (4) of that article are to be taken into consideration by the President before permitting introduction of the Bill which enjoins that the proceedings of the Supreme Court and the High Court should be in the language other than in English (Article 349).
10. Under Article 217 (3) any question as to the age of the judge of the High Court will be decided by the President in consultation with the Chief Justice of India, and his decision will be final.

Since India has a written Constitution, it is the Constitution that is supreme and it is obligatory on the President to exercise his powers in such a manner that there is no infringement of the Constitution.

"It is noteworthy that the Constitution uses a variety of words in relation to the powers and functions, some of which necessarily involve the use of personal discretion"[45] 'Satisfaction' is a word which juristically means the exercise of personal discretion by the dignitary vested with the power.

The words are, "is satisfied" (Articles 123, 347, 352, 356, 360); "is of the opinion" [Article 124(3)]; "Consent" (Article 127); "determine" (Article 128); "deem necessary" [Article 124(2)]; "notifies intention" (Article 108); "decision" (Article 103); "pleasure" [Article 72(2)]; "if it appears" (Article 263); "previous sanction" (Articles 304, 349);""assent" (Article 111); "it shall be lawful to hold" (Article 365); recognise" [Article 366(22)].

The President is also vested with supra-ministerial powers. "Some of the powers of the President were supra-ministerial where the ministry could not be relied upon to advise him".[46]

1. Dismissal of the Prime Minister
2. Dismissal of a Ministry
3. Dismissal of Lok Sabha
4. The exercise of the powers of the Supreme Commander.

"Patanjali Shastri, the Chief Justice of India, has argued that the President is free to reject Ministerial advice as no limitations can be put on his powers except a specific provision of the Constitution."[47]

The Presidents on different occasions in the past have asserted themselves and made the ministers apologise or yield. The President Rajendra Prasad was kept in the dark about the whole crisis connected with the resignation of General Thimayya. When the President came to know of it, he reprimanded Krishna Menon, the Prime Minister's friend and protege. Krishna Menon apologised.

The President Prasad discovered that the Prime Minister (Nehru) had launched a practice of ignoring him altogether in the matter of appointment of the highest state officials, governors and ambassadors. The President to his mortification came to know of all these through daily newspapers. Denouncing the practice, he wrote to Nehru without mincing words, "You are laying down bad precedents. A President who did not like you could have given you a lot of trouble."[48] "The matter was ultimately discussed in the Cabinet and it was decided that the files relating to high appointments were to be submitted to the President before the issuance of final orders. "Thus it is clear, a strong President who is prepared to give up his office can ensure that his views are given proper attention by the Cabinet."[49]

We must note the words, "could have given you a lot of trouble." Manifestly only a person with powers can give a lot of trouble. A powerless person prefers to keep silent.

We have so far dealt with only the normal powers

of the President. If we take up his 'Emergency powers', sky is the limit. "It is possible to contend that the Constitution does not sufficiently guard against the President becoming a dictator."[50]

"The President at any time, either on receipt of a report from the Governor, or otherwise could assume to himself all or any of the powers of the Governors of all the seventeen states at a time and convert the Indian Union into a unitary state in accordance with the provisions of the Constitution and not by *coup d'etat.*"[51]

Even Ambedkar admitted, "The emergency provisions were liable to be misused by the Executive and that there was no check against this abuse."[52]

Evidently, the sanctions to prevent the President from exercising arbitrary authority must be conventional and political rather than legal.[53]

The clause of impeachment implies that the President has discretion to use and where he fails to use it in accordance with the constitutional requirements, he is liable to be impeached. If he is always to act according to the advice of his ministers then the maxim 'King can do no wrong' can be applied to him. The President in such a case can do no wrong and hence cannot be impeached. "If the President is always to act on the advice of his ministers, the question of his impeachment does not arise."[54]

In Britain every document signed by the King is countersigned by the Minister indicating thereby that ultimately the responsibility is that of the Minister who will be rapped in Parliament if anything goes amiss. In India no such practice is followed implying thereby that a Minister alone is not responsible, the President shares the responsibility. In the absence of any written provision containing his powers he can act as some of the Heads of States in other countries have done and we can do nothing.

"President Hindenburg of Germany with a scant courtesy and without hearing him (Brunning) said, "Now

I can have a Cabinet of my friends." Hindenburg muttered and Chancellor "Brunning parted from him for the last time."[55]

"The President of France General De Gaule used his power of dissolution as a threat in order to prevent the Parliament from dislodging the Cabinet installed by him."[56]

It is now clear beyond doubt that no one says that the President has been given no powers. Everyone admits it that he has been invested with a large number of powers. Those who want to see him act as a figure-head expect of him not to use those powers except on the advice of his Council of Ministers. Upto this day almost all of our Presidents have tried to avoid crossing swords with the Prime Minister even on vital issues. Most of them were in the evening of their life waiting for the last journey to start. Almost in all cases, both the President and the Prime Minister hailed from the same party having little area of conflicts. They have given the impression that with minor reservations they have connived to accept the doctrine that the President is a Constitutional Head.

Pandit Nehru because of his strong position and aggressive nature had reduced Dr. Rajendra Prasad as well as Radhakrishnan to a figure-head, "If Nehru's charismatic personality kept the Presidency eclipsed, there is no reason to believe that the office will remain dormant for all time. With a weak Prime Minister and with a lean majority behind him, the roles may be reversed."[57]

Shankhdhar envisions an important role for the President in case of grave national crises. "In case he feels strongly on an issue of immense importance to national interest, he can also impose his will on the ministers who act during his pleasure. He has a real choice in the making of a Prime Minister in case the Parliament does not throw up a single party to command a majority in Parliament. Through the Prime

Minister of his own choosing he can guide the selection of other ministers. Perhaps in times to come there is a distinct possibility of a political pattern to crystallise, which would bring out the latent authority of the President into the open."[58]

After studying all this we are convinced that the Constitution and its conventions have thrown up the President as a national leader. As such, he has a significant role to perform.

In support of my contention I may quote Sir Ivor Jennings:

> "Dr. Rajendra Prasad seems to have been following British conventions with some fidelity, but there is nothing in the Constitution which requires him or his successors to do so, and one of them may well say that he is not bound by the Constitutional practices followed in a foreign monarchy and that he proposes to carry out the law and the law alone."[59]

According to lawyers' view the Constitution has made the President "a despot and he can under it be a 'dictator' or an autocrat in certain circumstances."[60]

In order to arrive at some worthwhile conclusion we must familiarise ourselves with the second school of thought that believes in the Constitutional role of the President. Dr. Ambedkar, the father of the Indian Constitution, says, "In the Draft Constitution there is placed at the head of the Indian Union a functionary who is called the President of the Union. The title of this functionary reminds one of the President of the United States. But beyond identity of names there is nothing in common between the form of government prevailing in America and the form of government proposed under the Draft Constitution. The two are fundamentally different. Under the Presidential system of America the President is the Chief Head of the

Executive. The administration is vested in him. Under the Draft Constitution, the President occupies the same position as the King under the English Constitution. He is the head of the state but not of the Executive. He represents the nation but does not rule the nation. He is the symbol of the nation. His place in the administration is that of a ceremonial device on a seal by which the nation's decisions are made known.[61]
T.T Krishnamachari said:

> "So far as the relationship of the President with the Cabinet is concerned, I must say that we have, so to say, completely copied the system of responsible Government that is functioning in Britain today; we have made no deviation from it and the deviations that we have made are only such as are necessary because our Constitution is federal in character."[62]

Bannerji, Anil Chandra:

> "The Constitution, of course, does not expressly provide that the President is bound to act in accordance with ministerial advice. But the implications of the various provisions of the Constitution point to one direction—and to one direction, the President must accept ministerial advice."[63]

Basu, D.D.:

> "Our country has thus a constitutional President superimposed on the Parliamentary system of the British type."[64]

Pt. Nehru :

> "Our Constitution was basically modelled on the British Parliamentary System and that the position

of the President in India was similar to the position of the King in England."[65]

Chitaley and Rao:

"Thus the President has been made a formal or Constitutional Head of the Executive and the real executive powers are vested in the ministers or the Cabinet."[66]

V.N. Sirivastava:

"Obviously then, persuasion, not compulsion, is the normal instrument of Presidential authority."[67]

A.K. Sen

Speaking in the Lok Sabha A.K. Sen asked members to remember that the President "acted on the advice of the Cabinet" and to be more scientific, "on the advice of the Prime Minister.[68]

B.N Rau:

"One can conceive of no better future for the President of India than that he should be more and more like the monarch in England, eschewing legal powers, standing outside the clash of parties and gaining in moral authority."[69]

H.V. Kamath:

"We expect our President to be a Constitutional President and that he would always act upon the advice or direction of Parliament."[70]

C.D. Deshmukh:

> "I am sure no President will act without the consent of the Cabinet and no Cabinet will act without the consent of the majority of the House."[71]

Hanumanthaiya:

> "In this connection, the President is given the position of reigning and not ruling. The President here is more or less analogous to King of England."[72]

Sardar Patel:

> "Both these Committees (Union Constitution Committee and the Committee on the Model Provincial Construction) met and they came to the conclusion that it would suit the conditions of this country better to adopt the Parliamentary system of Constitution, the British type of Constitution with which we are familiar."[73]

Alladi Krishnaswami Ayyar:

> "The Union Constitution Committee and this Assembly have all adopted what may be called the Cabinet system of Government."[74]

Dr. Rajendra Prasad:

> "We have adopted more or less the position of the British monarch for the President....his position is that of a Constitutional President."[75]

H.M Jain:

> "They wanted to invest the President with dignity though not with power."[76]

Dr. Appadorai, the Director of the Indian School of International Studies, New Delhi, held that the provisions of the Constitution do not leave any discretion to the President to act independently of the advice of the Council of Ministers, except in two matters: (1) the choice of the Prime Minister and (2) when the Government of the Indian Union cannot be carried on in accordance with the Constitution.[77]

"Shri B.N. Rau who in his earlier writings was advocating that the President had discretionary powers, reversed his stand later on and maintained that the President was bound by the advice of his Council of Ministers."[78]

Dr. Rajendra Prasad's susceptibilities were sometimes wounded by Nehru who wanted to make the President realise that he (President) could not do certain things. Dr. Rajendra Prasad wanted to refurbish the Rashtrapati Bhawan according to his taste. As the cost involved was great, Bimanesh Chatterji, President's Secretary, was sent to the Finance Ministry where he was advised to get the approval of the Prime Minister. When the advice of the Finance Ministry was conveyed to the President, he remarked with ruffled look, "That is surprising."

Pandit Nehru one day came to Rashtrapati Bhawan to attend a meeting. He called Bimanesh and said, "What changes the President wishes to be made in his study and his living apartments may perhaps be covered within the grant allotted to your office, but make sure that no changes are made in the state rooms and in the guest wing."

"Dr. Rajendra Prasad had expressed his desire on more than one occasions to have two more official residences, one in South India, in Madras, Hyderabad or Bangalore where he could spend a month or so every year and the other in a place close to the capital where he and his family could spend a quiet week-end. The proposal for a resort at Walipur in Bulandshahr was rejected by the Prime Minister."[79] President Rajendra Prasad was very much upset when he found that spying was being practised at Rashtrapati Bhawan, "I do not know how information about this house reaches the Prime Minister's ears in a distorted form. He seems to have received some completely incorrect information about my talks with the guests at the tea parties. I have never told any person that I want to set up a Parliamentary Review Committee to study the question of Presidential powers."[80]

We have so far studied the two extreme views. But there are some writers who try to find out a via media or the middle course between the two.

Talib Rashid:

> "The powers were vested in the Indian President and their true extent depends not on the scheme of the Constitution but on its express provisions."[81]

Seervai, H .M.

> "The existence of the Council of Ministers responsible to the House of the People and, therefore, removable by it, makes it impossible for the President ordinarily to override the Government but in the very "unlikely event" of a Council of Ministers being bent upon subverting the Constitution, the President has certain reserve powers and is obliged by his oath to exercise them."

R.G. Chaturvedi points out that a situation may arise wherein the President will be guilty of violation of the Constitution not because he has refused to abide by the advice of his ministers but because he has followed an advice which does not reflect the views of House of the People, because the President is individually responsible to both the Houses.[82]

It will be pertinent to recall the decision of the Supreme Court in Golak Nath *vs*. State of Punjab wherein Justice Wanchoo declined to refer to the debates in the Constituent Assembly on the ground that they were not legitimate aids to construction.[83]

It will be appropriate to refer to the Supreme Court judgement in the case of Ram Jawaya Kapur *vs*. State of Punjab, "The expression 'aid and advice' in Article 74 may apparently suggest that it is left to the President to accept the advice or ignore the same and thus the decision on all matters will be of the President himself."[84]

Two words have been used, 'powers and functions' while referring to the President in the Constitution. Had it been the intention of the Constituent Assembly to include in the word function both powers and duties the word 'function' alone could be sufficient to substitute the long expression of powers and functions. It may be explained here that function is a perpetual process, a ceaseless everyday business whereas power can only be exercised at stated times or emergent situations. Function means capacity and not power.

It will be, therefore, in the fitness of things to admit that both the extreme views have some grains of truth. To be on the safer side we shall have to choose the middle path. Whenever it occurs to the President to perform some executive function, it is always right on his part to refer the matter to the Council of Ministers for their assistance and considered opinion; and whenever the Council of Ministers feels that the President ought to exercise certain functions in certain circumstances, it would be essential for them to advise the President on the same.

"He resembles neither the American President nor the British Queen. Irish President is a poor resemblance. Like a pendulum, President of India swings between the positions of the Presidents of the Fourth and Fifth Republics. Nevertheless, unlike pendulum, he cannot be kept at rest in the middle."[85]

"The Indian President was intended to be a model of his own and not the copy of any constitutional institution or experiment of other countries. He is not a mere title page for the Indian Constitution."[86] Constitutionally, the President supposed to be above party politics is the centre of many hopes. The citizen looks to him for the protection of his fundamental rights. The states look to him for the protection of their state rights, autonomy and political, cultural, administrative balance. The judiciary looks to him for fairness and independence. The whole nation looks to him for protection in emergency.

"The President as far as possible should act as a liaison between the Government and the opposition."[87]

Every Prime Minister knows that the President has lots of powers and can create trouble for him if the latter chooses to do so. At the same time he (Prime Minister) expects him (President) not to use any of his powers except upon his (Prime Minister's) advice. Consequently, every Prime Minister has tried as far as he could to see that the President of his choice was elected.

In India the Presidential election has till 1977 been virtually a party affair. The candidate chosen by the monolith Congress had been sure of success. It was that party which because of its all-India character had its own President. Pandit Nehru wanted Rajagopalachari as the first President of the Indian Republic but most of the Congressmen were in favour of Dr. Rajendra Prasad and with the help of Sardar Patel they elected him against the wishes of Nehru.

In 1957, Jawaharlal did his best to keep Rajendra Prasad out of Presidentship. He even made public speeches insinuating that men in high positions had love for power. "This time Maulana Azad out-manoeuvred Jawaharlal by making the offer of Presidentship to Rajendra Prasad on behalf of the High

Command and seeing to it that the offer received publicity."[88]

Dr. Rajendra Prasad always being conscious that he belonged to the same party to which the Prime Minister belonged, tried his best to avoid conflict even though he was provoked to the extent of agony on different occasions.

Rajendra Prasad knew it fully well that any clash with Nehru would enervate the Congress. It is often conceived that it was Rajendra Prasad who under acts of grave provocation gave his utmost cooperation to Nehru in order to make Parliamentary Government a success. Had a man like Nehru succeeded to Presidentship and Rajendra Prasad to Prime Ministership, the case would have been different. "It is contended in this context, rather seriously, that had Jawaharlal Nehru been President of India, the character of our executive would not have remained Parliamentary."[89]

In 1969, Indira Gandhi in order to have a President of her own choice split the Congress Party. Sanjiva Reddy was the official nominee of the Syndicate. Indira revolted, supported the candidature of V.V. Giri who was the acting President. She demanded conscience vote or freedom of vote for Congressmen. J.B. Kripalani had criticised her severely for setting dangerous precedents. There was a neck to neck race and V.V Giri won. The Syndicate expelled Indira Gandhi from the Congress dividing the party into Congress (I) and Congress (0). The Prime Minister who was having all the powers in her hands made it a prestige issue and tried all underhand means to see that Sanjiva Reddy was defeated and V.V. Giri elected. "The electors of West Bengal were threatened with President's rule and Andhra Pradesh with the dissolution of the Assembly if they did not vote for Giri."[90]

Shri V.V Giri actually acted like the Prime Minister's President by shutting his eyes to the erosion of healthy traditions. Mr. Ray a junior Supreme Court judge was promoted to be Chief Justice of India superseding three senior judges. There was hue and cry in the country. The press unequivocally denounced this unhealthy practice. President Giri, it is said, was, himself opposed to the supersession but he surrendered even though he knew that he was right.

In 1973, President Giri was reported to have addressed the Prime Minister expressing his unhappiness over the Government's handling of the situation in Andhra Pradesh.

As a former leader of the Railwaymen V.V Giri was much concerned about the railway strike in May 1974. He wrote to the Prime Minister urging her to see that the dispute should be settled amicably and without any harm to railway employees. The Prime Minister and her ministers resented such exhortations to them as an interference with their duties and responsibilities. The President kept quiet even though the railway strike was suppressed with iron hands.

Fakhruddin Ali Ahmad was the second Prime Minister's President. He was made President when Indira Gandhi was at the peak of her glory. He was thankful and indebted to her. It was Indira Gandhi's belief that being a Muslim (belonging to minority) President Ahmad will never be able or willing to lead a revolt against the Prime Minister. The subsequent events proved that she was right. He signed the declaration of Emergency in 1975 without verification whether the matter was discussed by the Cabinet. The Emergency was clamped and the ministers came to know of it through the radio or the newspapers. When Subhadra Joshi, an M.P., met Ahmad Sahib complaining against family planning excesses and demolition of houses at Turkman Gate, the President expressed his helplessness in the matter as the Prime Minister did not heed his advice.

"Ahmad Sahib earned the wrath of Sanjay Gandhi,

when he (President) pleaded for the transfer of the District Magistrate of Muzaffarnagar in U.P. who was instrumental in spilling the blood of innocent people through police firing because they opposed the Sanjay inspired programme of family planning. It so happened that all these victims were Muslims, and for pleading that justice should be done to them, Sanjay branded Ahmad Sahib as "communal and "Pakistani" and showered upon him the choicest invectives and diatribes that were available to him. He resolutely opposed the transfer of the District Magistrate as this step would cause setback to his programme."[91]

The President was asked on February 10, 1977 to direct the Armed Forces Chief to take over the administration, suspend the Constitution and postpone the general elections. He was shocked so much so that he got the third fatal heart attack. Instead of acting to set things right he died.

The dangerous trend of having Prime Minister's President set in motion by Indira Gandhi was stemmed in 1977. Shri Sanjiva Reddy was elected unanimously as the President of the Indian Union. The President has been given powers in the Constitution and he is expected to act as and when the exigency demands. "If the role of the President in the Government of the country is merely ornamental, then surely poor India can ill-afford to maintain him at such a frightful cost."[92]

"To sum up, the President of India is to be an adviser, a brake, and arbiter and not a protagonist... Thus, the President is the repository of a 'reserve power' to prevent the breakdown of the Constitution and not a device to help in the establishment of a Presidential despotism, veiled or open."[93]

"The Presidency and the Prime Ministership, to be true, is a joint venture, a partnership of powers and responsibilities of a big political concern that is India. The President, of course, functioning within the constitutional framework, cannot do without a House of the People for a long time and without a Council of Ministers at all, both of which normally lie behind the Prime Minister. The Prime Minister cannot function unless he has the cooperation of the President because of his legal powers."[94]

To conclude, we can affirm that no one denies the fact that the President has large powers. Even those who want to see the President in the role of a ceremonial head admit this fact, but they also appeal to his good sense not to use those powers except on the advice of his ministers. Ambedkar also once said that the President would be a reasonable man. That's why a mature and old man is selected as the President who can be expected to act like a nominal head because he has lost the pep and nerve of life; who has no ambition left. "What is a President after all?", Dr. Radhakrishnan used to say in private, "anyone who is nearing seventy and has lost his own will power is fit enough to be the President of India."[95]

REFERENCES

1. Jain, H.M., *The Union Executive*, p. 14.
2. Constituent Assembly Debates, Vol. IV, p. 805.
3. *Ibid.*, p.713.
4. Munshi, K.M., *The President under the Indian Constitution*, p. 32-33.
5. Rau, B.N., *India's Constitution in the Making*, 1966, p. 66.
6. C.A.D. : 10th December, 1948, p. 969.
7. *Ibid.*, p. 985.
8. Chatterji, Bimanesh, *Thousand Days with Rajaji*, 1973, p. 57.
9. *Ibid.*
10. Chaturvedi, R.G., The President and the Council of Ministers, in the *Journal of Constitutional and Parliamentary Studies*, New Delhi 1971, p. 10.
11. Markandan K.C., The Office of the President of the Indian Union—A Probe into the intentions of Founding Fathers, *Journal of Constitutional and Parliamentary Studies*, July-September, 1969, p. 68.

12. Basu, D.D., *Introduction to Constitution of India*, Vol. II, p. 417.
13. Quoted from the memoirs of H.R.H. the Duke of Windsor.
14. Markandan, K.C., *op. cit.*, p. 68.
15. C.A.D. VIII, pp. 215-16.
16. Iyer, Alladi Krishnaswami, C.A.D. X, p. 270.
17. Chaturvedi, R.G., The President and the Council of Ministers in the *Journal of Constitutional and Parliamentary Studies*, New Delhi, 1971, p. 17.
18. Rout, Bishnu Charan, *Parliamentary Studies*, Feb-March, 1967, p. 18.
19. AIR, 1955, S.C. 549.
20. Prasad Papers—*Rajendra Prasad to Nehru*, July 24, 1948.
21. Mishra, R.N., *The President of the Indian Republic*, 1964, p. 61.
22. Chaturvedi, R.G., The President and the Council of Ministers in the *Journal of Constitutional and Parliamentary Studies*, New Delhi, 1971, p. 39.
23. Munshi, K.M., *Indian Constitutional Documents*, Vol. I, Pilgrimage to Freedom (1902-1950), 1967, p. 290.
24. Chatterji, Bimanesh, *The Presidential Predicament—Rajendra Prasad Remembered*—Affiliated East West Press Pvt. Ltd., New Delhi, 1974, p. 37.
25. *Ibid.*, p. 37.
26. *Ibid.*, pp. 39-41.
27. *Ibid.*, p. 41.
28. Pandit, H.N., *The Prime Minister's President*, S. Chand & Co. 1974, p.13.
29. Munshi, K.M., *Indian Constitutional Documents*, Vol. I, p. 289.
30. Durga Das, *India from Curzon to Nehru and After*, p. 335.
31. Lakshmi writing in '*Uttar Pradesh*' of April, 1963.
32. Gupta, M.G., *Aspects of Indian Constitution*, Central Book Depot, Allahabad, p. 197.
33. Asoka Chanda, *The Hindustan Times*, May 14, 1967.
34. Pandit, H.N., *Prime Minister's President*, S. Chand & Co. New Delhi, 1974, p. 14.
35. Giri, V.V., President of India, *The Illustrated Weekly of India*, July 31, 1977, pp. 8-10
36. Inderjit, Historic but unpublished, *The Tribune*, July 19, 1977.
37. Rehmany, F.A.A. (Additional Private Secretary to the President), The Last Unhappy Days of Fakhruddin Ali Ahmad, *Organiser*, January, 14, 1978.
38. A Special Correspondent—Advice to the President—The Letter

and Spirit of the Constitution in the Parliamentary Studies of September 1968, pp. 15 - 17.
39. Asoka Chanda, *The Statesman* of March 31, 1967, p. 8.
40. Munshi, K.M., *The President under the Indian Constitution*, 1963, p. 9.
41. Shukla, V.N. *Commentaries on the Constitution of India*, 3rd edition, 1960, p. 438.
42. Santhanam K., *The Statesman*, May 1, 1967, p. 8.
43. Subba Rao, K., *The Tribune*, August 15, 1969, p. 4.
44. *The Statesman*, New Delhi, July 9, 1967, p. 8.
45. Munshi, K.M., *The President under the Indian Constitution*, p. 44.
46. Munshi, K.M., Powers and Functions of the President, *The Hindustan Times* (Republic Day Supplement), 26 January, 1956.
47. Punjabi, K.L., *Rajendra Prasad*, Madras, 1960, p. 161.
48. Pandit, H.N., The Prime Minister's President, p. 18.
49. Santhanam, K., The President of India, *The Journal of Constitutional and Parliamentary Studies*, July-Sept. 1969, p. 1.
50. Gledhill, Allen, *The Republic of India*, 1951, p.1.
51. Dash, S.C. President as the Instrument of Bundesexekuntion, *The Journal of Constitutional and Parliamentary Studies*, Oct.-Dec. 1969, p. 37.
52. C.A.D., Vol. IX, p. 177.
53. Bomball, K.R., The President of India — Limits of Discretion — *The Indian Journal of Political Science*, July-Dec. 1966, p. 28.
54. Srivastava, G.P., *Journal of Constitutional and Parliamentary Studies*, Vol. III, No.4., Oct.-Dec. 1969, p. 68.
55. Bennet, Wheeler, *The Nemesis of Power*, 1953, p. 245.
56. Pickles, Dorothy, *The Fifth French Republic*, 1960, p. 146.
57. Shankhdhar, M.M., On the Office of the President, *Journal of Constitutional and Parliamentary Studies*, Vol. I, July- Sept., 1967, No. 3, p. 85.
58. *Ibid.*, p. 85.
59. Jennings, Sir Ivor, Crown and Commonwealth in Asia, *International Affairs*, Vol. 32, No. 2, April, 1956, pp. 144-145.
60. Gupta, Madan Gopal, *Aspects of Indian Constitution*, p. 161.
61. C.A.D. VII, p. 32.
62. Krishnamachari, T.T., C.A.D., X, p. 956.
63. Bannerji, Anil Chandra, *A Survey of the Indian Constitution*, p. 79.

64. Basu, Durga Das, *Commentary on the Constitution of India*, 3rd ed., Vol. I, p. 417.
65. Pt. Nehru, *The Statesman*, Calcutta, 16th December, 1960.
66. Chitaley and Rao, *The Constitution of India*, 2nd ed. 1970, p. 822, (The All India Reporter Ltd. Publisher).
67. Sirivastava, Vishnu Narain, *Indian Journal of Political Science*, April-June 1966, pp. 26-36.
68. Sen, A.K., *The Statesman*, 18 April, 1957, p. 4.
69. Rau, B.N., *The Constitution of India in the Making*, p. 382.
70. Kamath, H.V., C.A.D., VIII, p. 205.
71. Deshmukh, C.D., C.A.D., VIII, p. 211.
72. Hanumanthaiya, C.A.D., VII, p. 996.
73. Pate, S., C.A.D., IV., p. 580.
74. Aiyyar, A.K., C.A.D., XI, p. 956.
75. Dr. Rajendra Prasad, C.A.D., XI, p. 988.
76. Jain, H. M., *The Union Executive*, p. 141.
77. Das, B.C., *The President of India*, 1977, p. viii.
78. Rau, B.N., The Cabinet and the President, *The Hindu* of May 14, 1957.
79. Chatterji, Bimanesh, *The Presidential Predicament*, Rajendra Prasad Remembered, pp. 15 and 41.
80. *Ibid.*, p. 61.
81. Talib, Rashid, President's Powers, *The Hindustan Times* of August 17, 1969, p. 19.
82. Chaturvedi, R.G., *The President, and the Council of Ministers*, The Institute of Constitutional and Parliamentary Studies, New Delhi, 1971, p. 22.
83. A.I.R., 1967, S.C., 1643, 1682.
84. A.I.R., 1955, S.C., 549.
85. Qureshi, Zaheer Masud, *The President of India*, 1962, p. 43.
86. Mukherji, Justice P.B. The Critical Problems of the Indian Constitution—Chaman Lal Setalvad Lectures, November, 1966.
87. Das, B.C., *The President of India*, 1977, p. xi.
88. Munshi, K.M., Indian Constitutional Documents, Vol. I—Pilgrimage to Freedom (1902-1950), 1967, p. 287.
89. Lal, J.N., Relations between Indian President and Prime Minister in *Modern Review* of January, 1971.
90. Qureshi, Zaheer Masud, *A Study for Presidential Elections*, Vikas, 1973, p. 133.
91. Rehmaney, F.A.A., The Last Unhappy Days of Fakhruddin Ali Ahmad, *The Organiser* of January 14, 1979.
92. Kulkarni, V.B., *My Country and My Rulers—Powers of the President*, p. 247.

93. Sirivastava, Vishnu Narain, Indian Presidency in *Indian Journal of Political Science*, April-June 1966, pp. 26-36.
94. Dr. Lal, Dr. J.N., Relations between Indian President and Prime Minister in *The Modern Review* of January 1971.
95. Pandit, H.N., *The Prime Minister's President*, p. 52.

6
The Prime Minister and the Civil Service

"Bureaucracy is an irritating word."[1] Different writers have interpreted it in different ways. Early writers in the nineteenth century meant by it 'government by officials'. The French word Bureaux denoted office or department. There was a general fear that the people working in offices were gathering too much power in their hands and their activities were held to be fussy and meddlesome, cumbersome and mediocre. Prof. Laski writing in 1930 defined bureaucracy as 'a system of government', the control of which is so completely in the hands of officials that their power endangers the liberties of ordinary citizens. In our own day the word is often used generally to indicate too many regulations, delay, red-tape or inefficiency. "It may be defined as a systematic organisation of tasks and individuals into a pattern which can most effectively achieve the ends of collective efforts."[2] "Bureaucracy is an essential part of any political society. It is the keel of the ship of the state. Since ancient times it has been well organised in countries like Greece, Rome, India and China....Bureaucracy is often criticised but cannot be dispensed with."[3]

The Germans put a serious construction on it. In Germany even before the amalgamation of many separate states into the German Empire (after the Franco-Prussian War of 1870), the tradition of highly centralised government by professional officials was in existence. First the word was used for the growing power of these officials and then for the body of the officials.

The German writer Max Weber, the giant among the thinkers in this field, wrote in the end of the last century giving a new dimension to the discussion. He used the word in a different sense meaning a method of organising administrative staff. He described what he considered must be the best. He seemed to have conceived of administration as being a matter of using knowledge and then applying correct rules and procedures to solve day-to-day problems (all based on written documents). He used the word 'rational' to mean the method which should inevitably ensure that all this was actually done. By this he meant ideal type of bureaucracy. He knew that the ideal type never existed in exactly the form in which he conceived it. His concept helps us to understand the true nature of an administration, a measurement to gauge. Weber's ideal type had ten characteristics which are set out clearly in Martin Albrow's book '*Bureaucracy*'. These are as follows:

1. Officials are personally free (*e.g.* they are not the personal servants of any member of government)—they carry out only the duties of their office.
2. There is a hierarchy of offices.
3. The functions of the offices are clearly specified.
4. Officials are appointed under a contract.
5. They should be selected on the basis of professional qualification with ideally a diploma gained by an examination.
6. They have a salary graded according to the position in the hierarchy and usually pension rights and they can always resign and in certain circumstances be dismissed.
7. The official's post is his sole or major occupation (*e.g.* he does not at the same time carry on a business or practice his profession privately).
8. There is a career structure and promotion is possible.

9. The official may appropriate neither the post nor the resources that go with it (*e.g.* he may not sell it, as commissions in the Army were once sold in this country, or leave it to his son).
10. The official is subject to a unified control and disciplinary system (*e.g.* there is some form of code of conduct applicable to all officials in the same group).[4]

Weber's concept was applicable to the highly centralised German system. In modern democracies it appears to be too rigid and rule-bound. However, it is still interesting to consider how far our practice of public andministration corresponds to Weber's ideal type of bureaucracy.

Our form of organisation has some of the features of Weber's 'ideal type' of 'bureaucracy'. The digression has been necessitated by the modern conditions. Weber seems to have seen it as the application of a code of instructions, and the carrying out of orders which came down the hierarchy from those having the authority to give them. We can accept Weber's definition only as a landmark. We may quote here a practical definition given by Prof. Peter Blan, Columbia University, U.S.A., from his book *Bureaucracy in Modern Society*.

> "The type of organisation designed to accomplish large-scale administrative tasks by systematically coordinating the work of many individuals is called a bureaucracy."

By the beginning of the present century bureaucracy in the form of a body of public officials was accepted as something that was necessary in any modern state. Salaried people were a necessary concomitant to the service of the state. The very fact that they were salaried and spent their whole time on their work meant that they acquired special skills and experience. They thus become naturally more powerful and isolated from the common man.

Before 1780 conditions did not exist in Britain where the concept of civil service as we understand it now could be made applicable. There were no fixed tenures. Some administrators drifted on for extraordinarily long periods. Thomas Pratt, for example entered the treasury as a boy of seventeen in 1724 and was still drawing his salary eighty years later. Many of those who served the Crown in an administrative capacity did so for a long time or even for the whole of their working lives. It was sometimes very difficult to get rid of administrators even when guilty of flagrant neglect of duty. "Patent officers had much more security of tenure than twentieth century civil servants and much more than most people would think desirable."[5]

Naturally, a person working on the same post for half a century will acquire such a specialisation as will serve like a cocoon to step outside of which becomes a sin. "The Civil Service is, by European standards, an over-specialised, parochial, closed cooperation."[6]

In 1833 Northcole and Trevelyn were appointed in Britain to examine the organisation of all the government departments, especially the arrangements for recruitment and promotion. The object of the examination as mentioned in the treasury minutes of appointment was that the business of the public should be done in the best and most economical manner. Six months later the famous report was presented which became the foundation of modern civil service.

The work in the top posts is very difficult. Decisions made here may affect the lives of every one of us. Mistakes and errors of judgements can have far-reaching unpleasant consequences. People filling these posts can determine the tone for the whole service, especially the civil servants in the local offices whom members of the public meet every day, regarding many matters concerning their life. It, therefore, becomes imperative that the top posts ought to be filled by some of the best brains in the country through an impartial interviewing body.

The term 'civil servant' was first used in India in contrast to the military servants of the East India Company. The term when first used in Britain meant the same thing. We find a reference to it in Palmerston's memorandum on relations between the Secretary of War and Commander-in Chief dated 1811, where he speaks of the former as 'a civil servant of the Crown'. To make it clear that no distinction is to be drawn between civil and political service, he alludes to Secretary's civil character as a political servant of the Crown. This usage never took root. In 1847 it was inscribed on a memorial plaque of Lt. Col. Sir George Gipps R.E., a reference to his honourable and useful career in the military and civil service of his country although he had never held a civil service appointment in the modern sense. The earliest document to embody the modern distinction is a treasury circular dating 1816, which speaks of servants in the civil service of the country and so eligible for superannuation as distinct from political servants.

There were governments in India in the past and there were servants too, but there was no organised body of servants who were recruited on the basis of merit and were allowed to enjoy certain rights in order to be able to discharge their duties sincerely and faithfully. The recruitment was made on religious, political, filial and caste basis. A civil servant could go on his post as far as his health permitted. A civil servant in many cases bequeathed his post to his son. The Britishers modernised the services and gave them a new shape. The civil servants during the British time were one of the main props of the British Empire.

The East India Company wanted efficient and able persons who could run the British administration in India smoothly. It was, therefore, thought appropriate to devise examination system to select the best. To attract the ablest and the best handsome salaries or prospects were offered. Llyod George called the Indian Civil Service the steel frame of the British Government in India.

The future of a country depends not so much on its construction, as on the quality of its administration. It is the experience of knowledgeable persons that there is no subject more important than administration. One writer goes so far as to say that the future of the civilised government and indeed of the civilisation itself rests on our ability to develop a science and philosophy and practice of administration, competent to discharge the public functions of a civilised society. Jeremy Bentham's noble ideal of the "greatest happiness of the greatest number" cannot be realised without an able, upright and dedicated bureaucracy.

The Britishers had a thorough understanding of this fact. They, therefore, carefully devised methods to attain to high standards of probity and efficiency in their administration in India. They were convinced that a combination of integrity, efficiency, devotion and loyalty provided true basis for enlightened government. In those days good family background was also considered one of the qualifications. "A number of Indian families, with long traditions of learning at home, prided themselves on seeing their sons holding a place in the top storey of the country's administrative edifice. The revenue collectors of those days were the monarchs of their districts."[7]

Many Indians rose to high positions and did their duty with courage and independence unmindful of the consequences. For instance, C.D. Deshmukh as Finance Secretary told the British Governor of an Indian province that his A.D.C. would not be entitled to allowance for accompanying his (Governor's) wife to a sea port to see her off. "He also fearlessly told the Prime Minister of a province in 1938 that he could not order a superintending engineer to help in the construction of the Congress camp"[8] Paul H. Appleby wrote in his report on the Indian Administration: "India in these services shares with Britain the distinction of having the best body of generalist civil servants in the world."

Sardar Patel was the foremost amongst the Congress leaders to realize the importance of civil servants to assist the country in the task of its social and economic reconstruction. Sardar being a shrewd and practical statesman reposed full confidence in their loyalty and honesty. He appealed to them to serve their motherland with devotion. Speaking in Bombay in October 1949, he silenced the critics of civil services by saying that outsiders cannot appreciate their work. "Many of them are loyal workers and patriots and are working with us day and night. All that we have been able to achieve, whether it be in the sphere of States or in Kashmir or in other theatres, has been possible because of their loyalty and whole-hearted support"[9]

Sardar was sagacious enough to plan the dissolution of I.C.S. and replace it with I.A.S. (Indian Administrative Service), considering their great worth he urged Rajagopalachari, Rajendra Prasad and Nehru to give constitutional guarantees to civil servants with regard to the security of their service.

Consequently, he was against the interference of politicians both in the recruitment and control of services. He said, "An efficient, disciplined and contented service assured of its prospects as a result of diligent and honest work is a *sine qua non* of sound administration."[10]

The distinguished civilian Shri H.V.R. Iyengar wrote that he once took a decision which was not in accordance with the Sardar's point of view, but he was never made to regret his action. "When the matter subsequently came before the Cabinet, he (Sardar Patel) told them that the decision was his, and there the matter ended. The incident made a striking impression on me."[11]

Another eminent civilian officer H.M. Patel, close to the Sardar, described the Deputy Prime Minister as a tower of strength to the civilians."When he (Sardar) died in December 1950" Patel (H.M.) said,

> "All the civil servants, from the Under Secretary upwards, met in the central hall of Parliament in New Delhi with Sir Girja Shankar Bajpayee in the chair to mourn his death. After paying eloquent tributes to his statesmanship, they passed a resolution pledging their devoted service to the nation. Only the Sardar could command such a tribute."[12]

Nehru, on the other hand, was distrustful of the Indian Civil Service. He was not prepared to recognise the intellectual eminence of its members. "The standard of the service" according to him, "was necessarily one of mediocrity". It was strange that more members of the Nehru family entered this service than perhaps those of any other Indian family. Nehru was of the opinion that the civil service was at best a necessary evil which had to be tolerated. The idealist in Nehru nourished a conception of an Indian civil servant in his own image. "The basic test of an officer of new India should be whether he can draw out the cooperation of the people. If the official who is incharge of that cannot do it, does not matter how able or clever he is; he is just not suitable for the task....The services must gradually cease to think of themselves as some select coterie."[13]

Lesser men in power signally failed to realise the value of the services for the nation. Many politicians in the states underrated All India Services and tried to humiliate upright and assertive officers.

An I.A.S. officer who had worked with much distinction to modernize the administration of Hyderabad after the Police action in September 1948, had to seek premature retirement after some time as he could not get on with a minister who combined arrogance with pigheadedness.

"We have now reached a situation in the government of the country when ignorant are leading the ignorant."[14]

The ministers in the states did not follow Sardar Patel in proper evaluation of the services. They rather followed Nehru who described the services as a "Jungle". The Administrative Reforms Commission characterised it as an "Octopus".

An I.A.S. officer was working as the head of a department in a state. "There was a change of government and a well-known public leader became his minister who was not highly educated in the formal sense but he was shrewd."

He said to the officer: "This is my first experience as minister. Please advise me as to how I should conduct myself." "Well, Sir", the officer replied, "You should, as a minister, restrict yourself to policy matters and leave administrative matters, particularly personnel matters, to the secretary and myself."

The minister smiled with a mischievous twinkle in his eyes and remarked, "I would like to reverse the roles. You take care of policy matters. I shall deal with appointments, promotions, punishments and transfer of the staff."[15]

This has become the order of the day in the states.

> "When I was the head of a department, its portfolio was assigned to a new minister. He sent me a long list of non-Gazetted staff of inspectors, sub-inspectors, etc, whom he wanted to be transferred. This was a matter entirely within my purview and he was well aware of it. I wanted to avoid a confrontation and so I pointed out in writing the objections as regards effecting transfers of some of them."
>
> "He came on tour to the place where my

headquarters were located. I went to see him. I found that he was visibly annoyed. He told me, with ill-grace, that I could do as I pleased. I partially complied with his wishes. But what stumped me completely was that after some time he asked me to return the list. Obviously, he wished to obliterate the evidence of his having transferred in a matter that was outside his jurisdiction. He did not know that in my note on the file, I had recorded, that the minister had desired me to make this transfer."[16]

Another interesting episode. An Inspector General of Police once found that a Home Minister was directly passing orders of transfers of inspectors, sub-inspectors, head-constables and even constables. The I.G. was considerably perturbed over this. He and his Home Secretary approached the minister and pleaded: "How can discipline be maintained in the force, sir, if subordinate police officers bypass me and are directly entertained by you?"

The Home Minister replied: "I appreciate what you say but we have our compulsions. Anyway, I shall abstain in future."

For some time, there was an improvement but things became chaotic again as elections drew near. The minister was using thanedars to influence voters.[17]

A lady Deputy Commssioner was phoned by a Chief Minister to tell her that she should ensure that so and so is elected. The ballot boxes were lying sealed under safe custody with the police keping guard over them. She could do nothing. She was very much upset. When the counting took place, the gentleman in question lost heavily. To her good luck, her state had a new Chief Minister after the elections.

Even though Nehru had little appreciation for bureaucracy yet he tolerated it taking it as a necessary evil.

"In 1947, Pandit Nehru inherited the bureaucratic

apparatus from the foreign rulers when they left, and he kept it as it was."[18] The inherited apparatus was invented by the British Government for our suppression and maximum exploitation. After partition an urgent need to overhaul it completely was felt. The changes were never attempted or undertaken. Pandit Nehru could have altered the system in such a way as even an illiterate could reap the benefits accruing from the policies of free India. "It would be idle" he writes, "to deny the good qualities of the I.C.S. for we are not allowed to forget them, but so much bunkum is said about this service that I sometimes feel that little debunking would be desirable. The American Economist Veblan has called the privileged classes 'the kept classes.' I think it would be equally true to call the I.C.S. as well as the other imperial services the 'Kept Classes.' They are a very expensive luxury."[19]

The Civil Service structure remained almost the same upto Lal Bahadur Shastri. The deterioration which had set in the states had yet made no inroad at the centre. The inroad was, however, made after the elections of 1971 when Indira Gandhi emerged with thumping majority on her own and became 'the most powerful woman in the world'.

Our early political leaders like Jawaharlal Nehru, Vallabhbhai Patel, Rajaji, Dr. Rajendra Prasad, Maulana Azad, Rafi Ahmad Kidwai and Govind Vallabh Pant were first-rate politicians with integrity. They appreciated the part that the services were playing and they thought it essential to advise them, to encourage them on all matters and to leave them free to implement the policies of Government, once they were approved by the legislatures. The administrators were not intimidated to express themselves freely. Even if there were differences between the ministers and the civil servants it was taken, in the right spirit, as a part of the game.

"I still recollect the difference of opinion I had with Rajaji on decontrol of textiles whilst I advised strongly against it because I was afraid that in the then prevailing situation decontrol might result in rise in prices, thus creating difficulties for the poor consumers. When after repeatedly being asked to reconsider the matter I stuck to my position, Rajaji expressed his sorrow that whilst he expected me to take the burden of control off his shoulders, I was not helping him to do so. In reply I said that the matter was quite simple. He could get another Textile Commissioner to advise him to decontrol, and I offered to proceed on leave to facilitate him doing so. Not only did he firmly turn down my offer but he accepted my view and the control remained. He told me that he greatly appreciated my firmness on a matter which I sincerely thought to be of importance to the people. Thereafter, my relations with him not only improved but became one of affection and regard on both sides which persisted till his death. I had a similar disagreement with Sardar Patel on another matter, *viz.* of advice to Pandit Jawaharlal Nehru as his Principal Secretary. Here again, Sardar accepted my view and in fact appreciated my stand. Sardar very often used to say that services were the tools of the politicians and that it will be very wrong for the politicians to blunt these tools.[20]

Prime Minister as the Chief Administrator

A Prime Minister in a Parliamentary democracy has to recognise the importance of Civil Service. Pandit Nehru used to keep the portfolio of Foreign Affairs with him. He had direct connections with the Foreign Affairs Department. He would also keep in touch with senior officers of the other departments bypassing ministers sometimes. In Britain also the Prime Minister likes to maintain contact with the senior civil servants. "The Prime Minister also holds the office of First Lord of the Treasury. It is testimony to the fact that whosoever controls the strings controls the administration....This is the only Ministry with two permanent under secretaries, one of whom is the Principal Civil Servant and other is incharge of the economic work of the department. The senior of these Under Secretaries is also head of the Cabinet office and in that capacity he may well see more of the Prime Minister than any other man".[21]

The special feature of the civil service is that while the masters change, the servants remain the same.

Ministers may come and Ministers may go, but civil servants go on forever. Our administrative set-up is based on the British system. The relationship, in Britain between the political set-up and the services may be explained by an illustration.

A summit meeting, attended by Stalin, Roosevelt and Churchill, was held towards the close of the Second World War. It was followed by another but by that time the war was over and in Britain, Attlee had replaced Churchill as the Prime Minister. It was noted by Stalin and Roosevelt with some astonishment that at both the meetings, the same staff, including the personal staff, had accompanied the British Prime Minister.

> "When I succeeded Mr. Churchill as Prime Minister and returned to the Conference at Potsdam, I took with me precisely the same team of civil servants including even the principal secretary, as had served my predecessor. This occasioned a lively surprise among our American friends who were accustomed to the American system whereby the leading official advisers of the President and the members of his Cabinet are usually politically of his own colour."[22]

The thing is not so simple as it is described to be that the politicians are to lay down the policy and the services are duty-bound to carry them out faithfully without mental reservations. The relation is quite complex with many undertones and overtones.

No Prime Minister can work alone. He has to select a team of experienced persons who can help him in his task of formulation of policy.

Mr. Wilson has said that he favours people with 'earthy' experiences, *e.g.* promising civil servants from the ministries such as Agriculture and Power as well as budding diplomats from the foreign office. "Hand-picked private secretaries of top calibre may quite properly exert some influence over the Prime Minister's thinking. What is important is that they should not be yesmen"[23] "Llyod George once reminded Winston Churchill during the latter's war-time premiership, how important it was for a Prime Minister to be surrounded by people who would stand up and say 'No, No, No"[24] "No small part of Mr. Macmillan's success as a Prime Minister was the candid advice he could always expect from such Private Secretaries as Timothy Blight and John Wyndham."[25]

"A civil servant who first finds out what his Minister wants to do and then advised him accordingly is a bad civil servant."[26]

The successful implementation of Prime Minister Nehru's secular policies depended on the earnest application by civil servants. The communal riots in Bengal affected *Goalas* and *Majhis* of Bihar, most of whom had gone to Calcutta and all over East Bengal. They had suffered heavily and had all come back from Bengal crying for revenge against the local Muslims. "I had foreseen that the trouble would break out in Saran ....I talked to all my officers and convinced them that any communal riot in a Hindu majority area would go to prove Jinnah's contention that the Hindus and the Muslims were two separate nations and could not live together, and, therefore, it was the duty of police officers fo all ranks to see that communal riots did not break out in a Hindu majority district like Saran....When the wave of communal riots swept across Saran district, policemen of all ranks, including the village chowkidars, rose like one man and fought the advancing flames, and we had the satisfaction of putting down the disturbances with a strong hand without asking for any assistance."[27]

> "The Civil Service is also said to be dominated by the Prime Minister. As Government expanded its activities, there has been a growing need to centralise and coordinate the administration to ensure coherence of policy."[28]
> "Thus the Prime Minister controls his party, Parliament, the Cabinet, and the Civil Service. But he can also control to a great extent the succession to his position."[29]

Prime Minister vis-a-vis Cabinet Secretariat and his own Secretariat

It cannot be gainsaid that tremendous is the power that a Prime Minister possesses. Not only he but his secretaries also come to have an unprecedented accretion of powers around them. Nrhru's secretary John Mathai had become very powerful as all matters, including confidential ones, passed through him. Mr. Jha had become next to Prime Minister Lal Bahadur Shastri in powers and prestige. Indira Gandhi had her own powerful persons, P.N. Haksar, Yashpal Kapur and R.K. Dhawan. Morarjibhai had his own man V. Shankar.

"Mr. Haksar was the virtual Prime Minister during the time of Indira Gandhi. All the moves to consolidate and strengthen her authority emanated from him."[30] Even the 'stray thoughts' which she read at the crucial A.I.C.C. session at Bangalore were penned by him. "The strategy to bring down the opposition governments in many states was devised by him. Even the Congress split of 1969 was engineered by him."[31] Mrs. Indira Gandhi owed all her successes to his fertile brain. As long as he remained with her she went on ascending the ladder of name and fame. Yashpal Kapur and R.K. Dhawan were like bullies. They had less brains but more of aggression, sometimes to the point of crudeness.

The Research and Analysis Wing (RAW) headed by Kau, another Kashmiri Brahman, was transformed into a personal spy agency of Indira Gandhi. Mrs. Gandhi must have carefully assessed the dossiers on her colleagues and ministers in the states from her own sources of intelligence besides information supplied by the Central Intelligence Bureau. "From the RAW and the Governors of states, who maintained their own dossiers, copies of which were supplied to her....she knew of every skeleton in every cupboard. She maintained every bit of evidence that could be used as material to silence her critics in the party....She had her spies everywhere."[32]

The Secretary to the Prime Minister rapidly emerged as the most influential civil servant of the Shastri Transition.[33]

The origins of new secretariat may be traced to Shastri's reliance, some say, dependence, on the advice of civil servants during his tenure as Home Minister and even earlier.

The justification of the new secretariat and its formal functions were explained by Jha (Private Secretary to the Prime Minister, Lal Bahadur Shastri) in a candid and revealing interview a few months after his appointment. "Two factors were cited for its creation; the difference in the manner of the work and decision making of the two Prime Ministers; and the fact that Nehru held a specific portfolio while Shastri does not.... whenever a proposal was put to Nehru, outside the sphere of external affairs, he would answer promptly, 'yes', I agree or 'no', 'I have doubts', and he would pass the matter on to the appropriate Ministry for detailed consideration; later, when this issue came before Cabinet, he would put his mind to it; and not infrequently at that late stage Nehru would reject the proposal with the result that the effort in preparing the material would be wasted....The new secretariat was designed to prevent this inefficient way of conducting government business, by keeping the Prime Minister advised throughout. Stated somewhat differently, Jha remarked that Nehru took decision quietly and Shastri acts slowly."[34] Mrs. Gandhi's downfall is sometimes attributed to her parting of ways with Haksar who had a row with Sanjay Gandhi on Maruti affair. A Prime Minister must not offend his or her civil servant on personal grounds. "He (British Prime Minister) cannot afford to offend the civil service, whose services he needs in order to execute his abrasive counter revolution."[35]

There have been cases where the Prime Ministers fell because they did not take their secretary into confidence. "There was a case in which the Attorney General was prosecuting a communist for inciting the troops to insurrection, and he was told to stop the prosecution because the Cabinet didn't like it. Ramsay Macdonald, who was the Prime Minister, having stated that he was not consulted or implicated (which as the Cabinet ministers made clear was a lie) tried to challenge the record. The result was a deadly and elaborate minute from the Cabinet Secretary (at that time Hankey) to the Prime Minister—which leaked widely in Whitehall. Macdonald was forced to make a partial withdrawal which led to the fall of the Government."[36]

The above incident is a pointer to the importance of the Cabinet secretariat. "The Cabinet Secretary can browbeat a Prime Minister. There are officials in Whitehall who are very powerful in their own right, and one of the centres of power is the cabinet secretariat. I would say the Secretary to the Cabinet is to the Prime Minister what a Permanent Secretary is to a departmental chief."[37] In addition to the Cabinet secretariat every Prime Minister forms an informal group of advisers whom he trusts most. Indira Gandhi like the U.S. President had her 'Kitchen Cabinet' comprising Chandra Shekhar, Mohan Dharia, I.K. Gujral, during the first part of her regime. Similarly, Llyod George in Britain had his 'garden suburb' (small group of informal advisers), academics working in temporary huts in the garden of 10, Downing Street. Churchill had his 'statistical section under Prof. Lindemann (Lord Cherwell)', Mr. Wilson had his 'Policy Unit'.[38]

Macaulay highlighted the value of the civil service in his speech before the House of Commons that "even the character of the Governor-General was less important than the characters and spirit of the servants by whom the administration of India was carried on".[39]

Nehru because of his inborn dislike of the servants sometimes committed such acts as were tantamount to disgrace or offence to them. As a result, he along with the nation had to suffer.

In October, 1962 war with China the Indian troops were deliberately sent to doom. They were led by Brigadier Brij Mohan Kaul, Nehru's favourite, who had, according to J.P. Dalvi, superseded at least six officers to become Chief of the General Staff. Though he was Sandhurst trained for infantry, he had never served with a combat arm before so that he fully deserved to be put in the category of those Indian Generals who were picturesquely described by Prof. Galbraith as amiable frauds.[40]

Such a dangerous trend of supersession started by Nehru was viewed with apprehension by the Civil Service. They (services) were prepared to give of their best to Nehru also if he sought their cooperation. It is unfortunate that this great man had an inborn suspicion of the bureaucracy although he became responsible for its growth into what he himself called a "Jungle".[41] Nevertheless, Nehru had to yield before the courageous stand taken by some bold officers. "The reports of the Intelligence Bureau, which maintained that trouble in East Pakistan was continuing, were very upsetting to the Prime Minister, because these indirectly supported the criticism levelled against him for signing pact (with Liaqat Ali, Prime Minister of Pakistan). At last the Prime Minister lost patience and passed one of his severest strictures against the Intelligence Bureau. The Director, Sanjivi, was out of the country and, as I was the senior most Deputy Director, all these reports used to be processed and signed by me. He almost accused the officers, who were collecting the information and were compiling the reports, as being prejudiced. Naturally, the officers in West Bengal who were contacting the refugees were all Bengalis and so he suspected that they were swayed by the high feelings prevailing in West Bengal. The fact that I had a Bengali name must have also prejudiced him against me as Bengalis were usually opposed to the pact. Iyengar, to whom these remarks had been sent, showed them to me and I was extremely upset....we had invariably mentioned that the reports which were being passed on to the Government had been collected from refugees. The statements of the refugees must be exaggerated and one could easily dismiss as much as fifty percent as exaggerations and distortions. Yet if one believed only fifty percent of the reports, it would appear that things were not as smooth in East Pakistan as one could wish them to be....How could we be expected at the same time to fabricate reports that everything was normal in East Pakistan when it was not. I then took up the question of the Prime Minister's remarks against me, particularly his expression of doubt about my honesty and integrity.

"The Home Secretary was very disturbed. I, however, maintained that unless these remarks were withdrawn, I could not serve under the Government

> of India whose Prime Minister distrusted me....I maintained that these reports gave a fair picture of the situation in East Pakistan....We could not cater reports to his liking....I concluded by saying that if the remarks against me were not withdrawn I might be relieved immediately from my post and sent back to my state.
>
> "Iyengar (Home Secretary) on directions from Sardar Patel met the Prime Minister and remained with him that night from 10 p.m. to 1 a.m. ....The result of all this talk was that the Prime Minister wrote a note that his previous day's remarks should be considered as not having been written at all".[42]

Nehru admitted the importance of the civil service in his heart, outwardly though he criticised them.

The honour and grace of civil service depend not upon any constitutional guarantee but on the inhering qualities of service men *i.e.* sincerity, integrity, boldness and frankness. Civil servants with these qualities earn respect for the whole service. Some of the Civil servants saved big disasters by tendering sincere, impartial and rational advice to the Prime Minister or the Minister as the case may be.

"In April 1950, serious communal riots swept East Pakistan (now Bangladesh), as a result of which lakhs of Hindus were driven out of their homes and were forced to come as refugees to West Bengal and other parts of India, and there were repercussions of these riots in certain parts of West Bengal and Calcutta. At one time Sardar Patel was very much exercised over the treatment of the minority in East Pakistan. But on the day the Cabinet was due to meet to take a final decision, I was called by H.V.R. Iyengar, the Home Secretary and he asked about my views in this matter. He said Sardar Patel was fully prepared for this (attack on Pakistan) and Defence Minister was also ready. There was support from several other Cabinet ministers like

Dr. S.P. Mukerji, but Pandit Nehru was not in favour of any such move and a decision was to be taken in the Cabinet meeting to be held that afternoon. I opposed this idea. My reasons were that there were not sufficient Indian troops in the Eastern theatre to be able to sweep through East Pakistan. The huge river system of East Pakistan would block even the best army in the world unless it had prepared to negotiate the rivers. The Indian army had not had the time to make such preparations. There were many areas in Barisal, Faridpur, Noakhali, Chittagong and other districts where troops would take months to reach and in the rainy season, which would soon come, such areas would be completely inaccessible except through ordinary boats—and the boatmen were all Muslims. In any case the Indian troops would have to be withdrawn within a few days under the orders of the Security Council and this would bring about more serious repercussions on the minority in East Pakistan. The main battle, if it came, had to be fought in the plains of the Punjab and at no stage would India be in a position to withdraw a considerable number of troops from the Western front. The best course would be to come to an agreement with the Pakistan Government to allow all Hindus, who wanted to evacuate, to come out with their assets and make arrangements for their rehabilitation.

"Iyengar agreed with me. He said that these views coming from a Bengali officer had much weight. But the next day Iyengar informed me that in the Cabinet meeting Sardar Patel did not suggest that troops should be moved into East Pakistan....Then the Nehru-Liaqat Ali pact was signed."[43]

It is on the frank and free discussion by civil servants that the security of the country depends. Sarder Patel knew of this when he emphasised the need of an independent civil service. He observed, "Today my secretary can write a note opposed to my views. I have given that freedom to all my secretaries." I have told them, "if you do not give your honest opinion, then you had better go. I will bring another secretary.... I will never be displeased over a frank expression of opinion. That is what the Britishers were doing with the Britishers. We are now sharing the responsibility. You have agreed to share responsibility."[44]

> "There is no reason why he (civil servant) should not tell the Prime Minister that this plan is absurd and he will, because it is his duty to do so, although he must try his best to make it work, and thus rebut his own case."[45] The civil servant will probably have long-term view of a problem as he has no election in view. He has no political ambitions, he believes in a smooth and comfortable career. He is guided more by the common interest and less by party politics. He will not be afraid of giving the Prime Minister unpalatable advice if he thinks it is a good advice.
>
> "It is possible that the two men will dislike each other and find it difficult to work together, in which case the civil servant might be persuaded to retire. It is, however, more likely that they will learn to understand and like each other, because of the qualities that have brought them to the top. The boldness of one will be balanced by the steadiness, almost cautiousness of the other. The emotional party approach of one will be offset by the objective, rational attitude of the other. The constant exchanging of views, the frequent discoveries by one that the other was right, the knowledge that each can trust the other, breed an intimacy of relationship that is a source of strength."[46]

Early in 1951, the new Home Minister, Chakravarti Rajagopalachari directed his secretary to prepare new rules and rgulations for security arrangements of the Prime Minister. Handoo was the Deputy Director in charge of security and he used to travel with the Prime Minister. He prepared the main draft and gave it to B.N. Mullick who after study placed it before the Home Minister for approval. Rajaji (then Home Minister) after making some changes handed it back to B.N. Mullick telling him to get it approved by the Prime Minister.

The question was who should go to the Prime Minister with that draft. The Home Secretary requested the Home Minister to carry the draft to the Prime Minister, but Rajaji directed Mullick to go to the Prime Minister as he had prepared the draft. He would be able to explain all the implications better.

> "I did this reluctantly as I was apprehensive of a sure flare-up on that day when I raised the subject that night with the Prime Minister and gave him the papers. He looked at them cursorily and then returned them to me. At the same time he said quite firmly that he was not going to be kept as a museum piece in a glass case. He would go wherever and whenever he wanted and security could take care of itself. That apparently was the end of the matter so far as he was concerned.
>
> "I was in difficulty. I could not go back to Rajaji with an admission of failure. So, mustering courage, I replied that I entirely agreed with his sentiment that he could not be a museum piece. I further agreed with him that he should be free to go wherever he wanted and stressed that this was the outlook with which the draft of security rules had been framed. He looked a little astonished and said: 'You are going to restrict my movements by framing all sorts of rules and trying to shackle me and then you say, I can go where I like'. I told him that he could not for long remain the beloved leader of the country if he shut himself up in a fort inaccessible to the people at large, but there was nothing in the rules drafted by us which consigned him to such

loneliness. Pandit Nehru relaxed. He took the papers back from me, made some suggestions and ultimately returned the draft to me, saying in his matchless style, 'You can do what you like.' I asked him whether I could tell the Home Minister that this draft had been approved, and if it had, then I requested him to initial it. He asked me whether the Home Minister had seen the draft. On my replying in the affirmative, he enquired why the Home Minister himself had not brought the draft to him. I told him that the Home Minister felt that as I had prepared the draft I would be able to explain the implications better. Pandit Nehru laughed and said, 'So the Home Minister selected you to bell the cat,' and put his initials on the paper."[47]

Mrs. Gandhi like her father had a tendency to gather powers in her own hands so that she could dominate effectively. "In the new set-up Mrs. Gandhi took under her direct charge the Ministries of Home Affairs and Information and Broadcasting besides General Administration, Planning and Atomic Energy. This combination of Home and Information with Premiership was as unprecedented as it was indicative of the shape of things to come."[48] Mr. Y. B. Chavan was given Finance but he felt crippled when economic intelligence and company affairs were taken away from him.

She made her secretariat more significant by the addition of Shri P.N. Dhar as economic adviser. Shri Dhar was recalled from Moscow and was placed as chairman of the Policy Cell in the Ministry of External Affairs with the rank of a minister. This appointment overshadowed the External Affairs Minister, Shri Swaran Singh, reducing him to the position of a dignified clerk and "made Shri D. P. Dhar, a close confidant of Mrs. Gandhi, *de facto* Foreign Minister."[49]

In the inner circle of Mrs. Gandhi incidentally all

the confidential advisers were Kashmiri Brahmans. "The Prime Minister's secretariat which now included Shri P. N. Dhar, Shri P. N. Haksar, Shri R. N. Kao besides Shri D. P. Dhar and Shri T. N. Kaul, who acted as her advisers in regard to foreign affairs, now began to act as a super-cabinet."[50]

The Prime Minister through the Cabinet secretary gives his own bias to the minutes of the meeting. He would dictate to the Cabinet secretary and the secretary would take it down. "There was no question of the phrasing being left to civil servants; if it were; it would be their decision, so he (Nehru) dictated it....This was what went into the minutes. So, since he was the dictating man, he was more or less summing up the discussion. So that, at any time, if it were referred to, it would be what he had dictated."[51]

The decisions alleged to be arrived at after discussion in the Cabinet meetings are virtually his decisions. The decisions are already taken in the inner Cabinet before they are placed before the Cabinet. The senior colleagues or the close advisers whom the Prime Minister has already consulted speak a few words in favour of the proposal. The junior colleagues gauging the trend say nothing. The Prime Minister after explaining a point here and there declares that the proposal as far as he thinks has been accepted. He knows it that during the dictation of notes to the Cabinet Secretary he would mould it to suit his purpose and the Cabinet Secretary, a senior I. A. S. officer, will help him greatly in this respect. Outwardly Nehru gave the impression that he was allergic to civil servants but inwardly he realised that their services could not be dispensed with. "More specifically, Nehru often called meetings with officials, sometimes at the junior level, without informing their political chiefs....he (Shastri) too meets with officials at the secretary level — but he invariably sends a copy of the minutes to the Ministers concerned."[52]

"The pressure of the Civil Service upon a Minister especially the Prime Minister is relentless, like the tide that is always coming in."[53] They won't leave a gap in the Prime Minister's diary. If there is one, they will try to fill it with another official engagement.

Richard Crossman noted in his diary, ten days after taking office for the first time in October 1964:

> "At first I felt like someone in a padded cell, but I must now modify this. In fact, I feel like somebody floating on the most comfortable support. The whole department is there to support the minister. In his tray come hour by hour notes with suggestions as to what he should do. Everything is done to sustain him in the line officials think he should take. But if one is very careful and conscious, one is aware that this supporting soft framework of recommendations is the result of a great deal of secret discussions between the civil servants below. There is a constant debate as to how the minister should be advised or, shall one say, directed and pushed and cajoled into the line required by the Ministry. While Ministry has its own departmental policy and this policy goes on while ministers come and go."[54]
>
> "If we think of the civil servants as marine animals and the politicians as fishermen operating on the surface, we shall have some idea of the relationship between the two."[55]

The civil servants are apt to take a long view. They know that the fate of the politicians is likely to be changed within five years. They also know that any ideological enthusiasm to carry out the mandate may be blunted by failure, electoral unpopularity and sheer exhaustion. So, they may concede something under the first impact of an election victory. But when that is over, they revert to their entrenched departmental positions and policies against change.

Senior officials probably prefer ministers who, if they wish to unravel the options, rely on reading through the files rather than on oral communication.[56]

"Civil servants claim to prefer a Minister who puts them on their mettle, annotates their papers, poses shrewd questions in office meetings, disputes received departmental assumptions and throws out ideas for further considerations. In part, they are happier with a Minister, who is an intelligent prober and who makes a contribution to policy, because that is the way the Constitution is supposed to work. Sir Stafford Cripps, Labour's Chancellor of the Exchequer from 1947 to 1950, was mentioned by several more senior civil servants as fulfilling his constitutional role to perfection. He would appear in the office each morning by 9 a.m. with all his papers read and annotated. He also wrote papers himself and these served as a means of effectively 'getting his mind known' in the department. It was said of him that he mastered advice and briefs like a good barrister and then let his mind play on good things and expanded on what the department had given him."[57] R. A. Butler in Britain may be taken as an example of a Minister who clearly approximated to the ideal type. He was an intelligent layman minister. His oral summaries of points raised at departmental office meetings were held to be extremely valuable. He would think over things privately and arrive at some provisional decision which was communicated to his close political friends, to his wife and possibly to interested groups only. Thereafter he waited for their reactions. If the reactions were not found to be favourable and he felt so, he would cancel that decision. "Surprisingly Mr. Butler acquired the reputation among his colleagues of being something of a political divining rod."[58]

"When I was the Chief Minister of Madhya Pradesh, my Chief Secretary came up with an interesting comparison. He said that secretaries were like 'Arab horses' who could do wonders with good masters but would throw off the bad ones."[59]

After becoming Communication Minister at the Centre Shri S.D. Sharma told his secretary that he would not be issuing any oral orders. "A minister can function well with relation to his secretary and can achieve results only if he puts in hard work, studies the file before him and possesses the capacity to take a decision."[60]

"They (Civil servants) prefer a 'difficult', minister to one who is of no account. They like to have someone who will put up a fight, someone in whom they can have some pride."[61]

The civil servants like those ministers who know their minds, who can get things done at the Cabinet and in parliament, who can provide strong leadership. "It is my general experience that if the Minister incharge knows what he wants and is intelligent in going about it, he can command the understanding, cooperation and support of his servants."[62] A minister who can't master paper can't be master of his department.

A minister must defend his subordinate in the meetings of the Cabinet as well as of the House. A minister who does not know how to defend those who work under him and shifts the blame to them loses name, and cooperation from them. "Now and again the House demands to know the name of the officer responsible for the occurrence. The proper answer of the minister is that if the House wants anybody's head it must be his head as the responsible minister, and that it must leave him to deal with the officer concerned."[63]

Where the mistake made by an official is ordinary one and involves no important issue of policy, and where no claim to individual rights is seriously involved, the minister should have no hesitation in acknowledging the mistake and the responsibility though he is not personally at fault.

However, where a civil servant does a deed of which the minister disapproves and the mistake is of serious nature, then there is no obligation on the part of the minister to accept the responsibility.

The minister is supposed to be more in touch with the common man than the civil servant. Mr. C. R. Attlee always found the late George Tomilson say, "Well, what do you think of this, George?" He would answer: "It looks all right, but I've been trying to persuade my missus about it for the last three weeks and I can't convince her."[64]

William Harcourt also corroborates Attlee's stand. "The minister exists to tell the civil servant what the public won't stand." A minister has no right to issue unethical, immoral or illegal orders. If he happens to give such orders, the civil servant is the only remedy. The official should have enough courage to tell to him that he is wrong. "The administrator should take care not to degenerate into a sycophant. He should point out weaknesses, otherwise his master, the people, will be ruined....The minister on his part should take care not to disturb the line of authority in passing orders."[65] "A civil servant must advise without any fear. I would imagine that the Ministers would find it extremely difficult to take such improper decisions if they are called upon to overrule a civil servant who points them out."[66]

The power goes to the head of most of the ministers. They arrogate to themselves the right to decide what ought to be done, when, where and how. "The politician is likely to pay more heavily for his aversion to unpalatable advice. Once he has established a reputation for not liking to face the facts, he will be told only what he wants to hear. When the crash comes—it always does come—we will be treated to the familiar refrain, 'The bureaucracy has let us down'."[67]

During Mrs. Gandhi's time the civil servants were

highly pressurised into complete submission. "It was known that civil servants were expected to display their loyalty to Mrs. Gandhi and later to look smart about doing Sanjay's bidding and that those whose stomachs turned at this spurious interpretation of a civil servant's role, were dropped out and relegated to oblivion. We know that senior civil servants, some superannuated, led the commitment bride ride the crest career-wise."[68]

Ministers who are more concerned about their reputation in Parliament give much importance to civil servants who are effective at preparing answers to Parliamentary questions and speeches for delivery on the floor of the House of Commons. Ministers who care more for their public reputation and who wish to project their attractive image outside Parliament always choose "a few advisers with a shrewd sense of publicity and a knack for assisting him in headline catching."[69]

A minister expects from the civil servants the following;

1. Legal implementation of party objectives and programmes.
2. Advice on a range of alternative objectives, priorities and programmes in cases in which firm commitments have been made.
3. Expert advice on the possible and probable problems and consequences of implementing alternative policy programmes.

No minister can do without civil servants. Rather every sensible and far-sighted minister knows the advantage of having a set of civil servants with him. The weakness in a minister is often balanced by an experienced group of sincere advisers. "If a minister lacks the capacity to evaluate complicated policy option the existence of such a permanent secretary may at least prevent a bottleneck and increase the probability that decisions will be taken reasonably, promptly and the department's business despatched."[70]

No government whether past or present has ever been run without the aid of civil servants. The Chinese philosopher Lin Yutang said: "A natural man loves his children, a cultural man loves his parents." In the same vein a civilised government must love its civil servants.

"In essence, the civil servant is a truck-driver who doesn't own the truck he drives. The politician is the owner. Assuming a certain honesty of purpose, which is not rare even amongst civil servants, occasions arise when the driver has to tell the owner that any further progress down a particular road will result in a broken axle. A real truck owner, paying 22 percent to the finance company, will accept the advice."[71]

A minister must not stay too long in a department. If he does so, he becomes a creature of the department. "He ceases to be a Minister at all and becomes a sort of second permanent secretary."[72] "Even otherwise, a minister has to defend his department often in the Cabinet as well as in the Parliament. He spends a good deal of time defending what the department has done, and quickly becomes identified with its existing activities rather than with new initiatives."[73]

Though the training backgrounds of the Ministers and the Civil Servants are different yet their combination presents the complete picture. "The political backgrounds of ministers do not train them in policy analysis. The Houses of Parliament provide training in verbal, negotiating and debating skills, and 'constituency welfare' There is little Parliamentary training in the specific functions of government....Skill in administration is not naturally regarded as a qualification for ministerial office."[74] Their job demands strength of personality and skill in public advocacy. The Civil Servant, on the other hand, is an assessor of conflicting arguments, a dispassionate and uncommitted technician. This combination is nothing but a division of labour. "This division of labour is maintained by the devices of civil service anonymity and ministerial answerability."[75]

The civil service constitutes a conservative influence. They have to consider whether the new may not be more upsetting than the old.

"But the formation of policy is a joint effort—a team work, the work of constant discussion. The partnership should be alive and virile, rival ideas and opinions should be fairly considered, and the relationship of all should be mutual respect, with the understranding that the Minister's decision is final and must be loyally and helpfully carried out."[76]

To simplify things we give it out that it is the minister who makes the decision and that it is the civil servant who carries out that decision Actually decision making is not as simple as it appears to be. The vast experience, the high degree of educational level, the intellectual eminence of the civil servant are bound to influence the minister greatly at the time of arriving at a decision. "The theory of political administrative relationship is that the paid official exercises much more power in the formulation of public policies than the formal description of his responsibilities suggests."[77] It is the civil servant who collects data, tabulates it, discusses pros and cons of a proposal and in the end record his considered opinion. "A great deal of legislation builds on past administrative practice and accumulated experience. The details of much new policy are conditioned by what is administratively and politically impossible. The contacts which have developed between Civil Servants and organised interests provide information on the need for reforms. In this sense much of the legislation which the Cabinet is willing to sponsor comes from the permanent staff of the department."[78] It would not be inappropriate to say that there is a sizeable number of ministers who are run by their departments. Those who run their departments are there but they are a few ones.

The civil servants are slow in action because of being cautious, they appear to be conservative because they do not believe that every new idea is a passport to heaven. They are most sinned against than sinning. "The press, for the most part, tend to regard him either as an idle parasite or as a meddling busybody....Even today he is often thought of as a consumer of many cups of tea, enjoying a sheltered life."[79]

Whereas the minister may tend to place the interests of his party above national interests knowing it fully well that his ministership inheres in the strength of his party. A Civil Servant, on the other hand, has no party interests and has been trained to think in the interests of the people, has little inclination to deviate from his path. "Civil servants are not passive by nature they are do-gooders. They're Benthamites at heart. They want to reform the world."[80] "I have no brains myself. I don't need them. Other people (*i.e.* civil servant, advisers ect.) have brains. I have judgement."[81]

"It is necessary to have in any administration a proper combination of experts and men of the world."[82]

The considerably changed nature of modern society requires a differently equipped civil servant who may not be generalist but must know the intricacies of modern technology and industry. "Civil servants today have to be equipped to tackle the political, scientific, social, economic and technical problems of our time.... They have to keep up with the rapid growth of new knowledge and acquire new techniques to apply it. In short, the civil service is no place for the amateur. It must be staffed by men and women who are truly professional."[83]

The present system is a system of checks and balances. Churchill was once asked whether this political system was the best. He replied, 'can you tell me of something better'? "This system consists of rationalised checks and balances. The legislature is a check on the minister. The next important check are the officials themselves and the ultimate check are the people.[84]

REFERENCES

1. Smith, Evid Russel, *Modern Bureaucracy — The Home Civil Service*, Longman Group Ltd. 1974, p.1.
2. Dey, Bata K., *Bureaucracy, Development and Public Management in India*, Uppal Publishing House, New Delhi, 1978, p.1.
3. Chunder P.C., *Foreword to Bureaucracy, Development and Public Management in India* by Bata K. Dey.
4. Weber, Max, *Essay in Sociology*, Oxford University Press, 1946.
5. Parris, Henry, Constitutional Bureaucracy, University of Durham, Minerva Series of *Students Handbooks* No. 23. General Editor Brian Chapman, George Allen and Unwin, London.
6. Chapman, Brian, *British Cabinet Observed*, Allen and Unwin, London, 1963 pp. 23-24.
7. Kulkarni, V.B., *My Country and My Rulers*, p. 198.
8. Punjabi, K. L. (ed.), *The Civil Servant in India*, Bharatiya Vidya Bhawan, 1965, p. 4
9. Ahluwalia, B.K., *Sardar Patel : A Life*, Sagar Publications, Janpath, New Delhi, 1974, p. 222.
10. *Ibid.*, p. 222.
11. Iyengar, H.V.R., *A Historical Review*, three lectures delivered at Bharatiya Vidya Bhawan in 1966, p. 40
12. Interview with H.M. Patel on May 10, 1967 by V.B. Kulkarni.
13. Mullick, B N., *My Years with Nehru—1948 to 1964*, p. 192.
14. Kulkarni, V.B., *My Country and My Rulers*, p. 203.
15. Politicians *vs.* Civil Servants, *Caravan*, July (First), 1978, pp. 15-16.
16. *Ibid.*, p. 16.
17. *Ibid.*, p. 16.
18. Sharma, Radheyshyam, *Who After Morarji?* Pankaj Publications, New Delhi, 1978, p. 11.
19. Moraes, Frank, *Nehru: Sunlight and Shadow*, Jaico Publishisng House , Bombay, 1964, p 59.
20. Dharam Vira, Administrator and the Politician, 14th Shri Ram Memorial Lecture, January 10, 1979, at FICCI, New Delhi, p. 3.
21. Benemy, F.W.G., *The Elected Monarch*, p. 150.

22. Lord Attlee, on 'Civil Servants, Ministers, Parliament and Public, in the *Civil Service in Britain and France* edited by W.A. Robson, Hogarth Press, 1956, p. 16.
23. Mosley, R.K., *The Story of the Cabinet Office*, Humanities Press, Routledge and Kegan Paul, New York, 1969, pp. 76-77.
24. *Ibid.*
25. *Ibid.*
26. Patel, H.M., *The Illustrated Weekly of India*, November, 6, 1977, p. 10.
27. Mullick, B.N., *My Years with Nehru 1948-1964*, Allied Publishers, 1972, p. 10.
28. Jones, G.W., The Prime Minister's Powers — Editor Anthony King — The British Prime Minister, p.174.
29. *Ibid.*, p. 175.
30. Thakur, Janardan, *All the Prime Minister's Men*, 1977, p. 21.
31. *Ibid.*
32. Ghose, S.K., *The Crusade and End of Indira Raj*, Intellectual Book Corner, 1978, pp. 231-32.
33. Brecher, Michael, *The Succession in India — A Study in Decision-making*, Oxford University Press, 1967, p. 115.
34. *Ibid.*, p.116.
35. Crossman, Richard, *Three Lectures on Prime Ministerial Government*, Jonathan Cape, London, 1972, p. 23.
36. Crossman, Richard, *Three Lectures on Prime Ministerial Government*, Jonathan Cape, London,1972, p. 49.
37. *Ibid.*
38. Blake, Robert, *The Office of Prime Minister*, p. 49.
39. Macualay, Speech in 'The House of Commons' on Indian Affairs, dated 2.8.1922.
40. Kulkarni, V.B., *My Country and My Rulers*, p. 138.
41. *Ibid.*, p. 142.
42. Mullick, B.N., *My Years with Nehru 1948-1964*, Alliled Publishers, 1972, pp. 16-17
43. *Ibid.*, pp.14-15.
44. Tyagi, A.R., *The Civil Service in a Developing Society*, Sterling Publishers, Delhi, 1969, p. 56.
45. Benemy, F.W.G., *The Elected Monarch*, p. 150.
46. *Ibid.*, p. 150.
47. Mullick, B.N., *My Years with Nehru 1948-1964*, Allied Publishers, 1972, pp. 32-33.
48. Madhok, Balraj, *Murder of Democracy*, p. 117.
49. *Ibid.*

50. *Ibid.*
51. Brecher, Michael, *The Succession in India — A Study in Decision-Making*, Oxford University Press, 1967.
52. *Ibid.*, p. 106.
53. Haines, Joe, *The Politics of Power*, p. 34.
54. Crossman, R., *The Diaries of a Cabinet Minister*, Vol. I, Jonathan Cape, 1975, p. 31.
55. Crossman, R., *Three Lectures on Prime Ministerial Government*, Jonathan Cape, London, 1972, p. 22.
56. Headey, Bruce, *British, Cabinet Ministers*, George Allen and Unwin Ltd., London, 1974, pp. 142-143.
57. Headey, Bruce, *British Cabinet, Ministers*, George Allen and Unwin Ltd., London, 1974, pp. 142-143.
58. *Ibid.*, p. 86.
59. Sharma, S.D., Politicians *vs.* Civil Servants, *Caravan*, July (First), 1978, p. 17.
60. *Ibid.*, p. 18
61. Attlee, C.R., Civil Servants, Ministers, Parliament and the Public in India, *Journal of Public Administration*, Vol, I, No. I, Jan-March, 1955.
62. Minogue, Martin, (ed.) *Documents on Contemporary British Government*, p. 174.
63. *Ibid.* 175.
64. Attlee, C.R., Civil Servants, Ministers, Parliament and the Public in India, *Journal of Public Administration*, Vol. I, No. 1, Jan-March, 1955, p. 100.
65. Ray, S.S., Politician's Version, Politician *vs.* Civil Servants, *Caravan*, July (First) 1978, p. 17.
66. Patel H.M., *The Illustrated Weekly of India*, November 6, 1977.
67. Murthi, V.K., *In the Larger Personal Interest*, p. 105.
68. Sehgal, Nayantara, quoted by Murthi, V.K., *In the Larger Personal Interest*, p. 105.
69. Valentine Herman and James E. Alt (eds.) *Cabinet Studies*, p. 122.
70. Valentine Herman and James E. Alt (eds.) *Cabinet Studies*, p. 122.
71. Noronha, R.P., Family Resemblance between the Two, *The Illustrated Weekly of India*, November 6, 1977, p. 13.
72. Headey, Bruce, *British Cabinet Ministers*, George Allen and Unwin Ltd., London, 1974, p. 95.
73. Smith, Brian, Policy Making in British Government, p. 105.
74. *Ibid.*, 102.
75. Madgwick, P.G., *Introduction to British Politics*, p. 133.
76. Minogue, Martin (ed.) *Documents on Contemporary British*

Government, p. 175.

77. Smith, Brian, *Policy Making in the British Cabinet*, p. 100.
78. *Ibid.*, p. 101.
79. Attlee, C.R., Civil Servants, Ministers, Parliament and Public in the *Indian Journal of Public Administration*, Jan-March, 1955, p. 101.
80. Sampson, Anthony, *Anatomy of Britain Today*, Hoddar and Stoughton. 1965, p. 272.
81. Maples, Transport Minister, Quoted in the *Sunday Times*, June 18, 1961.
82. Bannerjee, D.N., Ministers and Civil Servants in Swarajya, Vol. 13, No. 13, Sept. 28, 1968.
83. Dey, Bata K., *Bureaucracy, Development and Public Management in India*, p. 53.
84. Ray, S.S., Politicians' Version, *Caravan*, July (First), 1978, p. 19.

7
The Prime Minister and the Nation

Prime Minister as Leader of the Nation

'The Prime Minister of India must typify the Indian nation by his behaviour, manners and living. He cannot win the hearts of the people if he cannot seek identity with the people whom he claims to represent. Mahatma Gandhi knew this secret very well and tried his best to live like a common Indian, ill-clad, ill-fed, humble, simple, non-aggressive and believing in God. The Indians, irrespective of caste, creed or class, looked upon him as one of their own. They responded generously to his calls of freedom struggle against the foreign rule. He fought against the most mighty empire of the time and shook it to its very foundations. Pandit Nehru also learnt this lesson from him; abandoned his western style of life and started living like a common man. Simplicity and honesty are the keynotes of Indian society. Mahatma Gandhi always emphasised that the ministers of free India should live like the man in the street. No minister should draw more than Rs. 500 a month. They should avoid all ostentation and must live and serve like a poor Indian.

Regrettably, the same Congressmen who had made sacrifices, served several imprisonments, lived a simple life while engaged in freedom struggle, changed their living style gradually after capturing power, creating an impression unwittingly on the people that the freedom meant only the change of masters.

Unfortunately, the rot started with Nehru whom the

people loved and believed in. "To be fair to Mrs. Gandhi all the ostentation did not begin with her but with Jawaharlal Nehru, who waxed eloquently about the poverty of the Indian peasant while permitting revelry by Congressmen."[1] Dr. Ram Manohar Lohia, the socialist leader, missed no opportunity of accusing Nehru of spending Rs. 25,000 a day on himself as Prime Minister "in maintaining a large retinue of assistants and bodyguards and a 'luxurious' standard of living."[2]

"The salary of the President is Rs. 10,000 per mensem but the travelling allowances of his two assistants are to the tune of rupees one lakh a month. The manifesto asserted that the daily expenditure of the government on the Prime Minister was Rs. 30,000 while as many as 300 million Indians could not spend more than twenty or twenty-five paisa per head per day."[3]

The degeneration once started is difficult to check. Like the hole in a tank it goes on increasing under the pressure of luxurious life-styles. "A.D. Gorwala points out that the Prime Minister and her colleagues live at a cost that would necessitate the possession of a taxable private income of at least twelve lakhs of rupees a year."[4]

The ministers who profess to be servants of the people belie their professions when we find them living like princes. "Earlier in May 1970, N. Dandekar, a retired civilian and an income-tax expert, had thrown a bomb-shell in Parliament by declaring, with all the weight of his specialised knowledge, that the salaries and various facilities that were given to a Central Minister amounted to as much as Rs 4.48 lakhs a year....one has only to visit them at their residences in New Delhi to realise how vast and unbridgeable is the chasm that separates them from the people."[5]

It is really very strange that our Prime Ministers have been talking loudly of socialism while maintaining themselves actually like princes. "The ruling elite today lives in a style which a majority of the members of the defunct princely order could not hope to attain in the heyday of their glory."[6]

The security arrangements are also out of proportion with the requirements of a democratically elected Prime Minister of a poor and backward country like India. We have failed to get rid of our inhering feudal mentality. "A former Chief Minister of Uttar Pradesh disclosed in January 1970, that the State Government had to spend Rs. 40 lakhs during the previous fifteen months on the security arrangements for the Prime Minister`s visit to that state. He added that one day`s visit by her cost the state exchequer as mch as one lakh of rupees."[7]

The heavy cost of security arrangements is undoubtedly an anathema, but the traffic clearance or diversions add insult to injury. "So, when a minister and other dignitaries move about, the world must not only know about it but must also feel it. In big and crowded cities, long stretches of roads are cleared of all traffic even during peak hours....Altogether it was quite an advertisement of the way in which senior ministers of a government claiming to be both democratic and socialist like to travel."[8]

"A mild stir was caused in Parliament in 1970 when a member asked whether a sum of Rs. 33 lakhs had been spent on chartering a plane for a brief visit of the Prime Minister to New York."[9]

The President of Vietnam, late Ho Chi Minh, lived all his life like an ordinary person in a hut. The most famous Prime Minister of Chandra Gupta Maurya, Chanakya, the architect of an empire, spent his whole life in a hut. But our modern Prime Minister and ministers feel irritated when their attention is drawn to these facts of history.

"Repeated suggestions that ministers should move into modest residences have fallen on deaf ears. On March 17,1970, the Prime Minister told the Rajya Sabha that their efficiency would suffer if they did so. She explained that in this country, unlike elsewhere, houses were places of work for ministers all the year round."[10]

The spacious bungalows (previously occupied by British rulers) in which they live proclaim their sense of superiority. "The maintenance of large bungalows costs the state a good deal. In July 1973 Parliament was told that a sum of Rs. 13,07,800 was spent on the repairs and maintenance of the bungalows of the Central Ministers. The expenditure in 1973-74, it was stated, would be Rs. 14,92,750. The water and electricity bills also run into lakhs of rupees."[11]

M.O. Mathai writing to Miss Padmaja Naidu, Governor of Bengal, criticized Indira Gandhi for her luxurious style of living. He submitted a long list of costly gifts retained by her without paying any amount to the State Treasury. It may be pointed out here that nobody is allowed to keep any gift from a foreign dignitary or a foreign government costing more than Rs. 200 unless one is prepared to pay to the Government of India entire market price of the gift. The gifts retained by her were as follows:

1. Expensive coat presented to her by the Soviet Government.
2. The pearl necklaces, ear-lobes and ring studded with pearls—these were not included in the list of jewellery in her wealth tax returns.
3. A silver cutlery set for twelve.
4. A German cutlery set for twelve (modern design).

There are some cases which she did not care to explain:

(a) Rs. 25,000 for the purchase of land in her name near Qutab Minar.
(b) Rs. 17,000 for the purchase of a Dodge Station Wagon.

(c) The entire expenses covering the trip of herself and her two children abroad (travelling by the polish luxury ship *S.S Batory* to Europe in 1953 and return by air plus the substantial foreign exchange expenses involved).

(d) The Finance Minister Sachindra Chaudhary advised Indira to use a small Government car in the interest of economy, she promptly had a new Hindustan car bought at Government expense exclusively for her trips to Parliament House to impress M.Ps. and retained the imported provocative, air-conditioned American luxury car for her other travels.[12]

"For Indira Gandhi's rest for two nights, the organisation had put up a typical Bengali peasant's hut on the austerity budget of some six lakhs of rupees (at Bidhan Nagar, Calcutta, December 1972)."[13]

A year after the disaster at NEFA, the Congress met at Jaipur. The correspondents of the *Hindustan Times* wrote, "Behind the *Pandal* was set up a *shamiana* mostly described as a "canteen" but which would have put to shame any well-provided restaurant."[14]

There are cases where Indira rewarded some of the persons at public expense for the personal services rendered to her by them. "She paid no salary to Usha Bhagat who tutored Sanjay. She got her (Usha) fixed up in some government post from where she (Usha) used to draw her monthly salary....Gopal Gupta was got out of the Air Force School for teaching science to Sanjay. Gupta was made producer in the Television Centre. He had on a number of occasions been abroad on public expense".[15]

Except Lal Bhadur Shastri who had a brief spell of Prime Ministership, all other Prime Ministers have failed to justify their claims to represent the poor and simple folks of India. "The Prime Minister must give the commom man the impression that he is a common man too. That is why he is in the House of Commons. He must speak language of the man in the street, who will then understand and trust him."[16]

We have amply seen what has been going on in our country. We shall now make an attempt to ascertain the life-styles of the Presidents and Prime Ministers of mature democracies. In Europe, the Presidents and Prime Ministers live in modest houses and never complain of decreasing efficiency. They drive small cars or use bicycles to attend their offices. "A.D. Gorwala drew attention to the sort of life that was being led by the Swiss President who, he said, "remaining in the modern suburban house he occupied before election, came in every morning to his office by bicycle or bus."[17] The life of British Prime Minister is noted for its simplicity and freedom from vulgar show...."drive in modest vehicles and are rarely noticed when they are travelling. Stanley Baldwin who was Britain's Prime Minister thrice, drove his own car which was so small that many dreaded the honour of travelling in it with him."[18] Such things are unthinkable in India. The people of mature democracies are very vigilant and touchy about simplicity and honesty. They do not tolerate even minor deviations from the right path on the part of their leaders. "There was a major sensation in the country when it was known that Ramsay Macdonald, Labour Prime Minister, had received a batch of shares from a friend to buy a car."[19] In India all of us appear to have accepted corruption as a part of our life. Instead of feeling ashamed and concerned we feel proud of our dubious dealings. We cannot trust our politicians as much as people of other country trust theirs. "On the whole Britain can trust its politicians. They are not always right but few governments are prepared to sacrifice the national interest as they see it in order to obtain a present party advantage."[20]

"In May 1974, Willy Brandt, Chancellor of West Germany upheld the finest tradition of Clean

Government, by resigning from his office following an uproar caused by an espionage scandal. His office had appointed Guenther Guilluame, an East German spy, as his assistant in spite of warnings by the intelligence service."[21]

Criticising the entrenched corruption under the patronage of Mrs. Gandhi, Jayaprakash Narain made a prophetic statement about the fall of Gandhi and her Congress. "The utter confusion, lack of direction and purposefulness, galloping corruption at all levels of politics and Government may suit Prime Minister Indira Gandhi's style of leadership, but it spells ruin for the Congress as a democratic organisation and for democracy itself."[22]

Now we come to the domestic policy pursued by our Prime Ministers. Under the leadership of Nehru India adopted a mixed economic system based on both public and private enterprise. Indian industry was classified into (a) those exclusively owned and managed by the state; (b) those run by both state and private enterprise, (c) and those left in the hands of private industrialists subject to some official controls.

The basic problem in India is to remove poverty and unemployment and the only course left open to tackle this ticklish issue is to produce more and more. Pandit Nehru was quite aware of this problem when he said, "The basic problem of India is the problem of economic development, because it was only through such development that all problems, social and economic, can be solved and the country can be made strong enough to defend itself, because defence today more than ever before depends on industrial background."[23]

A country's capacity to produce more and more can only lead her to prosperity. The case is just like that of a rich man and a poor man. The rich man tends to become richer because he has lot of money to invest. The poor man has no money to invest. It, therefore, become difficult for him even to live on the subsistence level.

In accordance with his professed faith in socialism Nehru took steps to nationalise Life Insurance business. The Life Insurance ordinance was promulgated in January 1956, when Shri Chintamani Deshmukh was the Finance Minister. Later, the Life Insurance Corporation Act was passed and came into force with effect from September 1, 1956 making the corporation an autonomous body and an investment committee was formed to recommend investments of L.I.C. funds.

Indira Gandhi nationalised Banks not out of socialistic fervour but out of her aversion to the Syndicate. She fell out with the Syndicate when they selected Sanjiva Reddy as a candidate for Presidency. She was afraid of Sanjiva Reddy for she looked upon him as a tool in the hands of the Syndicate. She was labouring under the misconception that on being elected as President, Reddy would sack her. In order to project her image as a great socialist she dramatically nationalised the Banks to capture the mind of the masses, and cleverly linked this move with her attempts at the removal of poverty. '*Garibi Hatao*' was her catchword. Her second tactic was to abolish privy purses of the princely order. Both the deeds added immensely to her stature among the masses. The man in the street hailed her as a friend of the common man. "A government will be judged by the performance of the Prime Minister. He has, therefore, to project an image of himself, which will be acceptable to millions of people."[24] But the fact remains that what she did was not motivated by any genuine concern for the common man, but to spite the nose of her enemies. "The claptrap about the defence of the small man will not stand even a minute's scrutiny because only a few months before, Morarji's budget proposal of taxing agricultural wealth of big farmers, a measure of far-reaching importance, was shot down by Mrs. Gandhi herself."[25]

The medium of projection was once the public meeting and the press, reporting the Parliamentary performances of the Prime Minister. Since 1959, television has supplanted both. Television though very useful in projecting the image has its own hazards. Every one today knows what Indira Gandhi, Morarji and Charan Singh look like. It may become difficult for any one of them to save himself or herself from the machinations of a meticulous assassin. It was not so in the days of Peel, "Who escaped assassination because the lunatic who intended to kill him shot his private secretary instead."[26]

Nehru was keen on achieving self-sufficiency in arms. He was quite clear in his mind how India could free herself from dependence on other countries. The real strength in the time of hostilities was the capacity our country possessed to meet all the requirements of our armed forces. "The Prime Minister was advised by Lord Mountbatten to go in for Gnat Aircraft as that would meet the requirements of the Indian Air Force. However, there was a stiff resistance from the Air Force and the Defence Minister. The Gnat producers in Britain had offered to help India to have her own factory to produce Gnats. Pandit Nehru was quite happy but the officials wanted to buy Oregon or Toofani from France.... He (Nehru) said that it was suprising that whereas every country wanted to produce her own war material, in India even very senior officials and ministers wanted to remain dependent on foreign countries and governments for military hardware."[27]

It was an ample testimony to Nehru's wisdom when during the Indo-Pak Wars of 1965 and 1971 the Indian simple and small Gnats played havoc with the sophisticated Sabre jets of Pakistan (supplied by America)

Pandit Nehru loved the people of India and the people loved him. It is said that Nehru possessed a charisma and drew crowds in millions wherever he went. He has referred to this fact in his autobiography. He liked to meet the people, to talk to them, to mix with them. His disregard of security measures sometimes created problems for the security officers. "He strongly protested against the stopping of traffic or the posting of constables along his routes though he admitted that there might be need for some arrangements at the place of his destination. He protested against the ostentatiousness in police arrangements....He once even went so far as to say that if this drain on public funds was not ended, he might have to stop functioning as the Prime Minister."[28]

He realised the importance of security but only upto certain extent. The security arrangements should be such as can ensure safety of his person, and not such as can isolate him from the people. He was so full of gratitude to the people of India that he could not contain himself to express it. "And yet there were occasions when the Prime Minister thought it necessary to throw all precautions to the wind and meet the people face to face. In these encounters he exhibited great courage and patience and ultimately his will prevailed."[29]

Pandit Nehru even in the midst of grave provocation acted bravely and courageously. These qualities added to his personal magnetism and helped the officers to control the situation without much use of force, on many occasions without any use of force. In July 1949, the Communists were up with arms to overthrow Nehru Government. Large-scale distrubances and police firings were the order of the day in Calcutta. The law and order situation was quite bad. Pandit Nehru arrived in Calcutta on July 14. He was received by a big crowd at the airport. Over a million of people gathered to hear him. The Communists tried their best to disrupt the meeting. They threw bombs at the dais where the Prime Minister was standing and speaking; they fired at the crowd and burst innumerable crackers. They also tried to hold rival meeting. "It was an amazing and breath-taking experience. So great was the magnetism of Jawaharlal Nehru that a million people sat enthralled by his speech imperturbed by all that was happening."[30]

Prime Minister as Chief Spokesman of the Nation, especially in relation to Foreign Affairs

When President Eisenhower visited India and all crowd control measures were smashed by the surging humanity in Connaught Place, and the whole cavalcade came to a standstill, the Prime Minister left the VIP car and mounted the pilot jeep directing the crowd to make way. The people were happy beyond measure seeing Jawaharlal acting as the pilot and made way for the cars to pass shouting '*Jais*' and waving to him. To see the magic, "President Eisenhower exclaimed that he had never seen anything like this."[31]

But this show of courage and bravery was not without its hazards. In the early years Handoo (Chief of the Security Staff) had to wrestle with him (Nehru) on many occasions when the latter jumped from the platform and rushed towards the disturbed place. In the melee Mr. Handoo got his clothes torn and sometimes even his pocket picked. Nehru laughed when he heard that Handoo lost his purse. Lal Bahadur Shastri had no personal magnetism. He, however, won the hearts of the people through his quick and timely decision against the onslaughts of Pakistan. Because of his tough stand against Pak invasion he earned the epithets of '*Veer*' (brave) daring and saviour of India. His life span was, however, quite short.

Indira like her father was gifted with a charismatic personality. Before Emergency she also attracted crowds in millions, and like her father jumped from the platform to meet the common man. In the elections of 1972 she did wonder by winning 80 percent seats of Lok Sabha. Her gallant role in Bangladesh War in 1971 made her darling of the people. Even Vajpayee, her opponent, hailed her as 'Durga' or 'Chandi'.

Nuclear explosion in May 1974, was another feather in her cap of achievements. "The explosion boosted the popularity and prestige of the Prime Minister."[32]

Morarjibhai lacked in personal charm. That is why he could not remain Prime Minister for long. He became Prime Minister on March 24, 1977 and resigned on July 15, 1979. Charan Singh could not last, even for a month. In the last week of July 1979, he was sworn in conditionally as the Prime Minister of India; could not face Parliament on August 20, 1979 and put in his resignation the same day.

No government worth the name can run the administration of its country without a well-organised Intelligence Bureau. Pandit Nehru was fully conscious of this fact. Addressing the Intelligence Conference on March 19, 1952, Nehru said,

> "It was obvious that for any organised government intelligence was the most important....All these groups and particularly the Marathas, who were full of courage, gallantry and dash, were totally ignorant of the geography of India and they did not even have proper maps; they had only vague ideas about this place or that. They did not bother to collect any information about the enemy. On the other hand the British had accurate maps and good information about the people of India, about each individual ruler, his weaknesses and foibles. They had their agents in every court, who won over important personalities of the ruler's entourage and thus got first rate intelligence about what was going on in that state. The highly organised Intelligence system of the Britishers led them to victory over the other contenders of power."

He often alluded to Changez Khan whom he

considered probably the greatest general in history. Changez Khan's army was not big compared to modern armies. Khan had his agents in all the states of Asia and Eastern Europe. He collected detailed information on each country before he invaded it. Even when his envoy was insulted in a country near Bokhara, he did nothing for nearly a year though he was very angry. He bidded his time and gathered all relevantly necessary information before he attacked. In this way he conquered the whole of Asia north of the Himalayas and also the greater part of North Western India and Europe as far as Austria.

Nehru also mentioned '*Arthashastra*' and said that it was astonishing what a complicated system of intelligence 'Chanakya' had built up. If intelligence was so important two thousand years ago, it had assumed much greater importance in the present age of swift communication and transport. In a war, a small army with better intelligence could beat a big army with little intelligence.

It will not be out of place to know about the smartness of our Intelligence. The Communists held a secret meeting at Calcutta in May 1951 in which the new line, called the Stalin line, was adopted. Subsequently, another meeting was held in October 1951 in which the decision to fight election was taken, "Moscow's caution that the documents must not fall into Nehru's hands was stressed on all the members who attended. However, the documents containing both the political thesis and the tactics fell into our hands and in due course I produced them before the Home Minister and the Prime Minister. The latter went through these documents very carefully. While going through the document he came across the passage containing the warning against its leakage. When he read this, Pandit Nehru laughed out and remarked that Moscow apparently did not know how smart our intelligence was."[33]

Reorganisation of states on linguistic basis was an error. The Congress had committted itself to it as far back as 1921. "Informed opinion was highly against the reorganisation of the states solely on the linguistic principle."[34] The princely states were to be integrated and the political map to be redrawn, but language could not be taken as the sole criterion for the new arrangement, Sardar Patel was also against the linguistic chauvinism. He "condemned the language bigots as the assassins of nationalism."[35]

Nehru borrowed the planning system from Russia. The Planning Commission working under his chairmanship gathered immense powers to determine the country's economic future dispite its constitution being non-statutory. The plans failed to achieve even fifty percent of the targets. That is why the subsequent Prime Ministers set no store by the plans considering the disproportion between the enormity of expense and the results attained.

Nehru was undoubtedly a great secularist but the exigencies of political situation forced him to come down. His daughter Indira Gandhi during her Presidentship of the Congress struck up an electoral alliance with the Muslim League in Kerala. She convinced Nehru that this was the only possible solution to struggle against the rising tide of communism in Kerala. The Muslims constituted an important minority and could influence the pattern of voting in many other states also. Over such unprincipled politics Nehru kept mum. In September 1970, Indira acclaimed the Muslim League of Kerala as a non-communal organisation, getting rebuff from the national President of Muslim League who vehemently rejected the thesis of non-communal character of his organisation.

During the regime of Indira Gandhi vote catching devices recognised no standards in professions. Deterioration and rot set in everywhere. Bitterly complaining against injustice of reservation of seats in Medical College, Bombay (110 out of 360) a medical expert writes: "In June 1973, a student from scheduled castes etc. with just 40 percent marks, obtained admission to a medical college while another student with 63 percent marks was permanently prevented from following the profession despite proven capabilities. Warning that such blatant discrimination will destroy one's faith in democracy."[36]

Nehru was quite fortunate in having Sardar Patel as his deputy. It was Sardar who fulfilled Nehru's dream of constitutional unity and national integration of the country. Patel because of his robust practical sense welded the 500 odd princely states into the general pattern of the country. It was he who solved the Hyderabad and Junagadh issues. Incorporating these states into the Indian Union he redrew the national map of India. Nehru because of his lofty idealism tried to tackle the Kashmir problem which stands unsolved till this day.

It is said that Nehru failed in his domestic policies. "Nehru's domestic policies were highly idiosyncratic. His aims were always lofty but attainment of most of them was either hampered or frustrated by his impractical idealism and vacillation."[37] The reason is not far to seek. Nehru's too much thinking mind halted his pace of activity. Literary minds had given him the epithet of 'Hamlet' of Asia. This can be easily corroborated by a quotation from N.V. Gadgil, a plain-speaking politician and Nehru's comrade in the national struggle for freedom. He held that "from the day Nehru joined the Wavell Government it became evident that he was incapable of firm decisions."[38] "Her (Indira Gandhi's) father failed because realism was not his forte and because he strongly believed that his personality could accomplish everything."[39]

Nehru by taking too much burden on his shoulders jumbled up everything. He wanted to accomplish much himself within the shortest possible time. He wanted to run fast but he committed the error of putting on the heaviest shoes. "Nehru had a keen sense of history but he learnt few lessons from it. He took upon himslf a volume of work which no human being could sustain with any degree of efficiency. He was Prime Minister, Minister for External Affairs, Chairman of the Planning Commission, President of the Indian National Congress for a number of years and a much-sought-after leader of the country."[40] If he had given some attention to British history, he would have learnt what A.J. Balfour, who had personal knowledge of the demands of the Premiership, said when Lord Salisbury wanted to combine the office of the Prime Minister and Foreign Secretary. "Writing to Chief Whip on October 18, 1900 Balfour suggested that the Queen should not agree to such an arrangement."[41]

Sri Prakasa pointed to the same shortcoming when he said that he (Nehru) had the serious failing of doing everything himself.

Churchill also suffered from the same malady. He also wanted to accomplish much single-handedly. It would be quite interesting to note how his colleagues commented on this trait of his character. Clement Attlee, Churchill's deputy during the Second World War, summed him up thus: "Fifty percent of Winston is genius, fifty percent bloody fool." Lord Waverly, equally close to the great man went further, and said: "Someone must hold his hand or he will blunder."[42]

Indira Gandhi except a short spell of glory (Nationalisation of banks, abolition of Privy purses, astounding victory over Pakistan in Bangladesh) generally failed in her domestic policies. Her '*Garibi Hatao*' (Remove Poverty) slogan proved to be a big hoax. Her economic policies made the rich richer and poor the poorer. Her dictatorial tendency, inherited from her father (Nehru used to contain it), created confusion all around and forced the opposition parties to unitedly stand against her. The imposition of emergency and the choice of wrong men surrounding her, led her towards her political crucifixion. Not one of them had the qualities even of a mediocre politician. Bansi Lal (famous for crudeness and barbaric depravity), V.C. Shukla, Barooah (Court clown—described so by J.P. Narain), Om Mehta, Yunus, S.S. Ray, D.P. Chattopadhyaya, Pranab Mukherji, not to speak of men like Yashpal and Dhawan, were all backroom boys whom the two (Indira and Sanjay) used for unbridled pursuit of power, devoid of all moral values. These were the men who rose to country's top positions and debased them all. So much mediocrity, so much grossness and insignificance of character would have been hard to find even in the minor courts of the Indian Renaissance.

Morarjibhai has utterly failed in his domestic policies. His inflexible nature and stress on wrong values (prohibition, cow-slaughter) has given birth to political chaos and patriotic bankruptcy. The poor country of India will have to undergo the electoral ordeal once again, after two and a half years at a great expense which she can ill-afford. Indira Gandhi's rise like sphinx from her own ashes is causing concern in the democracy-loving circles.

Chaudhari Charan Singh has perfected the technique of timely defection for self-aggrandisement. He has personal and burning ambition to become the Prime Minister of India. He lost the golden opportunity to emerge as the national leader to succeed Desai as and when the circumstances demanded. He has unconsciously and against his will reduced himself to be leader of a faction. He entered the shrine of history through the back door to carve out for himself a niche of honour but, to his dismay, he found that in haste he had entered the wrong place where he could not stay for long.

After discussing the domestic policies, now it will

be just appropriate to come to foreign policies pursued by our Prime Ministers. "The test of the success of a country's foreign policy", Nehru once remarked in conversation, "is its good relations with its neighbours.... By that yardstick his foreign policy would be rated as a failure. The five principles of peaceful co-existence which seemed to serve Nehru not only as a policy but as a dogma, were flouted and outraged by China's aggression."[43] Nehru's international prestige was quite high in the first decade of his term of office because he presented to curious world "a message which was challenging, even at times provocative, but always purposeful."[44]

His doctrine of Panchsheel approved by China and Russia caused a stir in the political circles of the world. His advocacy of non-alignment was misunderstood by Britain and America, especially America that was suffering from communist phobia, and in her zeal to contain Russia and China she was forming military alliances, pacts and distributing arms like sweets to her military allies.

Nehru did his best to help the Chinese Communist regime. Nehru refused to assist the corrupt and tottering Kuomintang regime of his friend Chiang Kai Shek. Writing to Mrs. Pandit Ambassador to the U.S., who was approached by Madam Chiang Kai Shek, he said,

> "I am quite convinced that if we stood up for the bankrupt government in China now, we would be condemned in India, and this would give a fillip to communism in India, strange as that sounds. The way to fight communism is not by armies, but by the adoption of progressive policies."[45]

On December 30, 1949, India recognised Communist China, Britain followed suit in January 1950. Nehru tried his best to cultivate friendship with China. India's Eastern and Western borders were always seething with trouble. Pakistan's hostility towards India was a known fact. Nehru, therefore, was very keen on making northern border secure. But inwardly he was having apprehensions because of China's revolutionary break with the past. Even after having inaugurated, jointly with Chou-En-Lai, the era of Indo-Chinese brotherhood in the summer of 1954, Nehru advised his colleagues to avoid complacency because in international affairs "one can never be dead certain and the friends of today might be enemies of tomorrow."[46]

This lingering suspicion never lessened his conviction that China might cause trouble in future. The robust commonsense of Patel and Tandon made them dislike Nehru's policy towards China. "Tandon publicly condemned Chinese intervention in Tibet and Korea."[47] Patel wrote a long letter to Nehru advising the Prime Minister "to regard China as an imperialist power and a potential threat to India's security on its northern and eastern frontiers."[48]

Nehru wanted to create a peaceful force which would act as a buffer between the warring camps. He tried to provide a common paltform for all those who did not believe in joining any bloc. The so-called non-aligned countries could meet after suitable periods to discuss world situation from an impartial and dispassionate angle. At the Bandung Conference "he (Nehru) was admonitory towards the delegates of aligned and Western-oriented countries—Pakistan, Iraq, Turkey, Iran, the Philippines, Thailand and South Vietnam."[49] Interestingly enough, he did not receive any rebuff from Chou or from any of the delegates of the aligned nations. Unexpectedly, he received it from the Ceylonese Prime Minister, Sir John Kotelawala who interrupted by making a scathing attack on Russian colonialism—Russian domination in central and eastern Europe. Chou and Nehru were both agitated. Nehru asked John Kotelawala, "Why did you do that, Sir John? Why did you not show me your speech before you made it?"

The Ceylonese Prime Minister rebuffed him with "Why should I? Do you show me yours before you make it."[50]

Nehru looked upon China as hornet's nest and did not want to disturb it. He could never dispel his inner fears of Chinese aggression at the opportune time. "He said that all through history China had been an aggressive country. Now it had acquired an aggressive political philosophy and was being governed by very agressive leaders who had waged an unceasing war during the previous twenty years. China did not believe in treating other countries on equal terms. Therefore, as soon as she succeeded in achieving a certain amount of economic and political stability, she would try to extend her influence and leadership, if not political suzerainty, over Asia. In this struggle for suzerainty in Asia, her biggest obstacle would be India. He said that Indian and Chinese cultures had been contesting for supremacy for hundreds of years in Central Asia, Tibet, Burma and countries of South East Asia. In these areas where the Indian influence had been supreme during the time of the Hindu and the Buddhist rulers, the Chinese extended their influence and began injecting Chinese culture when India became weak....The aggressive leadership of China might even take a short-cut and occupy these territories on some pretext or other and under conditions of occupation it would be easier to spread Chinese culture, and destroy the last vestiges of Indian culture. Communism or internationalism for the Chinese was only a cloak for furthering their own national interest....might even give large-scale assistance to the Communist Party of India and thereby to build up a strong Chinese lobby in the country."[51]

The Chinese picture of a highly industrialised state with a vast and growing population caused concern in Europe and elsewhere. Even the Soviet Union was worried. "Though Soviet Union was a friend of China and had given much help to her in the economic field, yet even in the minds of the leaders of that country there was a great deal of apprehension about the future of China. They would not break with China immediately, though the old sort of understanding and friendship that was expected of the alliance was no longer there and was not likely to be there in future."[52]

Even Napoleon two centuries back was aware of the 'Yellow Peril'. When asked about the Chinese awakening he prophetically replied, 'Let sleeping dogs lie, when China awakes, the whole world will be in trouble.'

The Chinese attack in 1962 on India, tolled the death-knell of Nehru's '*Panchsheel*'. Nehru was not taken unawares. We have already seen that he had his apprehensions but he did not expect the foray to occur so soon. The thing that shocked him most was the enormity of the debacle in NEFA, the galloping march of Chinese forces steam-rolling the Indian defences. Pandit Nehru then referred to the bad shock which India had received in the fighting in the Himalayas the previous winter and said that the Chinese had done well in the military sense. He referred to their training, their leadership and their tactics, which were all good, even brilliant. He then mentioned that the Chinese army had been trained in mountain warfare over long years of fighting and it was also a very big army, though not so well-equipped as compared to the Western armies, yet it was a very big army and it was backed by a vast country with its considerable resources.[53]

Nehru knew it fully well that the Chinese attack was motivated by the notion of political and cultural superiority, nourished for centuries by the Chinese. "Pandit Nehru said that it would be wrong to assume that the Chinese undertook this aggression only because they wanted some patches of territory, however important that territory might be. The real cause was something else. That something else was the basic conflict between China and India. India came in her way of domination in Asia, and so China wanted to remove India from her path."[54] Nehru did not like the American way of open hostility towards communism. According to him, India's strength did not lie so much in her armed forces as in her moral force. "Particularly referring to China, the Prime Minister said that it was impossible for America to overpower China because of latter's backwardness. In a backward country people were capable of enormous sufferings and the Chinese were used to dying in millions."[55]

The Chinese failed to cause disruption in India and could not accomplish the main objective of their attack. Hence. they declared unilateral ceasefire. They are occupying 12,000 square metres of Indian territory and no Indian Prime Minister has been able so far to retrieve the national honour.

Nehru's act of withdrawal of Indian forces from Tibet was a blunder on the part of his government. The Dalai Lama and his government were left alone to deal with the fierce Chinese dragon, and made our whole northern region vulnerable to their machinations. The Pakistani Eve that was created out of the ribs of Indian Adam was prone to playing in the hands of the Imperialist devil. Thrice Pakistan atacked India after having equipped her army with the most modern and sophisticated weapons received free from America as a part of the latter's policy to contain communism. It was only during the Prime Ministership of Indira Gandhi in 1971 that the unruly child of British conspiracy (Pakistan) against the Indian nationalism was taught a lesson of his life. Pakistan was cut to size and castrated not to challenge Indian honour again. Nehru had prophesied while he was alive that Pakistan born out of hatred against India would be compelled to attack India one day. "He felt that the Pakistani leaders would be compelled sooner or later by the force of their hatred campaign against India to commit aggression as otherwise they themselves would be overthrown."[56]

Ironically enough, Ayub Khan attacked India in 1965 and failed to grab Kashmir. As a result he was overthrown. In 1971 Yahya Khan again attacked India to grab Kashmir and to save Bengal, and in the struggle that followed he lost himself.

Indian relations with Nepal have always been cordial because of cultural and religious affinity. When visiting China in October 1954, "Nehru secured Chou's recognition of India's special position with regard to Nepal."[57] Consequently, Indian troops, money and skill began to pour into Nepal. Except a brief spell of mutual misgivings the general thread of friendly relationship remains unbroken.

Our relations with Britain are conditioned by our remaining within the Commonwealth. One of Nehru's chief reasons for joining the British Commonwealth was to avoid having to rely on America for capital goods and credit which would have been readily given by America, but on condition of India's aligning her foreign policy with that of the United States. "It would have been dangerous for us to isolate ourselves and risky for us to slope too much towards the U.S. in the present context. That would have made it more difficult for us at any time to play the role of a friendly neutral to any of the parties concerned."[58]

Our relations with America have not been so good as they ought to be. Mr. Dulles' (Secretary of State for U.S.) policy of formulating military alliances against communist countries and showing no sympathetic understanding of Nehru's non-alignment estranged Nehru's feelings. Pakistan's unscrupulous use of American weapons in their attck on India in 1965 in defiance of the repeated assurances of the American Presidents that the military aid to Pakistan would not be used against India, wounded the feelings of all Indians. During the Pakistani attack of 1971, President Nixon's tilt towards Pakistan injured the Indian susceptibilities beyond redemption. President Nixon even went to the extent of ordering the American 7th Fleet to enter the Bay of Bengal overtly to evacuate American nationals from East Pakistan and covertly to help Pakistan against India. In anticipation of trouble with Pakistan and American proclivity to help Pakistan, Indira Gandhi had already signed a twenty-year Treaty of Peace, Friendship and Cooperation with the Soviet Union in August 1971. As a sequel thereto and to counter the American threat (use of the 7th Fleet) a Soviet Fleet sailed from Vladivastack following on the heels of the U.S. 7th Fleet. Fortunately, Dacca fell before the arrival of the 7th Fleet in the Bay of Bengal and a showdown between America and Russia was averted.

It cannot be gainsaid that India has had leanings towards Russia. But it is equally true that Russia did much to earn these leanings. On Kashmir issue Russia always used her veto in the Security Council in favour of India whenever the Anglo-American bloc conspired to harm India's interests. The Soviet leaders acted astutely. "They made it appear that their aid was entirely selfless, designed to help India to stand on its own feet without having to depend on any foreign country. Khruschev took personal interest in the Soviet financed projects in India and would write to Nehru to remove impediments in the way of their quick completion.[59].

There was also a feeling in some quarters, which Nehru also shared, "that if the Soviet Union had not come forward with offers of large-scale economic aid, during the Second Five Year Plan, the Western countries would not have opened their purse strings as generously as they did."[60] The Americans complained that America gave much assistance to India even then Nehru inclined towards taking the side of Russia and that he was more appreciative of the Russian aid. Escott Reid, High Commissioner of Canada, received a telegram from Lester Pearson in December 1955, complaining that Soviet Union got more credit from Nehru by sending seven petroleum geologists at Government of India's cost than the Western countries had ever received despite a score of specialists they had sent to India.[61]

Inspite of Nehru's bias in favour of Russia, he minced no words in condemning Russia whenever the occasion demanded. He denounced Soviet intervention in Hungary. "Nehru told his members of Parliament that the majority of the people of Hungary wanted a change, political, economic, or whatever else and demonstrated and actually rose in insurrection to achieve it but ultimately they were suppressed....He made it clear that the Hungarian tragedy adversely affected the prestige of the Soviet Union among the non-aligned nations of the world."[62]

Following a brief spell of flirtation with the United States in the early months of her tenure Indira generally followed a moderately anti-colonial policy coming closer to Russia, the United Arab Republic and Yugoslavia. "During Arab-Israeli war of June 1967, she had come out firmly and unequivocally against Israel."[63]

The invasion of Czechoslovakia by Russia generated a furore in the Indian Parliament. Mrs. Gandhi made a cleverly-worded statement. She did not condemn the Soviet Union, only expressed sympathy with Czechoslovakia.

Unlike her father she kept the national interest to the fore in framing the foreign policy. When the Russians, in order to wean Pakistan from China, tried to please Pakistan by giving them military aid, India lodged a strong protest with the Russians reminding them that the Russian arms like the American arms would also be used against India. To offset Russian friendship with Pakistan, she initiated some moves to improve Sino-Indian relations. In her earlier years she played America against Russia, in her later years she played Russia against America, in between she tried to play China against Russia. She favoured the Arabs against Israel. Her foreign policy was born of her sense of realism. She vivisected Pakistan and took revenge of Indian partition. The astounding victory in Bangladesh where 90,000 Pakistani soldiers surrendered *en masse* (nowhere in the world, soldiers on such a large scale ever laid down their arms) raised India sky high. There is one field in which she did not make a single false move. In contrast to Mr. Nehru, whose policies lay in ruins when he left the political scene, Mrs. Gandhi's policies have retrieved to the maximum possible what was lost by her father.[64] It goes to the credit of Indira Gandhi that her bitter critic Shri A.B. Vajpayee, Foreign Minister in Janata Government followed the foreign policies laid down by Indira Gandhi with only minor variations.

Demagogy may be easy but real leadership is very difficult. More so in a democracy, "It is no easy matter to be the leader of a democracy even when there is a well established tradition of unity and independence. How much more difficult when the nation is an amalgam of religions, languages and cultures, when the overwhelming mass of the people are illiterate and miserably poor."[65]

A real leader who will lead India's march towards economic prosperity, moral strength and height of decency is yet to be born. India has been and continues to be a corrupt society. No Prime Minister has so far shown the courage, despite his or her loud professions, to deal with corrupt politicians, most effectively. Corruption has become the bane of Indian political and economic system. The success of internal as well as external policies is intimately linked with the solution of this problem. Any Prime Minister who can cut the Gordian knot will rule the roost and earn the title of real spokesman of the nation.

REFERENCES

1. Aiyar, S.P. and Raju, S.V., When the Wind Blows, *The Revolution of the Ballot-Box*, Himalaya Publishing House, Bombay, 1978, p. 52.
2. Durga Das, *India from Curzon to Nehru*, p. 373.
3. Vadilal Dagli (ed), Handbook of Election Manisfestoes, *Commerce*, 1971, pp. 77-78.
4. Gorwala, A.D., *Opinion*, January 2, 1973, p. 2
5. Kulkarni, V.B., *My Country and My Rulers*, p, 188.
6. *Ibid.*
7. *Times of India*, January 4, 1970.
8. *Times of India*, Notebook, June 6, 1974.
9. Kulkarni, V.B., *My Country and My Rulers*, p. 185.
10. *Ibid.*, p. 188.
11. *Ibid.*, p. 189.
12. Aiyar S. P. & Raju S.V. When the Wind Blows, *The Revolution of Ballot Box*, p. 50.
13. *Ibid.*, p. 52.
14. *Ibid.*
15. Agrawala, Chandra Prakash, *Indira Gandhi (Then and Now)*, p. 120.
16. Benemy, F.W.G., *The Elected Monarch*, p. 241.
17. Kulkarni, V.B., *My Country and My Rulers*, p. 193.
18. *Ibid.*
19. Hughs, Emrys, *Macmillan : Portrait of a Politician*, George Allen & Unwin,1962, p. 201.
20. Jennings, Sir Ivor, *The Queen's Government*, p. 131.
21. Kulkarni, V.B., *My Country and My Rulers*, p. 195.
22. *The Indian Express*, April 1, 1974.
23. Mulllick B. N., *My Years with Nehru — 1948 to 1964*, p. 166.
24. Madgwick, P.G., *Introduction to British Politics*. p. 64.
25. Sethi, J.D., *India's Static Power Structure*, Vikas Publications, 1969, p. xv (Introduction).
26. Blake, Robert, *The Office of Prime Minister*, p. 40.
27. Mullick, B.N., *My Years with Nehru—1948 to 1964*, p. 13.
28. *Ibid.*, p. 40.
29. *Ibid.*, p. 42.
30. *Ibid.*, p. 45.
31. *Ibid.*, p. 46.
32. Chakravarti, Saroj, *With West Bengal Chief Minister, Memoirs, 1962 to 1977*, Orient Longman, 1978, p. 447.
33. Mullick, B.N., *My Years with Nehru—1948 to 1964*, p. 61.

34. Kulkarni, V.B., *My Country and My Rulers*, p. 139.
35. *Ibid.*, p. 140.
36. Desai, H. G., Toward Health or Hazard — Medical Education, *The Indian Express*, 8 June, 1974,
37. Kulkarni, V.B., *My Country and My Rulers*. p. 139.
38. Gadgil, N.V., Under the Shadow of the Red Fort (original in Marathi), Chitrasala Press, 1964, p. 21. Also consult '*My Contemporaries*', p. 22.
39. Kulkarni, V.B., *My Country and My Rulers*, p. 146.
40. *Ibid.*
41. Young, Kenneth, *Arthur Balfour*, G. Bell, 1963, p. 191.
42. Lord Moran, Constable, Taken from his diaries, Winston Churchill: *The Struggle for Survival, 1940-65, 1966*, p. 774-77.
43. Moraes, Frank, *Nehru: Sunlight and Shadow*, p. 172.
44. *Ibid.*, p. 176.
45. Nehru to Mrs. Pandit, July 1, 1949, MPP.
46. Fisher, W. and Bandurant, Joan V., *Indian Views of Sino-Indian Relations*, pp. 83-4.
47. Pandey, B.N., *Nehru*, p. 331.
48. Patel to Nehru, November 7, 1950 as re-printed in Tahamankar's *Sardar Patel*.
49. *Ibid.*
50. Kotelawala, John, *An Asian Prime Minister's Story*, p. 187.
51. Mullick, B.N., *My Years with Nehru— 1948 to 1964*, p. 78.
52. *Ibid.*, pp. 168-169.
53. *Ibid.*, p. 219.
54. *Ibid.*, p. 217.
55. *Ibid.*, p. 73.
56. *Ibid.*, p. 79.
57. See Nehru's statement of November 8, 1954 in *Leader*, November 9, 1954.
58. *Nehru to Mrs. Pandit*, June 8, 1949, M.P.P.
59. Dutt, Subimal, *With Nehru in the Foreign Office*, Minerva Associates Pvt. Ltd. Calcutta, p. 240.
60. *Ibid.*
61. *Ibid.*, p. 239
62. Pandey, B. N., *Nehru*, p. 386.
63. Masani, Zareer, *Indira Gandhi—A Biography*, p. 189.
64. *Everyman's* (Weekly) New Delhi, Bombay, Madras, January 19, 1975, p. 8.
65. Grigg, John, quoted by D. R. Mankekar in; *Lal Bahadur — A Political Biography*, Bombay, Popular Prakashan, 1964-65. p. 12.

8
Assessment

Prime Minister's Authority

Prime Minister in the Indian Political system has become the cynosure of all eyes. Whereas the Constitution has placed all powers in the hands of the President, it is the Prime Minister who uses all of them.

We have already discussed in detail the real position of the Prime Minister in the previous chapter. We did not subscribe to the statement that the Prime Minister has replaced the Cabinet and that the Prime Ministerial Government has come into being. At the same time, we cannot deny the immense power and influence that he wields. A person who led a party to victory in the general elections has every reason to be proud of his political achievement. In other words, he can proclaim that the nation is behind him, and he is expected to fulfil the promises he made at the time of elections. Fulfilment of promises needs important decisions with promptitude, and decisions cannot be made without authority and authority he must wield as a logical conclusion.

The authority that a Prime Minister can exercise is in proportion to the strength of his personality. The powers that Nehru exercised could not be exercised by Lal Bahadur Shastri. Similarly, Morarjibhai Desai could not match Indira Gandhi in the vast powers and the enormous influence which she wielded. The nature of authority, therefore, varies from Prime Minister to Prime Minister. The power and status of the Prime Minister reached under Peel and Llyod George were high points to which no other Prime Minister has attained. In 1848, Gladstone told Peel : "Your Government has not been carried on by a Cabinet but by heads of departments each in communication with you."[1] "So far as power is in part a function of personality, Prime Ministerial power is not a constant factor. It varies according to the strength, style and aptitude of the individual Prime Minister and the ability, experience and determination of his colleagues. Some Prime Ministers are surrounded by experienced, able and powerful men and women. Some are not."[2]

Crossman lists three causes for the increase in the powers of the Prime Minister. "There has been the growth of the power of party which has reduced that of the individual M.P., diminished his chances of defying party orthodoxy and removed the real debate on political issues from the floor of the Commons to the secrecy of the Committee rooms upstairs. This enhances the power of the Prime Minister in his capacity as the party leader....Secondly, there was the ending of Cabinet informality by the creation of a secretariat to keep the minutes and circulate papers. This occurred soon after Llyod George became Prime Minister, and inevitably enhanced the Prime Minister's powers by giving him what was tantamount to a department of his own. Llyod George was also involved in the third of Mr. Crossman's suggested causes of change. The unification of the civil services, with the permanent under secretary of the Treasury at its head."[3]

The complexity of modern life has also added to the powers of the Prime Minister. The concept of social welfare has made the state interfere in almost every aspect of social importancc. "There is obviously one sense in which any modern Prime Minister has more power than Peel, Gladstone, Llyod George, or Neville Chamberlain, because government itself controls a far wider area of national life than it ever has before."[4]

Madgwick agrees with Blake when he says, "The growing complexity of government enhances the Prime Minister's position as coordinator."[5] "In peace time in this century and earlier, the Prime Minister in each decade has exercised, or has been able to exercise, more power than his predecessor. But this is because, over the whole period, governments have exercised more power and influence. The Prime Minister has shared in this increased power, and almost certainly has increased his share."[6] Foreign and international economic affairs are of overriding importance and demand special attention of the Prime Minister. P. Ratnam while writing on foreign policy-making echoes the same sentiment. The Prime Minister as a matter of routine consults the foreign minister, other Cabinet colleagues, party members, prominent visitors and one or two opposition leaders in the Parliament. "On the basis of this information the Prime Minister formulates foreign policies and determines most of the important, specific actions and policies to be followed by others. Thus it can be said without much contradiction that these policy decisions are one man's show."[7]

The general election is virtually the election for the selection of the Prime Minister. It is usually a personal contest between two rival leaders. It is the Prime Minister who advises the King for the date of next general election. "The Prime Minister makes the crucial political choice — the date of next general election."[8]

He possesses vast powers of patronage — making appointments and recommending dismissals. "A British Prime Minister has virtually no executive functions, except in the field of patronage."[9] This makes him free as a bird to exercise the power to intervene in the affairs of any department when he feels that the department is not functioning properly and is tarnishing the fair name of his government. What is true about the British Prime Minister is equally true about the Indian Prime Minister.

V. Lingamurthy writing about the status of the Prime Minister states : "The Indian Prime Minister has become one of the most powerful functionaries in the world, more by practice than by the letter of the Constitution.... The Prime Minister of India is the keyman not only in the Council of the Ministers and the Parliament but also in the Congress Party." Lingamurthy is so much alarmed over the rising position of the Prime Minister that he senses danger from him.... "one of the dangers to the Parliamentary government in India lies in the growing domination of the Prime Minister. Under Parliamentary system, no doubt the Prime Minister is the key-figure but in India he has become almost the sole figure."[10]

Benemy thinks that the Second World War increased the powers of the Prime Minister considerably "Prof. Max Belott, in a letter to the *Daily Telegraph*, expressed the view that the Prime Minister is now a dictator. Perhaps the Second World War hastened the process of constitutional evolution because Winston Churchill as Prime Minister of a nation fighting for life against a remorseless enemy assumed powers to direct the war that were unquestionably dictatorial. From time to time his control was challenged in the House of Commons, but whenever he demanded a vote of confidence, this was given to him with an overwhelming majority."[11] The reason for conferring dictatorial power on the Prime Minister in war time was the absolute secrecy without which no military operation could be a success. In India also immense powers were bestowed on the executive whose head is the Prime Minister, during the invasions of China and Pakistan.

Prof. Mackintosh also refers to the rising tide of Prime Minister's authority. "While British Government in the latter half of the nineteenth century can be described simply as Cabinet government, such a description would be misleading. Now the country is governed by the Prime Minister who leads, coordinates and maintains a series of ministers, all of whom are advised and backed by the Civil Service Some decisions are taken by the Prime Minister alone, some in consultation between him and the senior ministers while others are left to heads of departments, the Cabinet, the Cabinet Committees. The precise amount of power held by each agency, and the use made of the Cabinet depends on the ideas of the Premier and the personnel and situation with which he has to deal."[12] Brian Smith also points to the concentration of powers in the hands of the Prime Minister in the following words : "What is disputed, however, is that the power of the Prime Minister has increased in recent decades to the point of his being far from *primus inter pares* and becoming almost a Presidential figure or elected monarch.[13]

Built-in Checks, if any, on the Prime Minister

It is an acknowledged fact that the Prime Minister's power has increased considerably. One factor is the circumstantial changes, *i.e.* the complete nature of modern government, while the other is the Prime Minister's personality. Some of the Prime Ministers exploited the weakness of the Indian masses to intensify the effect of their personality. In Indian society hero-worship and idol-worship are widely prevalent. Nehru and his daughter Indira Gandhi made full use of this Indian trait. J.P. Narain also makes mention of this tragic fact, "The attitude of irresponsibility grows in the people who look out for heroes and miracle makers to solve their problems. It is out of such psychological situation that dictators are born."[14]

Pandit Nehru tried to concentrate more and more powers in his hands knowing fully well that he was regarded as one of the national heroes and that the people held him in deep affection. He could do what he liked and the people would not mind it. "Consciously, Pandit Nehru tried to suppress the streak of authoritarianism ingrained in him. But, he could not succeed very much in containing what was natural to him. Frank Moraes rightly noted that Nehru enjoyed the feeling of power; he had always been confident, but power gave him a new air of authority."[15] If the Prime Minister steals a pinch of salt, his ministers will steal in fistfuls. The Caesar in Nehru was forcing him to allow him full scope for expression. If the Prime Minister ignores the routine norms of behaviour, his ministers will also not lag behind. "There is at present a general tendency among the ministers to disregard the authority of the Standing Finance Committee and to adopt proposals of expenditure either without or in anticipation of its approval. Some greatest offenders in this respect are the ministers functioning under the immediate control of the Prime Minister. When the High Commissioner in London was appointed ambassador in Ireland, the Standing Finance Committee agreed on the understanding that there should be no expenditure other than the travelling expenditure. There was to be no building and no staff. This was agreed to by the External Affairs Ministry as a part of our economy campaign....It has now been decided by the Cabinet that the High Commissioner should be provided with a building and staff....this without the approval of the Standing Finance Committee and against its recommendations."[16]

This tendency of flouting rules and regulations gave birth to corruption. "It was no secret that this honest man (Pandit Nehru), in his final weariness, was well aware of the sycophancy and corruption that surrounded him and remained silent while it flourished because he was too vain to acknowledge it and too weak to fight it."[17]

Walter Crocker, one-time Australian High Commissioner in India, commented : "Nehru kept too much power in his own hands and so in effect he encouraged bad habits of dependence. Cabinet responsibility might have been collective in principle, but in practice, there was much more primus than *primus inter pares*, the position being made worse by the circumambient mixture of sycophancy and flattery."[18]

The Caesar in Nehru was contained by him. But the Caesar in Indira overwhelmed her and made her do errors which provoked the people in the general elections of 1977 to take up cudgels against her to drive her out of power and into political wilderness. "In 1966, a minister had come to me to seek my advice about leadership. I told him "do what you like but if she (Indira) becomes Prime Minister, she will ruin the country. I didn't know how long it would take and now you see she has ruined the country and has ruined herself in the process."[19]

The process that Indira Gandhi started to have a committed Judiciary, a committed Civil Service, committed Chief Ministers and committed Press, resolved itself into its logical conclusion—Emergency.

It was during her time that the Constitution was disfigured shabbily. "If now the dead framers of the Constitution were to come back alive after 27 years....they would not recognise the Constitution. The framework of the Constitution has been basically shattered and the substance and spirit have gone out of it. The inspiration behind the Constitution has drained out."[20] "The drastic changes effected in the Constitution before and during emerency (promulgated on June 25, 1975) have so grievously distorted the face of the Constitution that what remains of it bears little resemblance in spirit to the original document."[21]

Janata Party vehemently deplored the notorious 42nd amendment in the following words:

> "To call it an amendment is a misnomer. It is a betrayal of the testament of both that the founding fathers bequeathed to the people and it subverts

> the basic structure of the 1950 Constitution. It vitiates the federal principle and upsets the nice balance between the people and Parliament, Parliament and the Judiciary, the Judiciary and the Executive, the States and the Centre, the citizen and the Government."[22]

Indira Gandhi prompted by her own ambition for unlimited power did everything humanly possible to change the values which had been giving moral strength to the Congress as well as the government despite the minor lapses here or there. "What Indira Gandhi did was to encourage a code of loyalty with such rigid ramifications that like everything else, these became accentuated during the Emergency. Loyalty to the Congress was not enough, it had to be loyalty expressed in terms of unequivocal personal allegiance to her."[23]

Indira did not influence the economic trends to the benefit of the people. She rather used economic trends to retain and enlarge her political power. Nehru, contrary to this, had used political power to influence economic trends.

To raise huge funds for the party as well as for certian other activities she used every posssible source unscrupulously. Licences were cleared in a jiffy if money was paid into the party's coffers and, according to one estimate, the amount was as high as Rs. two lakhs for a single licence. Money from big business was pouring in through other channels even in 1969. The House of Birlas which had financed a state election had also gained immensely by the political support they got from Mrs. Gandhi's government. As one company executive proudly said, "Let the facts speak. The turnover of the Birlas was just 290 crores before Mrs. Gandhi became Prime Minister. By the time of Congress split it had shot up to Rs. 717 crores. All this during the time when Mrs. Gandhi was pleasing the communists. Isn't she a genius ?"[24]

Lure of lucre on the part of sons brought defamation and downfall of two powerful Prime Ministers. Raising crores of rupees by Sanjay Gandhi for his Maruti factory and other sister concerns spelt ruin for his mother Indira Gandhi. "The tragedy of the Nehrus has been an almost classic pattern: They proclaimed and believed in the principles of social democracy and sustained and promoted their party through the nastiest aspect of unbridled and dishonest capitalism. Congress has been sustained by corruption forever, by black money from the business houses."[25]

Indira Gandhi in spite of her good intentions and noble professions had a tryst with Devil and like Dr. Faustus bartered her soul for a handful of silver which turned out to be copper at the end. The dismal drama which ended with the elections of March 1977, provoked D.P. Mishra, one-time confidant of Mrs. Gandhi, to observe : "Nehru's monocracy brought about in 1962, India's humiliation at the hands of the Chinese. Indira Gandhi's absolutism produced the excesses of 1975-76 and culminated in her own defeat in 1977. What is more, it led to the eclipse of the Indian National Congress, an institution built by the sacrifices of countless Indian patriots and led by such stalwarts as Tilak and Gandhi. This Jawaharlal drama, with Sanjay as the final entrant, has all the elements of a Greek tragedy."[26]

Our studies lead us to believe that a Prime Minister if he or she stongly wishes, can manipulate to gather immense powers in his or her hands. "The powers under Part XVIII entitled 'Emergency Provisions' are so immense that the (Prime Minister) can, by a one-sentence proclamation, become a dictator."[27]

In Britain also the writers are pointing towards the tendency which results in the rise of Prime Minister's powers, "The British Prime Minister is in a practical sense a dictator, but a benevolent one. He has been trained to behave in accordance with the conventions of the Constitution. He knows that at the end of five years he must submit his fortunes to the hazard of an election."[28]

The only redeeming feature is the benevolent trait. But benevolence may disappear or may go under in certain circumstances. The trend as pointed above is full of dangerous potentialities. "The Queen has become the formal and ceremonial Head of State with the Prime Minister more and more openly acting as the true working Head of State."[29]

Indira Gandhi who ruled like a dictator during the 19 months of Emergency was reluctant to give up power even when she had lost everything. "On March 20, when almost all the results had been announced, Mrs. Gandhi, who was acting as the Prime Minister of the country did not resign nor relaxed Emergency, She waited if she could yet retrieve the position. The Congress and the CPI combine could not form the government and she could not be chosen as the Prime Minister. She then met the Army Chief, General T.N. Raina, seeking his help to remain in power but the General firmly expressed himself against committing "his men in partisan politics." Even the Border Security Forces and the General Reserve Police Chief voiced similar sentiments. The game was now all over. Shri Jatti the acting Rashtrapati then advised Mrs. Gandhi to resign and revoke Emergency lest the new Government may take advantage of it against the Congress Party leaders. Mrs. Gandhi harkened to his advice.[30]

Such is the attraction of this most powerful post that every worthwhile politician has his eyes riveted on it. "Such a position was never held by any Greek or Roman; and if it only lasts three months it will be worthwhile to have been Prime Minister of England."[31] Methinks Chaudhari Charan Singh must have read this quotation somewhere.

If such are the dangers attending on this most

important office of the nations, we must think of ways of plugging the loopholes of mischief. We must think in terms of curbs on the wild movements of this political dragon. We must think in terms of checks. If there are some already existing, well and good; if not, can we contemplate to devise some ?

The Independent Judiciary in a democratic country stands as a bulwark against the onslaughts of the Executive. The rights gruaranteed to the citizen by the state cannot remain secure if the judges are not free to decide on the merits of the case. The abolition of *zamindari*, the nationalisation of banks, the termination of privy purses were challenged in the courts of law and set aside. There was hue and cry in some quarters over the conservativeness and partiality of the judges. In America also the judges of the Supreme Court have been accused of blocking progressive legislative measures. Even President Roosevelt who failed to get his new deal approved in the first instance by the Supreme Court administered warnings to the judges. But nothing has happened so far. Whenever the Supreme Court invalidates some measure which is regarded as progressive, a storm of protest is raised, but soon the storm is over, the dust settles down and the nation reverts to its usual course. The independence of Judiciary is of utmost importance and the invalidation of even certain progressive measures in the march of history is a price that must be paid for the liberty that we cherish so much.

Prime Minister's Place in Nation's Polity

The politicians are also not above shady deals. The circumstances in which the nationalization of banks was attempted were not born of genuine concern for the welfare of the people. It was a cunning move by Indira Gandhi to hoodwink the people and settle scores with her political enemies. "By it (Ordinance) fourteen major banks were nationalized on the afternoon of Saturday, 21 July, 1969, notwithstanding the fact that the House of the People had been summoned and was to meet barely 36 hours later on Monday, July 23, 1969. The nationalization of banks cannot be covered by the words immediate action."[32]

The Government of Mrs. Indira Gandhi started the despicable practice of punishing the judges for not toeing the official line and giving instead impartial verdicts against the wanton acts of injustice committed by some of the over-zealous officials of her government. The boys in possession of the leaflets containing the speech by Mohan Dharia in Lok Sabha were promptly arrested by the police. They applied for bail, pending investigation and trial by the magistrate; to the Sessions Judge, and eventually to the Nagpur branch of the Bombay High Court. Mr. Justice U.R. Lalit ordered their release on bail on October 6, 1975. Rule 184 of the DIR forbade grant of bail to anyone accused of a breach of the Rules unless the court was satisfied, "that there are reasonable grounds for believing that he is not guilty of such contravention....The Judge held that in the whole leaflet there is no call for violence and the same was not seditious. Justice Lalit observed that in a prosecution under section 124-A of IPC, in respect of a writing or a speech, the entire material has to be considered as a whole and it has to be found out whether there is an incitement to public violence in such a writing or speech. We have also to find out whether it is possible to gather on the part of the author an intention or tendency to create disturbance or disorder to law and order.

Five months later, breaking all precedents the Government of India refused to confirm Mr. Justice Lalit as permanent judge of the High Court after he had served as Additional Judge for two years.[33]

"Mr. Justice A. N. Ray was today (April 4, 1973) appointed Chief Justice of the Supreme Court in succession to Mr. Justice S.M. Sikri who retired today. This is the first time in the history of the Supreme Court that Government of India departed from the established convention of appointing the senior most judge as Chief Justice....The appointment of Mr. A.N. Ray has led to the supersession of his three senior colleagues, Mr. Shelat, Mr. Hegde and Mr. A.N. Grover."[34] "Mr. S.M. Sikri, who retired as the Supreme Court Chief Justice earlier this week, said here (New Delhi) today that the supersession of three judges in the appointment of the new Chief Justice was a "big blow to the independence of Judiciary."[35] Every attempt was made to influence Justice Jagmohan Lal Sinha who was hearing the election petition against Indira Gandhi filed by Raj Narain.

"On a day during the week ending May, 23 1975 at 10.00 a.m. Justice Mathew, Ex-Chief Justice of Allahabad High Court, went to the house of Justice J.M. Lal Sinha and talked to him, in all secrecy, there was a rumour that if he favoured Mrs. Gandhi in his judgement, the next day he would be taken on the Supreme Court Bench, otherwise Mrs. Gandhi was very vindictive. Justice Sinha gave no heed to the rumours. He at the same time told Mathew that he was being spied but would not mind. This fact has been divulged by Sinha himself to the Home Minister Charan Singh. It is also reported that a few days before Justice Sinha delivered his judgement he was offered a sum of Rs. four lakhs and even more, if he decided the case in Mrs. Gandhi's favour."[36] Efforts were also made to bribe Shanti Bhushan, the lawyer engaged by Raj Narain. "It is also alleged by Prashanta Bhushan, the son of Shanti Bhushan that during the final stages of this long drawn case in a dinner party in May 1975, the Attorney-General Mr. Niren Dey wanted to lure away Mr. Shanti Bhushan by saying that everybody had a high opinion about him and a post of Additional Attorney-General could be created for him. But Mr. Bhushan gave no attention to it and remarked that he attached more importance to any contribution he could make in the political life of the country. At last June 12 dawned, and in packed court at 10.00 a.m. Justice Sinha delivered his most famous judgement."[37]

Another form of scuttling the independence of Judiciary is to appoint judges after retirement on political posts. Justice Fazal Ali after retirement from the Supreme Court was appointed as the Governor of Assam.

The independence of Judiciary like as in Western democracies must be maintained at any cost if the democracy is to survive. It should be made wellnigh impossible for any government to break the healthy convention of promoting the senior most judge to be the Chief Justice of India. No Justice retiring from a High Court or the Supreme Court should be appointed to any political post. Adequate financial security, however, may be provided to them.

"The clamour about committed Judiciary and bureaucracy, appointment of new Judges on the basis of commitment rather than merit and the allurement of post-retirement assignments has done all to seriously compromise the independence of the Judiciary."[38]

Another factor which added to the powers of the Prime Minister and needs a check was the practice started by Congress Prime Ministers to impose their own stooges as Chief Ministers on States irrespective of the fact whether they were members of the State Legislature or not. "She (Mrs. Gandhi) nominated the Chief Ministers for Madhya Pradesh, Rajasthan, Gujarat, Mysore, Bihar and other states, some of whom were not even members of state assemblies....They had no free hand in the matter of choosing their cabinet colleagues....The Chief Executive Councillor for Delhi (Radha Raman) was nominated by her even though he was not an elected member of the Delhi Metropolitan Council."[39]

The so-called hadicapped Chief Ministers were always on the run between Delhi and the state capital. Their main aim was to keep Mrs. Gandhi pleased at all costs and to suppress the natural leaders of the state. Such a sharp practice struck at the roots of Federalism and democratic traditions, stimulated conspiracies and rebellion in State legislatures. Much of the time of the Chief Minister was wasted in unnecessary and irrelevant activities, and no real work for the betterment of the people was done. With the formation of Janata Government at the Centre in 1977 this practice was minimised though it could not be eliminated.

Another important restraint on the increasing powers of the Prime Minister is his Cabinet. "Prime Ministers on a fair number of occasions have been overruled by their cabinets both before and since the ascent of the Prime Minister to pre-eminence."[40]

Although by the 1950s and 1960s the office of the Prime Minister had risen greatly in status, although the Prime Minister had acquired an authority different in kind from that of his colleagues yet he was not independent of the Cabinet. The Cabinet remained the sole source of political authority.

> "A strong Prime Minister can be very strong. He can sometimes commit the Cabinet by acts or words. But he cannot habitually or often do so."[41]
> "A Prime Minister could not, and never does, behave as if he could govern on his own—because this would undermine his position."[42]

He cannot ride roughshod over the wishes of his colleagues. "A Prime Minister must carry with him a number of his senior colleagues (who might claim his office.)"[43]

A Deputy Prime Minister also acts as a hurdle in the race of unbridled power; acts as a corrective to the

Prime Minister's shortcomings and enhances the effect of his qualities. He reminds the Prime Minister of the limits he should respect.

Sardar Patel was the Deputy Prime Minister in Nehru's Government and incharge of Home portfolio. He had given his report on the communal riots at Ajmer. Pandit Nehru sent his private secretary, H.V.R. Iyengar, to visit Ajmer to make an on-the-spot study of the situation there. There arose a conflict between the Prime Minister Nehru and Sardar Patel.

Sardar Patel rebutted the contention of Pt. Nehru that the Prime Minister could arrange an investigation of his own to get first rate information of the happening anywhere in the country. "I have found myself unable to agree with the conception of the Prime Minister's duties and functions. That conception, if accepted, would raise the Prime Minister to the position of a virtual dictator....But he has no overriding powers over his colleagues, if he and any, a Cabinet and Cabinet responsibility would be superfluous....He has accordingly the right to ask for information from the Minister concerned as well as the right to consult and advise on the lines of policy to be adopted and even the manner in which the policy is to be implemented. But the responsibility for the policy must be that of the Ministry concerned and the Minister Incharge."[44]

Sardar Patel got many decisions in the Cabinet as well as in the party against the stand of the Prime Minister. His Herculean task of cleaning the Augean stables of 500 princely states and welding them all into the Union of India stands as an outstanding monument to his political genius. His solutions of Junagadh and Hyderabad tangles stand as examples of ample testimony to his robust practical sense. Nehru handled the Kashmir question and turned it into a question mark forever. As long as Patel was there Nehru as Prime Minister remained within his limits. He could not override the wishes of his Cabinet as well as his party.

Only after Patel's death, Nehru could cross the '*Lakshman Rekha*' to stride like a leviathan. Another important barricade against Prime Minister's galloping ride is the independent Press. Realizing the importance of publicity and propaganda a Prime Minister calls a press conference from time to time to give information on some vital issues or to project his image, to reach the people through this important media. If the Press is not independent, correct and true news will fail to reach the people. Editorials and articles giving balanced and fair assessment of the achievements and failures of government will not appear. Distorted and garbled versions will be published in which no one will take interest. Rumours will be rife and exaggerated accounts will reach the people causing mistrust and suspicions. Belief in underground literature will increase. This is what happened during the 19 months of Emergency in India.

Indira Government imposed strict censorship on the press. All endeavours were made by her government to control the press from all angles. Only two names appeared again and again daily, Indira Gandhi and Sanjay Gandhi. People had lost interest in newspapers as all censored news had become boring. "*Samachar* had been constituted by merging four news agencies., the PTI, the UNI, *Hindustan Samachar* and *Samachar Bharati*. The merger was forced on the reluctant agencies so as to enable the Emergency Government to exercise tight control over the main sources of news to the newspapers....Alongwith the clout, monetary incentives too were offered to the news agencies to buy the loyalty of their employees. Before the merger, all four news agencies had been running at various levels of losses. In the case of the language news agencies, *Samachar Bharati* and *Hindustan Samachar*, The emoluments of their employees were dismally low. With the merger these were brought on par with the rest. The Government was willing to make available a susbtantial amount of fund to cover extra expenses. In 1976-77, the government gave a grant of Rs. 25 lakhs to facilitate the increase in pay and allowances, and Rs. 10 lakhs and Rs. 15 lakhs respectively to clear previous liabilities and making up the current deposit. The prospect at the then existing level of subscriptions was that the liabilities would increase thereby increasing their dependence on the government."[45]

Mr. B.G Verghese, the Chief Editor of *Hindustan Times*, wrote some articles advising Indira Gandhi to step down as Prime Minister in view of the verdict of Allahabad High Court against her. As a result, the Management of the *Hindustan Times*, Birlas under the obligation of Indira Gandhi, forced Verghese to leave and go. Those newspapers who could not prepare themselves to toe the official line preferred to pull down their shutters. *The Indian Express* remained under constant harassment.

The Additional Secretary in the Ministry of Information and Broadcasting deposed before the Shah Commission on October 20, that "all newspapers were classified into three categories friendly, neutral and hostile to the Congress government and those friendly to the government were freely given government advertisements and the cost of such advertisements in the years 1974-75 and 1976-77 went upto 1.4 crores and 2.19 crores. *National Herald* (Prime Minister's newspapers) alone was given advertisement valued Rs. 80,000. They also deposed that the rates of advertisement in Congress Souvenir were enhanced to Rs. 2,000 per page."[46]

It was only when the Janata Government was ushered in March 1977 that the censorship on the press was removed and its liberty restored.

Strong party leadership can also act as a check on the Prime Minister's powers. As long as Syndicate was there, Indira Gandhi could not ride roughshod over her colleagues in the Cabinet and members of the Congress

Working Committee. During the Second World War the inner Party revolt in the Conservative Party forced Premier Neville Chamberlain to resign in May 1940 and replaced him with Winston Churchill.

Madgwick recommends the selection of prosaic and unimaginative persons as Prime Ministers because such persons are good workers and reasonably ambitious "My (political judgement) own would be for the prosaic, unimaginative character of Mr. Attlee, because most of the time the nation's problems are solved by prosaic, unimaginative (but competent, cautious, tolerant) people. The eloquence and sense of drama and history may have its uses, at particular moments in a nation's history, but not often."[47] Bagehot called for a man of first-rate capacity and second-rate ideas.

The mass media of communication, Radio and T.V. are two-edged swords. On the one hand they enhance the status of the Prime Minister but if he is not doing well, they also corrode his authority and place a check on him. "The increased exposure of a modern Prime Minister on radio and television, which greatly raises his power when things are going on well, may rapidly undermine his prestige when things are going badly. Indeed the mere passage of time may weaken his position through the overfamiliarity of the public with his manner and style of address. It may well be that the mass media of communication, which have helped to raise the Prime Minister to greater heights than his earlier predecessors, may also have shortened his political life in comparison with them."[48]

Sometimes, the Prime Minister allows his powers to be limited in a particular field in the interest of the nation. The British Prime Minister has done so. "So far as honours are concerned, Prime Minister has allowed his powers to be restricted by the appointment of a Committee of three privy councillors who are no longer in active politics to examine all recommendations and to ensure that no decorations or titles are being conferred improperly."[49]

In spite of all these checks and balances, the powers of the Prime Minister remain unbounded in the sense that he can manage to cross all the hurdles and barricades if he is determined to do so. "The Prime Minister today is a man of enormous influence, with a frightening power over the life and death, the prosperity and happiness of men and women. This perhaps, is a source of immense satisfaction to him, but it is power that is purchased at a high price, which price is the heavy burden of never being off duty. His day is long indeed. Even when he goes to bed, the Prime Minister is liable to be wakened to be told of some sudden crisis somewhere about which he must make a decision and give an order."[50] His work like that of a woman is never finished. "The most convincing evidence of Prime Ministerial domination concerns his ability to manipulate office and decide on the deployment of the available political talent."[51] "The Prime Minister as Chairman of the Cabinet, the most important single member, clearly carries great weight."[52]

"This Constitution concentrates so much power and influence in the hands of the Prime Minister, in regard to the appointment of Judges, ambassadors or governors to such an extent, that there is every danger to apprehend that the Prime Minister may become a dictator if he chooses to do so. I think there are cases which ought to be removed from his political influence.[53] No one could prevent Indira Gandhi from becoming a dictator when she chose to become so.

Dr. Ambedkar also admitted that the Prime Minister is bound to become very powerful as the practice of Parliamentary government demands so. "If any functionary under our Constitution is to be compared with the United States President, he is the Prime Minister and not the President."[54]

It may be easy for a Prime Minister to try to assume dictatorial powers but it is extremely difficult for him to enjoy them for a long time. The concentration of all powers in his hands leads to the creation of Frankenstein's monster that may run out of control at any time and cause the death of its creator. Every sane Prime Minister knows of it and resists the temptation of driving at the maximum speed which is not meant for frequent and constant use because such a course is fraught with dangerous consequences. Dictatorial authority is like a two-edged sword. It helps the sowrdsman if used with caution but it may harm him if used with carelessness.

REFERENCES

1. Minogue, Martin (ed.), Documents on Contemporary British Government, Vol. I. *British Government and Constitutional Change*, Cambridge University Press, London, 1977, p. 88.
2. Smith, Brian, *Policy Making in British Cabinet —An Analysis of Power and Rationality*, Publisher, Martin Robertson, 1976, p. 97.
3. Blake, Robert, *The Office of Prime Minister*, p. 46.
4. *Ibid.*, p. 47.
5. Madgwick, P.J., *Introduction to British Politics*, p. 71.
6. Wilson, Harold, *The Governance of Britain*, p. 9.
7. Ratnam, P., Policy Making and Parliamentary Accountability with Particular Reference to India's Foreign Policy, *Journal of Constitutional and Parliamentary Studies*, Jan. - March 1975, p. 73.
8. Madgwick, P.J., *Introduction to British Politics*, p. 71.
9. Haines, Joe, *The Politics of Power*, Jonathan Cape, 30, Bedford Square, London, 1977, p. 8.
10. Lingamurthy, V., The Prime Minister in the Indian Polity, in *Modern Review* of Sept., 1959, pp., 194-196.
11. Benemy, F.W.G., *The Elected Monarch*, George G. Harrap & Co., London, 1965, p. 11
12. *Ibid.*, p. 11
13. Smith, Brian, *Policy Making in British Cabinet — An Analysis of Power and Rationality*. Publisher, Martin Robertson, 1976, p. 93.
14. Narain, J.P., *Organic Democracy in Studies in Indian Democracy*, S.P. Aiyar and R. Srinivasan, Bombay, 1965,

p. 334.

15. Murthy, V.K., *In the Larger Personal Interest : An Investigation into Indian Politics Since 1947*, Allora Publications, Darya Ganj, New Delhi, 1978, p. 5.
16. *Ibid.*, p.12.
17. James, Cameron quoted by Murthy, V.K. in '*In the Larger Personal Interest*', p. 39.
18. Walter Crocker quoted by Murthy, V.K. in '*In the Larger Personal Interest*', p. 71-72.
19. Mathai, John (Private Secretary to Nehru) quoted in *All the Prime Ministers' Men* by Janardan Thakur, p. 15.
20. Mukherji, P.B. (Justice), *The Indian Constitution : Change and Challenge*. p. 56.
21. Mirchandani, G.G., *Subverting the Constitution*, Abhinav Publications, New Delhi, 1977, p. 5.
22. Janata Party Election Manifesto, 1977.
23. Uma Vasudeva quoted in '*In the Larger Personal Interest*' by V.K. Murthy, p. 59.
24. Aiyar, S.P. and Raju S.V., *When the Wind Blows— India's Ballot Box Revolution*, Himalaya Publishing House, Bombay, 1978, p. 29.
25. Thakur, Janardan, *All the Prime Minister's Men*, 1977, p. 8.
26. Mishra, D.P., *In the Larger Interest* by V.K. Murthy, pp. 71-72.
27. Ram Gopal, *Undemocratic Elements in the Indian Constitution*, p. 186.
28. Benemy, F.W.G. *The Elected Monarch*, p. 21.
29. *Ibid.*, p. 35.
30. Darbara Singh, *Indian Politics*, p. 109.
31. Haines, Joe (Harold Wilson's Press Secretary), *The Politics of Power*, Jonathan Cape, London, 1977, p. 1.
32. Ram Gopal, *Undemocratic Elements in the Indian Constitution*, p. 183.
33. Agrawal, Chandra Prakash, *Indira Gandhi (Then and Now) and Janata*, pp. 27-30.
34. *The Hindu* of April 26, 1973.
35. *The Hindustan Times*, April 29, 1973.
36. Singh, Darbara, *Indian Politics 1968-1978*, Sandeep Prakashan, Ashok Vihar, New Delhi, 1978, p. 7.
37. *Ibid.*, p. 8.
38. Madhok, Balraj, *Murder of Democracy*, p. 119.
39. *Ibid.*, p. 127.
40. Minogue, Martin (ed.), *Documents on Contemporary British Government* p. 90.

41. *Ibid.*, p. 91.
42. *Ibid.*
43. Madgwick, P.J., *Introduction to British Politics*, p. 71.
44. Murthy, V.K., *In the Larger Personal Interest — An Investigation into Indian Politics Since 1947*, Allora Publications, Darya Ganj, New Delhi, 1978, p. 9-10
45. Sinha, Sachchidanand, *The Permanent Crisis in India--After Janata What* ? Heritage Publishers, New Delhi, 1978, p. 104.
46. Singh, Darbara, *Indian Politics*, p. 111.
47. Madgwick, P.J., *Introduction to British Politics*, p. 74.
48. Minogue, Martin (ed.), *Documents on Contemporary British Government*, Vol. I: British Government and Contitutional Change, Cambridge University Press, London, 1977, p. 90.
49. Benemy, F.W.G., *The Elected Monarch*, p. 157.
50. *Ibid.*, p. 178.
51. Smith, Brian, *Policy Making in British Cabinet — Analysis of Power and Rationality*, Publisher, Martin Robertson, 1976, p. 97.
52. Jones, G.W., *Development of the Cabinet in the Modernization of British Government*, Edited by William Thornhill, Pitman House, 39 Parker Street, London, p. 57.
53. Shaw, K.T., C.A.D., Vol. VIII, p. 234.
54. Ambedkar, B.R., C.A.D., VII, p. 998.

9
Prime Minister and Emergency Powers

The harrowing and bone-chilling tale of emergency lasting for 19 months constitutes the most significant and revealing chapter in the constitutional history of India. The Article 352 dealing with emergency powers was included in the Constitution after a long and critical deliberation in the Constituent Assembly. Our forefathers were fully conscious of the imperative need for such a provision under the compulsions of history. All of them almost agreed that a strong centre meant a free Inda and a weak centre a slave India. Every student of Indian history knows that whenever our central government became weak in the past, the fissiparous forces grew stronger and India lost her freedom. Agreeing to the incorporation of Emergency provision, many of them expressed their apprehensions that the emergency powers might be misused by unscrupulous politicians.

Shibban Lal Saxena stressing the need for emergency provision in the Constitution told the Constituent Assembly, "I do not think any person who takes the present position of the country into account can oppose this article."

T.T. Krishnamachari defended the chapter on emergency in the following words, "a sort of safety valve which is intended to save the Consititution."[1]

H.V. Kamath expressing his apprehensions warned that the Constitution may be subverted "not merely by agitators, rebels and revolutionaries, but also by those in office or in power."[2]

K.T. Shah severely criticised the provision and

warned against "arming the central Executive with excessive authority" and described it further as "unjustifiable of democratic freedom".[3] Dr. P.S. Deshmukh expressed his fears thus : "Ministers might utilise the powers vested in the President for electioneering purposes and declare an Emergency just on the eve of the elections and thus choke off the other party, and utilise the powers which are in the hands of the President for party ends."[4]

The original words on the need of emergency in the Draft Constitution were "war or domestic violence". These were amended to read "war, external aggression or internal disturbance".

The President is empowered to proclaim an emergency on personal satisfaction that a grave situation warranting it exists.

T.T. Krishnamachari, a member of the drafting committee, expressed his hope that the President himself will not declare emergency. "The whole scheme of this Constitution has been envisaged on the basis that the President is a constitutional head."[5] Our forefathers in order to help us preserve our national liberty gave us Frankenstein's Monster with the hope that the Monster would always obey us. But it rode the nation roughshod in 1975 under the guidance of Shrimati Gandhi, the most astute and wily Prime Minister India has seen during the last 32 years.

It is said in some quarters that the circumstances compelled Indira Gandhi to impose emergency. It is difficult to accept this proposition. On the other hand, it can be stated with confidence that it was she who was responsible for creating such circumstances as warranted imposition of emergency. The autocrat in her was very subtly working on the development of Personality Cult. After her astounding victory over Pakistan in 1971 and in the subsequent elections held in India she began to look upon herself as the uncrowned queen of India. She appointed her own judges, her own governors, her own chief ministers and her own party presidents. There was no one in the Congress who could have challenged her arbitrary use of authority. A meekly loyal group of politicians were posted at the key points in the Government as well as in the Party. They devoted themselves wholeheartedly to the building up of personality cult by nurturing the notion daily that Indira Gandhi was indispensable for the nation.

The Chief Minister of Maharashtra described her thus in January 1972 : "Mrs. Gandhi has made people proud of themselves as no other leader in the last thousand years has done."[6]

At a felicitation function held at Lucknow in January, 1972, the President of the Uttar Pradesh Congress Committee described the Prime Minister as the incarnation of Goddess 'Durga'.[7]

The President of the Bombay Pradesh Congress Committee paid her an illustrious tribute in the following words : "The new B.P.P.C. will be a people's party, a party of socialism. In B.P.P.C. there will be no leader, no followers. The party has only one leader — Mrs. Indira Gandhi. We are all soldiers in a vast army of socialists."[8]

While talking to newsmen in Bombay, the Union Law Minister observed that the norms for choosing candidates for elections to Maharashtra State Legislature from the metropolis would be "clear inclination on the candidate's part that he can be trusted to follow the Prime Minister's policies."[9]

Whereas Indira-worshippers were busy in nourishing personality cult, the spiralling prices, the mounting corruption was eroding the influence of the Congress over the masses. In due course of time Jai Prakash Narain felt compelled to launch a movement against the corrupt Congress politicians. Soon the Congress became a party of the minority if not in legislatures, at least amongst the electorate. "In the U.P. Vidhan Sabha election held in 1973 on the eve of the J.P. movement, the Congress had secured barely 29.18 per cent of the votes, 70 per cent of the voters had voted against the Congress and still the Congress was ruling because of lack of national alternative of the Congress party.[10]

The Allahabad judgement against Mrs. Gandhi proved to be calamitous for her. Raj Narain who had contested election in Rae Bareli against Indira Gandhi in 1971 elections had charged that the elections were fought with the twin weapons of unaccounted money power and official machinery which was at the disposal of the Prime Minister.

Jagmohan Lal Sinha of Allahabad High Court made history by declaring that Mrs. Indira Gandhi had been found guilty having committed a corrupt practice under Section 112(7) of the Representation of the People Act by having obtained the assistance of the gazetted officers of the State Government of U.P., *viz.*, the District Magistrate, Rae Bareli; the Superintendent of Police, Rae Bareli; the Executive Engineer, P.W.D., Rae Bareli; Engineer Hydel Department, Rae Bareli in furtherance of her election prospects in the manner indicated in the findings on Issue No. 2. He further found her guilty of having committed another corrupt practice under Section 123(7) of the Representation of the People Act by having obtained the assistance of Yashpal Kapur, a gazetted officer in the Government of India, holding the post of officer on special duty in the Prime Minister's secretariat for the promotion of her election prospects in the manner indicated in his findings on Issue No. 1. Accordingly, she stands disqualified for a period of six years from the date of this order as provided in Section 8A of the Representation of the People Act. June 12, 1975, the day of Judgement, shook the Congress (R) through its very foundations and maddened Mrs. Gandhi, "who having once tasted absolute power, prestige and popularity decided not to part with it"[11] The opposition stepped up its agitation against Mrs.

Gandhi demanding her immediate resignation. Shanti Bhushan, Raj Narain's pleader, said "It will be highly improper and contrary to all good conventions for the Prime Minister to continue to hold office after the High Court has found her guilty of corrupt practices."[12]

Instead of bowing before the deity of law she began her serious efforts to throw him out and demolish the temple of justice in addition. The thirty-ninth amendment was enacted in 1975. The purpose of the amendment was to take away the jurisdiction of the courts to entertain any dispute about the election of the Prime Minister, the Speaker of the House, the Vice-President and the President. The best construction on this amendment is that it sought to shift control in these matters from the courts to Parliament. "It was enacted solely for the purpose of protecting Mrs. Gandhi so that she did not lose her Parliamentary seat....The use of the power of amendment for these purposes is regarded as a total abuse of the power of amendment."[13] Oddly enough, it looks like as if Indira Gandhi had divined in 1973 what was going to happen in June 1975. To meet the challenge of catastrophic judgement in 1975, meseems, she had started as early as 1973 her endeavours at fortification of her defences. In April, 1973, Mr. Ajit Nath Ray was appointed Chief Justice of India superseding his three senior colleagues—Justices Shelat, Hegde and Grover. It was followed by the supersession of Justice H.R. Khanna in January 1977. After the appointment of A.N. Ray all the three judges had resigned in protest. K.S. Hegde, who was most forthright in the expression of his resentment, declared, "I had reason to believe that Mrs. Gandhi was greatly piqued by my decision in her election appeal. Ever since her agents were busy to build up a case against me."[14]

In a vain attempt to defend the indefensible the Government came forward with the most contradictory explanations. On May 4, the Prime Minister denied that the government bore any animus against Judiciary, "All that has happened is that we did not bow before the idol of seniority."[15] The Minister for Steel and Mines, the late Mohan Kumaramangalam, had made a categorical statement in the Lok Sabha, "the Government was interested in having a committed Judiciary."[16] The Law Minister H.R. Gokhle had earlier remarked that "The first Law Commission did not regard seniority as an absolute principle."[17]

"The curb on the powers of the High Court (through 44th amendment) was a step to give too much power to the Executive."[18]

Even Parliament was not spared. Various recognised institutions, rules and procedures, essential for the smooth running of Parliamentary institutions, were violently defied. Frequently, vital issues were pushed through without adequate scrutiny and debate. Long before the June Emergency was proclaimed, a crucial amendment was rushed through the House in less than a day. Mrs. Gandhi's role as leader was disappointing. "Unlike her father, who held Parliament in high esteem, she showed scant regard for the institution or its time-honoured conventions. She largely ignored her responsibility and was conspicuous by her absence from Parliament even on important occasions. To her still more discredit, she neither made any sincere effort to establish a rapport with the Opposition, nor did she play fair by it according to the rules of the game. Discussion on embarrassing issues was often shut out and various devices were employed to bar inconvenient questions."[19] The denigration of Parliament was also a subtle move on the part of Mrs. Gandhi. It was a portion of the large scheme which aimed at arming the Executive with more and more powers. "One will have to regretfully admit that Parliament today does not enjoy the high esteem that it ought to have."[20]

The Party President had lost his independent stance and was acting as though he were a courtier at the

Prime Minister's Darbar. D.K. Barooah's (Congress President) notorious slogan (Indira is India, India is Indira) smacked of fascist tendency. It bore some resemblance to the oath Rudolph Hess administered to young Nazis on 25 February, 1934, 'Adolf Hitler is Germany, Germany is Adolf Hitler'. A strong Party President who can think on his own can stall the Prime Minister's attempt to shin up the tree of power.

"In fact the so-called weakening of the Cabinet system started in India after the Chinese aggression in 1962 since when the Emergency Committee of the Cabinet started working like the war Cabinet of the British Government bypassing the full Cabinet and the Standing Committee of the Cabinet."[21]

Even long before Emergency was proclaimed, she had started dominating her Cabinet colleagues. Gradually she packed her Cabinet with very faithful persons who only knew how to wag their tails instead of their heads. Dr. L.M. Singhvi had observed in September 1973: "Institutionally, Cabinet Ministers are in the process of becoming in increasing measure the agents and delegates of the Prime Minister and less the supporting stones of the arch sustaining the Prime Minister. The Cabinet has become a registering body."[22] In such conditions freedom of speech becomes a casualty and fawning a virtue. "In both these machines (political and executive), loyalty has become the supreme virtue and independence of thought a dangerous adventure."[23]

The Press was completely gagged. Shri B.G. Verghese who had refused to toe the official line was harassed. He was Editor of the *Hindustan Times* a very popular newspaper in North India. The Birlas were controlling the paper and had no mind to enrage Indira Gandhi. A six-month notice was, therefore, served on him and he was relieved after the expiry of that period.

All this strangulation of Judiciary, Parliament, Cabinet, Party and Press was bound to culminate in the murder of democracy, and the murder did occur at night on June 25, 1975.

After the judgement of the Allahabad High Court, started the race of rallies. The opposition held rallies to show their strength to force Indira Gandhi to step down. Indira Gandhi with all the superior resources at her command staged rallies as a counter move to prove how indispensable she was for the nation. Since the nation wanted her, she could not bow down before the verdict of the Allahabad High Court. Nation is, after all, bigger than a court. On the 20th of June, 1975, a very mammoth rally was held at the Boat Club ground in New Delhi. The press described it as the biggest ever rally held in the capital and according to many estimates not less than ten lakh persons were brought to it. People from all over India were brought to New Delhi by special trains, cars and trucks for this huge gathering which was to demonstrate its support to the Prime Minister. "Judging by the press reports about 7,000 cars and more than 4,000 trucks plied between the Punjab, Haryana and New Delhi to bring Mrs. Gandhi's supporters to the capital. Not less than 10 crore rupees must have been spent on it. Very few people in Delhi took that particular rally seriously. Such meetings had become familiar sights in New Delhi in those days. The Prime Minister was in the habit of addressing such hired gatherings. The people of India imagined that this was one of such familiar sights."[24]

The above-mentioned meeting was a pointer to what was to follow in the coming months. "For the first time in the history of independent India all members of the Prime Minister's family sat at the stage, the people of India saw them, and Mrs. Gandhi addressed the mammoth meeting. Except the Congress President who gave his life's briefest speech of two and a half minute, no non-Nehru clan member was allowed on the dais. All other leaders were with their state contingents. Y.B. Chavan was with the Maharashtra unit deep into the masses. On the dais sat Mrs. Indira Gandhi, Rajiv Gandhi, Sanjay Gandhi and Rajiv's wife. Some Delhi papers expressed a little surprise over such a family gathering. The Prime Minister had announced to the people of India and the rest of the world that now onwards the members of the Nehru family would rule over India."[25]

Thereafter very much serious but hectic deliberations were on at the Prime Minister's residence. She was advised by Sanjay, Bansi Lal and S.S. Ray to impose emergency to deal with the agitation started by the opposition. S.S. Ray was for a short-lived emergency as he disclosed later on. At last came the most fateful night of June 25, 1975, most fateful for Mrs. Gandhi but the most momentous in the history of India. Mrs. Gandhi and her henchmen plotted against the nation and imposed a vigorous emergency on the country. Jaya Prakash Narain at that time was addressing a historic mass meeting at Ramlila Ground, Delhi.

J.P. announced to the people a programme of civil disobedience in the capital and other cities of the country. He repeated his exhortation to the Police and the Army not to obey illegal orders. He asked the students to walk out of classrooms to walk into jails.

He suggested to the Chief Justice of India, A.N. Ray not to sit on the Division Bench of the Supreme Court which would hear Mrs. Gandhi's appeal as he was obliged to the Prime Minister for his appointment.

"He said that the people should know that Mrs. Gandhi had uttered no less than 27 lies in the court during her evidence, that is, a lie every fifteen minutes."[26]

At about 8.30 p.m. Mrs. Gandhi accompanied by Siddhartha Shankar Ray motored to Rashtrapati Bhawan to intimate to the President her most significant decision to clamp down an internal emergency to meet the challenge of the opposition.

At 11 p.m. Home Minister Brahmananda Reddy was

summoned to the Prime Minister's house and told about her decision. Half an hour later a special high-powered messenger took the document to the President for his signature. Having been informed earlier about it, Fakhruddin Ali Ahmad duly signed it. Significantly, the proclamation bears no date.

Only Om Mehta, a 'Palace' confidant, knew about it that night. No other Cabinet minister was thought to be worthy of confidence.

It was not until 6 o'clock the next morning that the Cabinet was convened to be informed of Emergency in the country. The Cabinet was simply 'told' of what had already happened when all of them were asleep. Long before that, starting from midnight and in some cases earlier, opposition leaders were rounded up, Jaya Prakash Narain and Morarji Desai were woken up in their beds around 3 a.m. The arrests went on till late on June 26.

At the Cabinet meeting which lasted only fifteen minutes, "the assembled Ministers were shocked out of their wits. There was not a whimper. No one even asked a question let alone protest. After a couple of minutes Swaran Singh regained balance and tried to seek some clarifications. The External Emergency was already on the statute book, he said, could not the Government take the desired steps under it? Was there the need for the declaration of another Emergency? How long did the Prime Minister propose to continue these restrictions. The Prime Minister tersely drew Swaran Singh's attention to Jaya Prakash Narain's speech overnight, in the course of which he had threatened to *gherao* her house. Mrs. Gandhi also informed the Cabinet that strict censorship would be imposed in the country."[27] It was reported that some 400 warrants were signed overnight.

The reasons advanced by Mrs. Gandhi in justification of the Emergency were as under:

> "In the name of democracy it has been sought to negate the very functioning of democracy. Duly elected governments have not been allowed to function and in some cases force has been used to compel members to resign in order to dissolve lawfully elected Assemblies. Agitations have surcharged the atmosphere, leading to violent incidents. The whole country was shocked at the brutal murder of my cabinet colleague Shri L.N. Mishra. We also deplore the dastardly attack on the Chief Justice of India. Certain persons have gone to the length of inciting our armed forces to mutiny and our police to rebel. The fact our defence forces and the police are disciplined and deeply patriotic and, therefore, will not be taken in, does not mitigate the seriousness of the provocation. The forces of disintegration are in full play and communal passions are being aroused threatening our unity."[28]

Shri Jagjivan Ram deposing before the Shah Commission said, "The reason given by the then Prime Minister for imposition of Emergency was that she wanted to give a shock treatment to the country, and that through this treatment she wanted to improve the economic condition of the country.[29] A blanket censorship and mass incarceration deprived the opposition of the right to reply. All the engines of propaganda, radio, T.V. and news agency and the Press, as a whole were turned on at Government's command to damn the opposition. There was only one '*mantra*' to be repeated daily. 'Mrs. Gandhi is indispensable for the country in the unprecedented crisis facing it and that she alone can lift the country from the current crisis. Not untramelled by constitutional and legal obstacles she can take the country speedily to socialism, social justice and economic process.'

Jaya Prakash Narain wrote to her from Jail rebutting

the allegations levied by Mrs. Gandhi against him and the opposition leaders. But this letter remained unpublished until after 19 months, when the general elections were announced and censorship lifted in January 1977. He had written to say, "The very fact that you have to say something every day to justify your action implies a guilty conscience." He further said, "In a democracy the people do have the right to ask for the resignation of an elected government if it has gone corrupt and has been misruling. And if there is a legislature that persists in supporting such a government it too must go, so that the people might choose better representatives."[30]

Miss Carras elaborates her thinking about the imposition of Emergency in this way : "Mrs. Gandhi was impelled to take resolute action only when her will or dignity or beliefs were somehow assaulted. Viewed from that perspective, the Emergency decision was a 'defensive reaction' against threats to her self-esteem, resolve and her vision of India. But the manner in which the Emergency decision was reached and implemented clearly reveals Indira Gandhi's 'fatal leadership flaws'. Self-sufficiency, independence and autonomy which when displayed in good measure could be virtues became flaws. And they grew to be obsessively guarded ends in themselves rather than means to a healthy self-fulfilment."[31]

It can be safely stated that Mrs. Gandhi virtually gave up on June 26, 1975 and Sanjay took over from her and became *de facto* Prime Minister to rule like Charles I (the wisest fool) for 19 months. The Emergency was in fact a gift toy from a doting mother to her spoilt son who played joyfully with it. She fell out with all her well-meaning friends and supporters over Sanjay-Maruti affair. Siddhartha Shankar Ray's frank dialogue with her over Maruti affair brought about mutual estrangement. P.N. Haksar who was one of her main props entered into conflict with her when he touched the hot iron, Maruti affair. He was singed badly and lost his job. "She was perfectly rational but as soon as it came to Maruti and Sanjay, she would just clam up."[32] Sanjay and Maruti affairs became her most sensitive point so much so as to the extent of a tragic flaw in her character, which, according to Shakespeare, leads to the downfall of great heroes. And she would not listen to good advice where her personal life was concerned. "I was told by several individuals whose information was highly reliable", says Miss, Carras, "that prior to June 1975 she had been advised many times by friends and loyal supporters to put some physical and political distance between herself and her son, Sanjay, and certain other unsavoury characters. She consistently resisted these sound suggestions."[33]

During the night of 25 June, 1975 Indira's Government crossed the ethical bounds to indulge in Fascist game. "Power has been cut in Bahadurshah Zafar Marg, Delhi's Fleet Street, to ensure that no newspapers came out that morning."[34]

More than a lakh were arrested. Those who escaped arrest went underground to keep the movement alive. One of the major activities of the underground movement was preparation and circulation of bulletins, pamphlets, news sheets among the people. The well-known bulletins were : from Delhi—*Janavani* and *Mashal*; from Varanasi—*Darpan*; from Hyderabad—*Vajrayug*; from Bombay—*Asli Samachar*; Gauhati—*Satya Barta*. George Fernandes issued his own journal from his hideout, which bore a strong literary and poetic flavour. It was mailed regularly to Mrs. Gandhi.

"Seven thousand workers were arrested for circulating the underground literature. In the two-month *satyagraha* 80,000 were arrested — 15,000 in Karnataka, 9,000 in Kerala, 8,000 each in Bihar and U.P. and 5,000 in Delhi. *Satyagraha* was organised in 300 districts. The total figure of political prisoners of all kinds was 140,000."[35]

"All this sordid and gory drama of unscrupulous arrests, brutal killings and senseless murders by police, was enacted not to make democracy safe for India but to make Prime Ministership safe for Indira. Obviously, Mrs. Gandhi's intelligence sources, RAW and CIB, reported to her about the opposition's incapability to start any serious trouble for the government beyond a *dharna* outside the Prime Minister's house or Rashtrapati Bhavan. Yet Mrs. Gandhi kept on plugging the line in her public speeches that the opposition were plotting to paralyse the government and create anarchy in the country."[36] "Mrs. Gandhi converted her personal emergency into a national emergency. She resorted to extra-constitutional methods to stifle all opposition, to turn down the judiciary, to gag the press, to alter and amend the Constitution to give legality to her illegal acts. She wore the mantle of a dictator, exploited the benefits which flowed back to her as a result of proximity to the centre of power, closed her ears to the voice of sanity, and shut her eyes to the misdeeds of those who crowded around her. Obsessed with her critics who, she imagined, were out to destroy the very fabric of the nation."[37]

Many excesses were committed by the authorities, sometimes deliberately and sometimes unconsciously. Excessive power is bound to produce excesses. What else can it produce?

"In Kolhapur one Mr. Bhonsle was arrested and was kept in prison for the full emergency period. He never knew why he was arrested. Some investigations by the local political detenues revealed that the police wanted an RSS worker by name Bhonsle; when they could not get him, they arrested his name-sake, probably to tick off the list completely."[38]

"Mr. Prabhakar Sharma aged 65, a worker in the Sarvodaya movement, burnt himself to death at Surgaon outside Wardha in Maharashtra on October 11 in protest against Mrs. Gandhi's dictatorial methods of governm...t. Before killing himself Mr. Sharma sent a letter to Mrs. Gandhi explaining the reasons for his suicide with copies to S.D. Chavan the Chief Minister of Maharashtra and others....Quoting Gandhi's *Young India* Sharma said in his letter to the Prime Minister, "We must be content to die, if we cannot live as free men and women".[39]

An unconfirmed report said that several thousand people attended his funeral in spite of attempts by the police to stop them.

As already noted since Sajay took over from his mother, all Indira's ministers became ineffective. "The centre of power shifted from Indira's Cabinet to Sanjay's coterie. They were cut off from the happenings around them. Mr. K. Raghuramiah, the then Minister for Works and Housing, told the Commission on Tuesday that he was not aware of any decision taken by his Ministry to undertake demolition on such a large scale in Turkman Gate and other areas in Delhi during the Emergency. He also said that he was never kept in the picture about the demolitions, and that the decision to clear the slum in the Turkman Gate area was not taken by his ministry, and in fact he came to know about the decision after it had actually taken place."[40]

"Tapping and bugging was practised on large scale. One of her (Indira's) loyal "*Bhaktas*" once told me how the car in which he had been travelling had been bugged to test his loyalty. She had the secret bio-data of all important politicians and journalists on her finger-tips."[41]

Mr. Khandalwala while deposing before the Shah Commission stated, "the lists to be arrested were prepared in the Prime Minister's House." According to Mr. Kishan Chand (Lieut. Governor of Delhi), "Even before Shri Jaya Prakash Narain's rally on the evening of June 25, 1975, Mr. Bansi Lal had telephoned to his special assistant to get ready with arrangements for the confinement of Shri Jaiprakash Narain and Mr

Morarji Desai at Sona."[42]

As already pointed out the late President, Fakhruddin Ali Ahmad, was also sore at the imposition of Emergency. Being the Prime Minister's President, he found himself helpless to do anything in the matter. He felt let down, took it to heart and died of heart failure. "Mr. Karl Khandalwala (while deposing before Shah Commission) remarked that a fraud was playcd on the then President by Mrs. Gandhi when she had made out that there was no time to consult her Council of Ministers."[43]

The Emergency period is a gruesome tale of a people on whom were let loose the hounds of terror. "She was feared beyond reason. Most Congressmen, Ministers, M.Ps. and legislators felt tongue-tied in her presence. Pandit Nehru, her father, the tallest leader of our country, was respected even held in awe but never feared."[44]

Pandit Nehru, despite his arrogance and vanity, never treated his Cabinet colleagues or state Chief Ministers as his subordinates. Dr. B.C. Roy sometimes behaved as if he were superior to Nehru but the latter would never mind it. Most Congress M.Ps. and state Ministers never played the role of shameless sycophants. He never allowed anybody to touch his feet nor did he allow the performance of '*Arati*'.

The family planning drive was turned into a nightmare. The buses were held on the way and passengers forced to get down for immediate sterilization. Even thousands of unmarried young men were sterilized forcibly. Many died as a result of faulty operations. Resistance was offered at many places but it was met with bullets. "The only kind of sterilization that peasant had known before was the castration of his cattle. Now when men could be caught and forcibly sterilized, the implication became clear. In the eyes of the government the status of a poor man was no better than that of an animal."[45]

The most funny aspect of the tragi-comedy was the emergence of a raw, immature and hot-headed but mediocre character (Sanjay) on the stage, who ferreted, fumed, gesticulated foolishly, talked incoherently and disappeared suddenly.

At the age of thirty Sanjay Gandhi was *de facto* Prime Minister of India. He had access to Government files, made decisions on Government appointments, travelled in Government planes (47 times) and was given exposure on Government controlled radio (190 news items between January 1976 and January 1977). "In 1976 he was actually the person who first announced the postponement of elections, yet his only executive position was a member of the National Council of the Youth Congress, appointed without even having served the statutory three years as a primary member."[46]

Encomiums were showered on him by the various Chief Ministers. Chief Minister of Assam, "He was the 'energiser' of the Youth Congress". Chief Minister of Madhya Pradesh, "He the inspirer of self-confidence among people". Chief Minister of Maharashtra, "the rising star on the political horizon of India". Chief Minister of Punjab, "The great leader of the nation". The Chief Minister of Himachal Pradesh, "The only hope". Sanjay could not digest this eulogy, and began to behave like a man of destiny who was born to change the course of Indian history.

A resourceful correspondent of *Washington Post*, Mr. Lewis Simons, first correspondent to be expelled from India after the proclamation of Emergency, wrote a sensational piece in July 1975 in which he had maintained that "Sanjay Gandhi had already emerged as the successor of the Prime Minister and was ruling over India from her residence. No Chief Minister was allowed to see Indira direct. Everyone who wanted to see Indira had to meet Sanjay first to explore the possibility of an audience with her. All the key posts were filled in with Sanjay's men. Herdeo Joshi

(Rajasthan's Chief Minister) had gone to Delhi in the first week of July and wanted to see Indira Gandhi. He was asked to see Sanjay Gandhi to discuss his problems with him."[47]

Sanjay derived his strength not only from his mother but also from the coterie of men around him (Bansi Lal, V.C. Shukla, Om Mehta). Bansi Lal, the cussed and crude *jat*, called Indira a cow and Sanjay a calf. His theory was 'love the calf and control the cow'.

Some of the journalists, for some unknown motives, fed such like instincts. The Editor of *Blitz* described Sanjay's rise to power 'as history's own answer to our prayers'.[48] The Editor of the *Illustrated Weekly of India* declared 1976 'The Year of Sanjay Gandhi'.[49] The Editor of the Bombay Weekly *Current* held that 'What his city needed was the Sanjay Touch'.[50]

Such was the Emergency era wherein a few enjoyed all the freedom of speech whereas all others enjoyed the freedom of silence. In Bombay there were 75 performances mainly on the roof tops of an allegorical play in Marathi and Hindi, which could be termed as an interesting satire on Emergency. The story goes like this, many years ago there was a ruler in India who decreed that there should be no noise in his kingdom. If a baby or its mother uttered a sound at child birth the father was fined. One night a robber broke into the house of an old woman. A dog barked, waking the neighbours and the robber was caught. But the king's men arrested the dog and not the robber. The old woman was astonished. But, "Your Majesty", she complained, "should a thief be allowed to rob without any voice being raised against it? It was right and even the duty of the dog to register a protest." His Majesty replied, "In my kingdom a dog is not permitted to bark. He is only allowed to wag his tail."[51] Recently Mrs. Gandhi has been held guilty by one-man Manipur Emergency Excesses Enquiry Authority. The report says that Mrs. Indira Gandhi in collusion with the then Chief

Minister, Mr. R.K. Dorendra Singh, was responsible for committing atrocities on the people of the state during the emergency.[52]

The Gupta Commission report on Maruti published recently accuses Mrs. Gandhi of misuse of official machinery in furtherance of the interests of her son. It is a woeful tale of misapplication of state rules for self-aggrandisement. Crores of rupees were collected from motor dealers to supply them cheap small cars. When no cheap car was in sight and some of the dealers suspecting foul play met Sanjay Gandhi to demand back their deposits, they were arrested under MISA.

"The Indian events compressed within the span of the 19 months of the Emergency rule are characterised by the capture and exercise of political power by a small coterie in complete disregard of all norms of not only constitutional rule but also of enlightened self-interest of the ruling elite. The fact that a small band of illiterate or half-literate persons, either notorious for their immoral escapades, or absolutely faceless non-entities, were entrusted with seemingly unlimited powers over the life and death of 600 million population of the second most populous country in the world—a country which occupies a key position in the international geo-politics — carries its own verdict not only on the elite of this country but also on the statesmen of the world."[53] The Emergency will go down in history as an indictment of the whole nation that crawled and cringed but could not bite. "From June 26, 1975, onward, day by day, week by week, month by month, the Union Cabinet, the Indian Parliament, the haughty Indian Bureaucracy, the Supreme Court of India (with a few noble exceptions) and the state governments, as well as the multimillion strong Congress organisation increasingly succumbed to both the crude and subtle logics of the developing situation—and cooperated with the caucus to legitimise Indira Gandhi's coup against the Indian people, and acquiesced in the induction of her politically uncouth son as the Crown Prince cum joint Prime Minister and the gradual build-up of the surrogate power centre (Sanjay, Bansi, Dhawan)."[54]

Benemy says that the Prime Minister (British) in an emergency is just as powerful as the President.[55]

It can be averred that the Indian Prime Minister in an Emergency is far more powerful than the President. But the people are the most powerful. "The most backward and the abjectly poor people of the northern Hindi belt have shaped the history of India. They have removed their powerful rulers with one hard stroke. The like of this has simply not happened in the entire course of Indian history since the stone age."[56] The excesses during emergency and the present political crisis generated by power hungry politicians, the dissolution of Parliament and the new elections in December 1979 have again revived the controversy that the Constitution has failed, Nani Palkiwala has again pleaded for the Presidential form of government.

There is nothing wrong with the Constitution. It has not failed us, neither have we failed it. "However good a Constitution may be, it may turn out to be bad if those who are called to work it, happen to be a bad lot. However bad a Constitution may be, it may turn out to be good if those who are called upon to work it, happen to be a good lot. The working of a Constitution does not depend wholly on the nature of the Constitution."[57]

The democracy has survived. Those who wanted to emasculate it are no more. The Parliamentary government is again under heavy strain, it is hoped that the mature sense of the people displayed during 1977 elections will again come to the fore and place the derailed bogey on the right track. The political crises do occur in every country and are resolved by the people in accordance with their agreement on fundamentals, political notions, traditional and religious beliefs, social and economic concepts. If they cannot solve, it is their failure. I remember Shakespeare has said somewhere, "The fault does not lie in our stars but in ourselves that we are underlings".

REFERENCES

1. C.A.D., IX, p. 123.
2. *Ibid.*, p. 108.
3. *Ibid.*, p. 112.
4. *Ibid.*, p. 114.
5. *Ibid.*, p. 124.
6. *The Indian Express*, January 6, 1972, p. 1.
7. *The Times of India*, January 9, 1972, p. 1.
8. *The Indian Express*, January 17, 1972, p. 1.
9. *The Indian Express*, January 18, 1972, p. 1.
10. Naik, J.P., *The Great Janata Revolution*, S. Chand & Co., New Delhi, p. 2.
11. Jain, P.K., *The Glorious Revolution in India*, p. 142.
12. Shanti Bhushan's statement to the P.T.I. on 12 June, 1975.
13. Dhawan, Rajeev, *The Amendment : Conspiracy or Revolution*, Wheeler Publishing, Allahabad, 1978, p. 24.
14. *The Indian Express*, May 2, 1973.
15. Kulkarni, V.B., *My Country and My Rulers*, p. 52.
16. *The Times of India*, May 3, 1973.
17. *Ibid.*, August 4, 1971.
18. Jain, P.K., *The Glorious Revolution in India*, p. 158.
19. Sikri, S.K., *Our Developing Constitution*, p. 23.
20. *Main Stream*, Republic Day issue, 1975.
21. Chaudhary, Deepak B.R., Emergence of Prime Ministerial Government in India, *Modern Review*, November, 1968, p. 822.
22. Singhvi, L.M., *Journal of Parliamentary Studies*, October, 1973.
23. Chaudhary, Deepak B.R., Emergence of Prime Ministerial Government in India, *Modern Review*, November, 1968, p. 819.
24. Naik, J.P., *The Great Janata Revolution*, p. 14.
25. *Ibid.*
26. *Blitz*, June 25, 1977, p. 10.
27. *Ibid.*, p. 10.
28. *Ibid.*, p. 11.
29. Singh, Darbara, *Indian Politics*, pp. 161-162.

30. *Blitz*, June 25, 1977, p. 11.
31. *The Illustrated Weekly of India*, September 9, 1979, p. 27.
32. *Blitz*, July 30, 1977, p. 9.
33. *The Illustrated Weekly of India*, September 9, 1979, p. 27.
34. *Blitz*, July 2, 1977, p. 13.
35. *Ibid.*, p. 14.
36. *Blitz*, June 25, 1977, p. 12.
37. Murthy, R.K., *The Cult of the Individual*, p. xv.
38. Naik, J.P., *The Great Janata Revolution*, p. 44.
39. Rao, Amiya and Rao, B.G., *The Press she could not whip*, Bombay Popular Prakashan, p. 37.
40. Singh, Darbara, *Indian Politics*, p. 167.
41. Ghose, S.K., *The Crusade and End of Indira Raj*, Intellectual Book Corner, 1978, p. 231.
42. Singh, Darbara, *Indian Politics*, p. 170.
43. *Ibid.*
44. Ghose, S.K., *The Crusade and End of Indira Raj*, 1978, p. 231.
45. Sinha, Sachchidanand, *Emergency in Perspective*, Heritage Publishers, New Delhi, p. 70.
46. Handerson, Michael, *Experiment with Untruth : India Under Emergency*, The Macmillan Co. of India Ltd., 1977, p. 57.
47. Naik, J.P., *The Great Janata Revolution*, p. 20.
48. *Blitz*, November 27, 1976.
49. *The Illustrated Weekly of India*, January 23, 1976.
50. *Current*, October 30, 1976.
51. Henderson, Michael, *Experiment with Untruth, India under Emergency*, 1977, p. 23.
52. *The Hindustan Times*, September 28, 1979, p. 1.
53. Roy, Ajit, *The Meaning of the Indian Experience — The Emergency*, edited by Saral K. Chatterji, The Christian Literature Society, Madras, 1978, p. 5.
54. *Ibid.*, p. 6.
55. Benemy, F.W.G., *The Elected Monarch*, p. 228.
56. Naik, J.P., *The Great Janata Revolution*, p. 55.
57. Dr. Ambedkar quoted by Rajeev Dhawan in *Conspiracy or Revolution*, Wheeler Publishing, Allahabad, 1978, p. 34.

Bibliography

Agrawala, Chandra Prakash : *Indira Gandhi and (Then and Now), Janata*, Hindustan Exporters (Publications Division), Chandausi-202412 (U.P.), 1978.

Ahluwalia, B.K. : *Sardar Patel—A Life*, Sagar Publications, Ved Mansion, 72 Janpath, New Delhi, 1974.

Aiyar, S.P. & Raju, S.V. : *When the Wind Blows, India's Ballot-Box Revolution*, Himalaya Publishing House, 71, Juhu Road, Bombay, 1978.

Alderman, R.K., & Cross, J.A. : *The Tactics of Resignation*, Routledge and Kegan Paul, New York.

Anson : *The Law and Custom of the Constitution*, 5th edition.

Austin, Granville : *The Indian Constitution — Corner Stone of a Nation*, Oxford University Press, Bombay, Delhi, Calcutta, Madras, 1972.

Azad, Maulana Abul Kalam: *India Wins Freedom*. Orient Longman.

Bagehot, Walter : *The English Constitution*, Thomas Nelson & Sons, 1872.

Bannerji, Anil Chandra: *A Survey of the Indian Constitution*, A. Mukherji & Co. P. Ltd., 2 College Square, Calcutta.

Basu, Durga Dass : *Shorter Constitution of India*, S. C. Sarkar and Sons (P) Ltd., College Square, Calcutta, 1956.

Basu, Durga Dass: *Introduction to the Constitution of India*, C. Sarkar & Sons (P) Ltd., College Square, Calcutta, 1966.

Basu, Sajal (ed.) : *Underground Literature During Indian*

Emergency, Minerva Associates Publication Pvt. Ltd., 7B, Lake Place, Calcutta, 1978.

Bendre, Sudhir Laxman : *Undeclared Civil War in India*, Supraya Prakashan, 52, Warden Court Tank, Bombay.

Benemy, F. W. G. : *The Elected Monarch*. George G. Harrap & Co., London, 1965.

Bennet, Wheeler : *The Nemesis of Power*, 1953.

Berkeley, Humphary : *The Power of the Prime Minister*.

Bhargava, G.S. : *Morarji Desai — Prime Minister of India*, Indian Book Co., Delhi, 1977.

Bhat, P. N. : *Seminar on Constitutional Questions relating to the Power of Dissolution* (A Pamphlet).

Bhatia, Krishan : *Indira — A Biography of Prime Minister Indira*, Young Asia Publications, New Delhi, 1975.

Blake, Robert : *The Office of Prime Minister*, Oxford University Press, 1975.

Brecher, Michael : *The Succession in India — A Study in Decision Making*, Oxford University Press, London, 1967.

Chakravarti, Saroj: *With Bengal Chief Ministers*, Memoirs 1962 to 1977. Orient Longman, 1978.

Chapman, Brian : *British Government Observed*, Allen and Unwin, 1963.

Chatterji, Saral K. : *The Meaning of Indian Experience: The Emergency* Edited by Saral K. Chatterji. The Christian Literature Society, Madras.

Chatterji, Bimanesh: *Thousand Days with Rajaji*, 1973.

Chaturvedi, R. G. : The President and the Council of Ministers, *The Journal of Constitutional and Parliamentary Studies*, New Delhi, 1971.

Chitaley & Rao: *The Constitution of India*, (2nd ed.), The All India Reporter, 1970.

Crossman, Richard : *Inside View* (Three lectures on Prime Ministerial government) Jonathan Cape, 30, Bedford Square, London, 1972.

Crossman, Richard : *The Diaries of a Cabinet Minister, III*, Hamish Hamilton and Jonathan Cape, London.

Das, B. C. : *The President of India*, S. Chand & Co. Ltd., New Delhi, 1977.

Dey, Bata K. : *Bureaucracy, Development and Public Management in India*, Uppal Publishing House, 3 Ansari Road, Darya Ganj, New Delhi, 1978.

Dharma Vir, I. C. S. (Retd.): 14th Shri Ram Memorial Lecture, Wednesday, 1 January 1979 (FICCI) Building, Barakhamba Road, New Delhi-1.

Dhawan, Rajeev: *The Amendment, Conspiracy or Revolution*. Wheeler Publishing, Allahabad, 1978.

Drieberg, Trevor : *Indira Gandhi — A Profile in Courage*, Vikas Publications, Delhi, 1972.

Durga Das : *Sardar Patel's Correspondence, 1945-50*, Vol. IV, 1972.

Dutt, Subimal : *With Nehru in the Foreign Office*, Minerva Associates (Publications) Pvt. Ltd., Calcutta.

Earl of Oxford and Asquith: *Fifty Years of British Parliament*.

Fisher, W. and Bandurant Joan V., *Indian Views of Sino-Indian Relations*.

Gangal, S. C. : *Prime Minister and the Cabinet in India*, Navachetana Prakashan, Rajghat, Varanasi, 1972.

Ghose, Atulya: *The Split*, Calcutta, 1970.

Ghose, S. K. : *The Crusade and End of Indira Raj*, Intellectual Book Corner, 1978.

Ghose, Sankar: *Changing India*, Allied Publishers Pvt. Ltd., 1978.

Gledhill, Allen : *The Republic of India*, 1951.

Gupta, Madan Gopal: *Aspects of Indian Constitution*, Deptt. of Politics, University of Allahabad, Central Book Depot, Allahabad.

Gupta, Nirmala: *Bharatiya Sanvidhan Men Pradhan Mantri Ki Bhumika*, Rajpal & Sons, 1978.

Haines, Joe *The Politics of Power*, Jonathan Cape, London, 1977.

Handa, H. L. : *Rajendra Prasad : Twelve Years of Triumph and Despair*, Sterling Publishers Pvt. Ltd., AB/9, Safdarjang Enclave, New Delhi, 1978.

Handerson, Michael : *Experiment with Untruth — India under Emergency*, The Macmillan Co. of India Ltd., 1977.

Haneman, H. J. : *The Growth of Executive Power in Germany*, 1st edition, 1934.

Hanson, A. H. Douglas Janet : *India's Democracy*, Vikas Publishing House, New Delhi.

Headey, Bruce: *British Cabinet Ministers*, George Allen and Unwin Ltd., Ruskin House, Museum Street, London, 1974.

Henry, Parris: *Constitutional Bureaucracy*, University of Durham, Minerva Series of Students Handbooks No. 23, George Allen and Unwin, London, 1969.

Herman, Valentine, and Alt, James E., (eds.) : *Cabinet Studies — A Reader*, Mackmillan Press Ltd., London.

Herz, Carter and Runney: *The Government of Great Britain*, 1958.

Hughs, Emrys : *Macmillan — Portrait of a Politician*, George Allen and Unwin, London, 1962.

Iyengar, H. V. R. : *A Historical Review—Three Lectures delivered* at *Bharatiya Vidya Bhawan*, 1966.

Jain, Ajit Prasad : *Rafi Ahmad Kidwai.*

Jain, H. M. : *The Union Executive.*

Jain, P. K. : *The Glorious Revolution in India—An Analysis of Historical Foundations 1947-1977*, Gitanjali Prakashan, New Delhi, 1978.

Jennings, Ivor : *The Queen's Government.*

Jennings, Ivor, *Cabinet Government*, Cambridge University Press, 1959.

Jewell, R. E. C. : *Outlines of Public Administration*, Charles Knight & Co. Ltd., London, 1976.

Jones, G. W. : *The Modernization of British Government*, edited by William Thornhill, Pitman Publishing Pvt., Australia, 1975.

Joshi G. N.: *The Constitution of India*, Macmillan and Co. Ltd., St. Martin's St., London.

Kagzi, M. C. : *The June Emergency and Constitutional Amendment.*

Kale, S. B.: *Man of Crisis*. Sindhu Publications Pvt. Ltd., Bombay, 1969.

Kalhan, Promilla : *Black Wednesday — Power Politics, Emergency, Elections*, Sterling Publishers P. Ltd., A B/ 9, Safdarjung Enclave, New Delhi-16, 1977.

Kapur, R. P.: *Kamaraj, The Iron Man*, 1967.

Karaka, D. F. : *Morarji*, 1965.

Keeton, George W. (General Editor): *The British Commonwealth. The Development of its Laws and Constitution*, The Republic of India.

Keith, A. B. : *British Cabinet System*, 1952.

Keith, A. B. : *The King and the Imperial Crown*, 1936.

Khera, S. S. : *The Central Executive*.

King, Anthony, (ed.) : *The British Prime Minister*, 1969.

Kotelewala, John : *An Asian Prime Minister's Story*.

Kulkarni, V. B.: *My Country and My Rulers*, Jaico Press Pvt. Ltd., Bombay, 1977.

Lal, Kanwar : *Thank You Mrs. Gandhi*, Anupam Publications, New Delhi, 1977.

Laski, Harold J. : *Parliamentary Government in England*, 1938, 6th edition, 1959.

Lewis, Promila : *Reason Wounded*, Vikas Publishing House, New Delhi.

Lord Hill : *Both Sides of the Hill*, 1964.

Mackintosh, John P. : *The British Cabinet*, 1968.

Madgwick, P. J.: *Introduction to British Politics*, Hutchinson Educational Ltd., 3 Fitzroy Square, London, 1971.

Madhok, Balraj : *Murder of Democracy*, S. Chand & Co., Delhi, 1973.

Mahajan, V. D. : *The Constitutional History of India*. S. Chand & Co. P. Ltd., Delhi, 1971.

Mankekar, D. R. : *Lal Bahadur — A Political Biography*, Bombay Popular Prakashan, 1964-65.

Masani, Zareer : *Indira Gandhi — A Biography*. Hamish Hamilton, London, 1975.

Mellors, Collin: *The British M. P.*, Sexon House, Teakfield Ltd., Westmead, Farnborough, Hants, England.

Minogue, Martin : *Documents on Contemporary British Government.*

Mirchandani, G. G. : *Subverting the Constitution*, Abhinav Publications, E-37, Hauz Khas, New Delhi, 1977.

Mishra, R. N. : *The President of the Indian Republic.* Vohra & Co. Pvt. Ltd., 3, Round Building, 1964.

Mohan, K. T. J. : *Independence to India and After.* S. Chand & Co., Delhi, 1977.

Moraes, Frank : Nehru — *Sunlight and Shadow*, Jaico Publishing House, Bombay, 1964.

Mosley, R. K. : *The Story of the Cabinet Office, Routledge and Kegan Paul*, New York: Humanities Press.

Mukerji, Hiren: *Sarvapalli Dr. Radhakrishnan.* Popular Book Services, New Delhi.

Mukherji, P. B. (Justice): *The Critical Problems of the Indian Constitution* (Chaman Lal Setalvad Lectures, November, 1966).

Mullick, B. N. : *My Years with Nehru*, Allied Publishers, 1972.

Munshi, K. M. : *Indian Constitutional Documents*, Vol. I, II, 1967.

Munshi, K. M. : *The President under the Indian Constitution*, Bharatiya Vidya Bhawan, Chowpatty, Bombay-7, 1963.

Murthy, R. K. : *The Cult of the Individual—A Study of Indira Gandhi*, Sterling Publishers Pvt. Ltd., AB/9, Safdarjung Enclave, New Delhi, 1977.

Murthy, V. K. : *In the Larger Persona! Interest—An Investigation into Indian Politics Since 1947*, Allora Publications, Darya Ganj, New Delhi, 1978.

Naik, J. P. : *The Great Janata Revolution*, S. Chand & Co., Ram Nagar, New Delhi.

Nayar, Kuldip : *Between the Lines*, Allied Publishers, Bombay, New Delhi, 1969.

Nehru, J. L. : *Democracy — Welcome Address at Common-wealth Parliamentary Conference*, (95), India Branch Commonwealth Parliamentary Association, New Delhi.

Nehru, J. L. : *India's Quest*. Asia Publishing House, Bombay, 1963.

Neustadt, Richard E. : *The British Prime Minister* edited by Anthony King.

Nicolson, Harold : *King George the Fifth*.

Noorani, A. G. : *Ministers' Misconduct*, Vikas Publishing House (P) Ltd., Delhi, Bombay, Bangalore, Kanpur.

Pandey, B. N. : *Nehru*, Macmillan, London, 1976.

Pandit, H. N. : *Prime Minister's President*. S. Chand & Co., 1974.

Paras, Diwan : *Abrogation of Forty-second Amendment: Does Our Constitution Need a Second Look?* Sterling Publishers P. Ltd., 1977.

Pardasani, N. S. : *How India is Governed*, New Book Co., Kitab Mahal, Hornby Road, Fort, Bombay, 1942.

Patrick, Cosgrave: *Margaret Thatcher — A Tory and Her Party*, Hutchinson of London, 1978.

Pickles, Dorothy, : *The Fifth French Republic*, 1960.

Punjabi, K. L. (ed.) : *The Civil Servant in India*, Bharatiya Vidya Bhawan, 1965.

Punjabi, K. L. : *Rajendra Prasad*, 1960.

Pyare Lal : *Mahatma Gandhi*, Vol. I.

Quraishi, Zaheer Masud (Dr.) : *The President of India*, New Literature, Marina Arcade, New Delhi, 1962.

Rafeek, Ahmad Y., *Office of the Indian Prime Minister*, A Report on the research done under the U.G.C. Research Fellowship, Mysore University, 1964.

Ram Gopal : *Undemocratic Elements in the Indian Constitution*, Somaiya Publications P. Ltd., Bombay, New Delhi, 1977.

Rangachary, K., P. N. Bhatt, and K. K. Bhardawaj: *Seminar on Constitutional Questions relating to the Power of Dissolution of Lok Sabha*. The Institute of Constitutional and Parliamentary Studies.

Rau, B. N. : *Address to the Indian Council of World Affairs* on August 10, 1949.

Rau, B. N. : *The Constitution of India in the Making*.

Riddal, W. R. : *The Canadian Constitution in Form and Fact*, 1923.

Roy, Amal, *Inter-Governmental Relations in India*, Doctoral Dissertation, Asia Publishing House, Bombay, 1971.

Rao, Amiya and Rao, B. G. : *The Press She Could Not Whip*, Popular Prakashan Pvt. Ltd., Bombay.

Sampson, Anthony : *Anatomy of Britain Today*, Hoddar and Stoughton, 1965.

Sen, Ela. : *Indira Gandhi — A Biography*, Rupa & Co., Calcutta.

Sethi, J. D. : *India in Crisis*, Vikas Publishing House, 1975.

Sethi, J. D. : *India's Static Power Structure*, Vikas Publications, 1969.

Sharma, Radhey Shyam : *Who After Morarji?* Pankaj Publications, New Delhi, 1978.

Sharma, Sri Ram :*Parliamentary Government in India*, Central Book Depot, Allahabad, 1969.

Shashi Bhushan : *Feroze Gandhi* — Progressive People's Sector Publications (P) Ltd., New Delhi.

Sikri, S. L. : *Our Developing Constitution, Trends, Issues and Problems*, S. Nagin & Co., 1978.

Singh, Darbara : *Indian Politics - 1968-1978*. Sandeep Prakashan, Ashok Vihar, Delhi, 1978.

Singh, Nau Nihal (Dr.) : Jagjivan Ram : *Symbol of Social Change*, Sundeep Prakashan, New Delhi, 1977.

Sinha, Sachchidanand : *Emergency in Perspective*, Heritage Publishers, M-116, Connaught Circus, New Delhi.

Sinha, Sachchidanand : *The Permanent Crisis in India— After Janata What?* Heritage Publishers, M-116, Connaught Circus, New Delhi, 1978.

Siwach, J.R. : *The Indian Presidency*, Haryana Prakashan, Delhi, 1971.

Smith, Brian: *Policy Making in British Cabinet — An Analysis of Power and Rationality*, Martin Robertson, 1976.

Smith, Enid Russel, (Political Realities) *Modern Bureaucracy, The Home Civil Service*, Longman Group Ltd., 1974.

Stannard, H. : *The Two Constitutions*, 1950.

Thakur, Janardan : *All the Prime Minister's Men*, Vikas Publishing House P. Ltd., Delhi, 1977 and 1978.

Thornhill, William : *The Modernization of British Government*, Pitman House,, 39 Parker Street, London, 1975.

Turner, John E. : *Labour's Doorstep Politics in London*, The Macmillan Press Ltd., London, 1978.

Tyagi, A.R. : *The Civil Service in a Developing Society*, Sterling Publishers, 1969.

Walker, Patrick Gordon : *The Cabinet*, Jonathan Cape, 30, Bedford Square, London, 1970.

Weber, Max : *Essays in Sociology*, Oxford University Press, 1946.

Wilson Harold : *The Governance of Britain*, Weidenfield and Nicolson and Michael Joseph, 1976.

Young, Kenneth : *Arthur Balfour*, 1963.

Newspapers

The Hindustan Times
The Hindu
The Indian Express
The Patriot
The Statesman
The Times of India
The Tribune

Periodicals and Miscellany

Blitz
Constituent Assembly Debates — Relevant Volumes
Current
Everyman's
Mainstream
Minutes of the Congress Working Committee Meetings
Modern Review
Mrs. Pandit's Papers
Opinion
Parliamentary Studies
Prasad (Dr. Rajendra Prasad) Papers.
Swarajya
The All India Reporter
The Caravan
The Illustrated Weekly of India
The Indian Advocate
The Indian Journal of Political Science
The Indian Journal of Public Administration
The Journal of Constitutional and Parliamentary Studies
The Law Reporter

Index